GeoServer Beginner's

Share and edit geospatial data with this open source
software server

Stefano Iacovella

Brian Youngblood

[PACKT] open source
PUBLISHING   community experience distilled

BIRMINGHAM - MUMBAI

GeoServer Beginner's Guide

First published: February 2013

Production Reference: 1110213

Published by Packt Publishing Ltd.
Livery Place
35 Livery Street
Birmingham B3 2PB, UK.

ISBN 978-1-84951-668-6

www.packtpub.com

Cover Image by Brian Youngblood (brian@brianyoungblood.com)

Credits

Authors

Stefano Iacovella

Brian Youngblood

Reviewers

Pablo Rodríguez Bustamante

Daniela Cristiana DOCAN

Brett Gaines

Eric-Jan Groen

Antonio Santiago

Acquisition Editor

Usha Iyer

Lead Technical Editor

Dayan Hyames

Technical Editor

Jalasha D'costa

Copy Editors

Aditya Nair

Laxmi Subramanian

Ruta Waghmare

Project Coordinator

Amey Sawant

Proofreader

Aaron Nash

Indexer

Hemangini Bari

Production Coordinator

Shantanu Zagade

Cover Work

Shantanu Zagade

About the Authors

Stefano Iacovella is a long-time GIS developer and consultant living in Rome, Italy. He also works as a GIS course instructor.

He has a Ph.D in Geology. Being a very curious person, he has developed a deep knowledge of IT technologies, mainly focused on GIS Software and related standards.

Starting his career as an ESRI employee, he was exposed to and became confident with proprietary GIS Software, mainly the ESRI suite of products.

For the last 10 years, he has been involved with open source software and also the task of integrating it with commercial software. He loves the open source approach, and really trusts in the collaboration and sharing of knowledge. He strongly believes in the concept of open source, and constantly strives to spread it, and not only in the GIS sector.

He has been using GeoServer since the release of Version 1.5; configuring, deploying, and hacking it in several projects. Some of the other GFOSS projects he mainly uses and likes are GDAL/OGR libraries, PostGIS, QGIS, and OpenLayers.

When not playing with maps and geometric shapes, he loves reading about science, mainly physics and math, riding his bike, and having fun with his wife and his two daughters, Alice and Luisa.

I would like to thank many people who have helped me to make this book a reality.

A special mention for GeoServer's developers; they are the wonderful engine without which this book would not exist.

I would like to thank Usha Iyer, Dayan Hyames, Amey Sawant, and everyone else at Packt Publishing for all their hard work to get this book published.

My gratitude to Luca Morandini, a colleague and friend; he spurred me to take this challenge.

Last but not the least, I want to express my gratitude to Alessandra, Alice, and Luisa for their support and patience.

Brian Youngblood is a open source developer living in Montgomery, AL with more than a decade of experience developing, integrating, and managing high traffic websites.

Brian was the Online Operations Manager and Technical Lead at the Southern Poverty Law Center for over 12 years. The SPLC is a nationally recognized nonprofit, and its websites SPLCenter.org and Tolerance.org have continued to get sharp increases in visitors year-on-year, resulting in growth in its online operations with open source. The SPLC won two Webby Awards in 2002 and 2004.

Brian was also the founding partner and Chief Technology Officer for IntelliTours, a GPS-guided multimedia tour. He worked with several companies developing hardware and software including Alcorn McBride, Volkswagen, and Garmin. His work explored San Diego, Santa Cruz, Hawaii, and miles and miles of I-95 on the East Coast. Most notably, his work was featured on the cover of Entertainment Engineering magazine, Martha Stewart radio, the LA Times, and NPR.

Embracing the spirit of other open source communities such as Drupal, and a combined passion for scalable GIS solutions, led him to adopt GeoServer for rapidly changing geospatial data stores.

You can contact him at brian@brianyoungblood.com or follow him on twitter @brianyoungblood.

The GeoServer developers and community. So many have contributed to bringing this software to this point. Specifically, Andrea Aime, Chris Holmes, Gabrel Roldan, and David Winslow have fielded my questions on GeoServer's mailing list and in IRC. Their tireless commitment to the GeoServer project has helped me and so many others immensely.

Other contributors are also listed on the contributors page at http://geoserver.org/display/GEOS/Contributors.

Thank you Melissa Henninger for helping edit and proof chapters. To Bill Fitzgerald for his advice as a Packt author.

About the Reviewers

Pablo Rodríguez Bustamante is a geographer and an Environment and Geographic Information Systems (GIS) Consultant with experience in the field of water resource planning and natural hazards.

He has 4 years' experience in the field of GIT (Geographic Information Technologies) and thematic mapping, 3 years' experience in environmental consulting, and 2 years' experience in water planning issues and natural hazards.

He is a GIS specialist. He has expertise in EIA and Urban and Regional Planning.

He is fluent in Spanish, English, and Italian.

GEOCyL Environmental and Territorial Consultancy

GEOCyL is an environmental and territorial consultancy specializing in environmental studies, risk management, GIS development, land management, urban planning, geomarketing, and spreading knowledge about nature and our environment.

Our company optimizes various territorial areas in different sectors. For that, we use the newest technologies in geographical science concerning environmental and territorial issues. On the basis of GIS, we provide specific and optimized solutions for public authorities and/or private companies.

R&D lines (lines of research)

- Research referring to the management of natural hazards, which include drawing up of maps of risk, danger, and vulnerability through particular methodologies of risk analysis; technological advice and help concerning territorial planning and development of endangered areas to prevent or reduce the effect of natural hazards in order to protect the civilian population; and management of emergency bodies.

- Implementation of the GBI system (Geographic Business Intelligence) for greater profitability

◆ Analysis and optimization of geographical information and solutions.

I would like to thank my family and my GEOCyL partners (Eduardo Bustillo, Florian Schilling, ...), who always supported me, even in difficult times. Special thanks to my girlfriend Patricia and my friends.

Daniela Cristiana DOCAN is a lecturer at Technical University of Civil Engineering, Bucharest, Romania. She works within the Faculty of Geodesy, mainly in GIS and survey engineering.

Formerly, she worked for ESRI Romania and ANCPI (National Agency of Cadastre and Land Registration).

She obtained her Ph.D in 2009 in Civil Engineering, with the thesis "Contributions to quality improvement of spatial data in GIS".

While working for ESRI Romania, she has trained (as an authorized Instructor in ArcGIS by Environmental Systems Research Institute, Inc. (ESRI), Redlands, California, USA) teams from different states and privately owned companies. Also, she has created and administrated databases (geodatabase format) for different domains of activity.

For ANCPI (National Agency of Cadastre and Land Registration), in 2009 she created (for the first time in the field) a logical and physical datamodel for the National Topographic Data set on a large scale (TOPRO5). She was a member of different workgroups who elaborated the standards and technical specifications and the country report, in 2010 for INSPIRE (Infrastructure for Spatial Information in the European Community).

Brett Gaines is a GIS programmer and remote sensing analyst. He holds a B.S. degree in Geography with a specialization in GIS, along with a M.Sc. degree in GIS.

He stays on the leading edge of GIS and database technologies, and he is always eager to learn new things. He prefers challenging projects and solving tough geospatial intelligence problems.

Eric-Jan Groen is a Linux Professional from the Netherlands. Formerly, he worked at Automotive Navigation Data.

I would like to thank everyone who helped create this book in any way.

Antonio Santiago is a computer science professional with a keen interest in the subject. He is an extremely curious Software Engineer who loves programming and learning new things.

GIS is his preferred area of interest, mainly because of the amount of things it encloses: databases with spatial capabilities, servers, protocols and standards, desktop and web development, and scalability.

After working with different technologies, such as C, Perl, and PHP, he found his preferred language, Java.

In 2004, while on a weather radar project with the IDL language (Interactive Data Language), he started working with OGC standards and GeoTools/GeoServer projects.

Nowadays, he is more focused on the JavaScript language because of the great performance implementation of current browsers and the growing adoption of the HTML5 specification.

He has authored the book *OpenLayers Cookbook*, by *Packt Publishing*.

To my partner, Pilar, for understanding my passion for computers, and to my parents for igniting in me the spark to see the beauty of learning.

www.PacktPub.com

Support files, eBooks, discount offers and more

You might want to visit www.PacktPub.com for support files and downloads related to your book.

Did you know that Packt offers eBook versions of every book published, with PDF and ePub files available? You can upgrade to the eBook version at www.PacktPub.com and as a print book customer, you are entitled to a discount on the eBook copy. Get in touch with us at service@packtpub.com for more details.

At www.PacktPub.com, you can also read a collection of free technical articles, sign up for a range of free newsletters and receive exclusive discounts and offers on Packt books and eBooks.

http://PacktLib.PacktPub.com

Do you need instant solutions to your IT questions? PacktLib is Packt's online digital book library. Here, you can access, read and search across Packt's entire library of books.

Why Subscribe?

- Fully searchable across every book published by Packt
- Copy and paste, print and bookmark content
- On demand and accessible via web browser

Free Access for Packt account holders

If you have an account with Packt at www.PacktPub.com, you can use this to access PacktLib today and view nine entirely free books. Simply use your login credentials for immediate access.

Instant Updates on New Packt Books

Get notified! Find out when new books are published by following @PacktEnterprise on Twitter, or the Packt Enterprise Facebook page.

I would like to express all my gratitude, affecttion, and professional respect to Ruggero Faggioni.

He was a colleague and a friend. He helped me discover my skills; he gave me the opportunity to grow as a GIS consultant. In the years we worked together, he was not only a boss, but also a kind tutor, and he taught me a lot.

I would like to dedicate this book to Ruggero, unfortunately he isn't there anymore to read it, but I am sure he would have liked it.

Stefano Iacovella

I would like to thank Jon Fisher from Auburn University Montgomery who ultimately led me to pursue a career in the Information Technology field. His patience, mentoring, and willingness to share his knowledge planted the seed that continues to grow today.

To Jim Carrier, the founder and my partner at IntelliTours for sharing the passion to explore the world around us through the use of GPS, story-telling, and writing.

My grandmother, mom, dad, brother, sister-in-law, and two nephews. They have seen my highs and lows during the process of writing this book and provided encouragement when I needed it most.

Also, it would be remiss if I didn't mention my dog Cooper, who has never been too far from me and my keyboard as I have written this book over many long nights and weekends.

Brian Youngblood

Table of Contents

Preface	**1**
Chapter 1: GIS Fundamentals	**7**
What is GIS about?	7
The foundation of any GIS – spatial data	8
Measuring the world	9
Projecting a sphere on a plane	10
Understanding coordinate systems	12
Commonly used coordinate systems	12
Universal Transverse Mercator system	12
Web Mercator	13
Spatial Reference Identifier (SRID)	13
Representing geometrical shapes	14
Modeling the real world with raster data	16
Representing the world	17
Time for action – exploring OpenStreetMap	20
Adding more colors to your maps	23
Choropleth maps	23
Proportional maps	25
Time for action – making your thematic map	26
Summary	29
Chapter 2: Getting Started with GeoServer	**31**
Installing Java	32
Time for action – checking the presence of Java on Windows	32
Time for action – checking the presence of Java on Ubuntu	34
Time for action – installing JRE on Windows	35
Time for action – installing JRE on Ubuntu	36
Installing Apache Tomcat	38
Time for action – installing Apache Tomcat on Windows	38

Time for action – installing Apache Tomcat on Ubuntu	**42**
Time for action – configuring Tomcat as a service on Ubuntu	**45**
Installing GeoServer	**48**
Time for action – deploying GeoServer on Tomcat	**49**
Implementing basic security	**51**
Time for action – improving security settings	**52**
Summary	**53**
Chapter 3: Exploring the Administrative Interface	**55**
Understanding the interface	**55**
About & Status	**57**
Server Status	57
Locks	58
Connections	58
Memory Usage	58
JVM Version and fonts	58
JAI usage and configurations	58
Update Sequence	58
Resource Cache	59
Configuration and catalog	59
GeoServer Logs	59
Contact Information	59
About	60
Time for action – manually reloading configuration	**60**
Data	**61**
Layer Preview	61
Time for action – OpenLayers preview	**62**
Time for action – KML preview	**63**
Workspaces	64
Time for action – creating a workspace	**65**
Stores	66
Layers	68
Layer groups	69
Styles	69
Services	**70**
WMS	71
Time for action – limiting the SRS list from WMS	**71**
WFS	73
WCS	73
Settings	**73**
Global	73
Verbose Reporting	73
Enable Global Services	74

Proxy Base URL 74
Logging Profile 74
Log to StdOut 74
Log location 74
Time for action – changing your logging configuration **74**
JAI 75
Tile Caching **76**
Security **76**
Settings 77
Users, Groups, and Roles 77
Data 78
Catalog security 78
Services security 79
Demos **79**
Time for action – exploring Demo requests **80**
SRS List 83
Time for action – filtering the projection list **83**
Summary **85**

Chapter 4: Accessing Layers **87**
Layer types **88**
OpenLayers **88**
Time for action – exploring OpenLayers options **89**
Working with tiles 90
Exploring the Web Map Service output formats **92**
AtomPub 92
GIF 92
GeoRSS 93
JPEG 94
KML (Plain) 94
KMZ (Compressed) 94
PDF 95
PNG 95
SVG 95
TIFF 95
Web Feature Service **96**
CSV 96
GML (plain text) 96
GML2 (compressed GZIP) 97
GeoJSON 97
Time for action – parsing GeoJSON **97**
Shapefile 98

Extra output options	**98**
GDAL and OGR output	99
TEXT/HTML	99
Time for action – using the GetFeatureInfo freemarker template	**99**
Using WMS Reflector	**101**
Time for action – using WMS Reflector	**102**
Summary	**103**
Chapter 5: Adding Your Data	**105**
Configuring your data	**105**
Configuring vector data sources	**106**
Adding a properties file	106
Configuring an external Web Feature Service	107
Adding shapefiles	107
Time for action – adding shapefiles	**107**
Using PostGIS	110
Time for action – installing PostgreSQL and PostGIS	**110**
Time for action – loading data in PostGIS and publishing them in GeoServer	**116**
Configuring raster data sources	**120**
ArcGrid	120
GeoTiff	120
Gtopo30	121
ImageMosaic	121
WorldImage	121
Configuring an external Web Map Service	121
Exploring additional data sources	**122**
Using Oracle	122
Time for action – adding Oracle support in GeoServer	**122**
Using MySQL	123
Time for action – adding MySQL data source	**124**
Summary	**126**
Chapter 6: Styling Your Layers	**127**
Understanding Styled Layer Descriptor	**127**
Editing styles	**128**
Exploring the standard structure of a style	**129**
Time for action – viewing GeoServer bundled styles	**130**
Loading data for styling	**133**
Working with point symbols	**134**
Time for action – creating a simple point style	**134**
Time for action – adding a stroke value	**137**

Time for action – dealing with angles and transparency   140
Time for action – composing simple shapes   141
Time for action – using external graphics   144
Linestring symbols   146
Time for action – creating a simple line style   146
Time for action – adding a border and a centerline   148
Time for action – using hatching   149
Time for action – using dashed lines   151
Time for action – mixing dashing lines and markers   153
Working with polygon symbols   155
Time for action – creating a simple polygon style   155
Time for action – using a graphic filling   157
Time for action – using hatching with polygons   158
Adding labels   160
Time for action – labeling points   161
Time for action – labeling lines   163
Time for action – labeling polygons   166
Thematic mapping   168
Time for action – classifying roads   169
Setting visibility   173
Time for action – enhancing thematic roads map   173
Putting it all together   175
Time for action – grouping layers   176
Summary   178

Chapter 7: Creating Simple Maps   **179**
Exploring Google Maps API   180
Time for action – adding a GeoServer layer as overlay   180
Time for action – adding a GeoServer layer as a base layer   185
Using pre-calculated maps   187
Time for action – adding a GeoServer cached layer as overlay   187
Time for action – customizing Google basemap   189
Interacting with the user   193
Time for action – intercepting the Click event   193
Using OpenLayers   196
Time for action – integrating GeoServer and OpenLayers   196
Time for action – using GeoRSS with OpenLayers   199
Exploring Leaflet   201
Time for action – using Leaflet with GeoServer layers   201
Summary   203

Chapter 8: Performance and Caching   205

Exploring GeoWebCache   206
Time for action – configuring GeoWebCache storage   206
Time for action – configuring Disk Quota   209
Setting caching defaults   212
    Direct integration   212
    WMS-C   212
    TMS and WMTS   213
    Default layers options   213
    Default Cached Gridsets   214
Configuring gridsets   215
Time for action – creating a custom gridset   215
Configuring tile layers   218
Time for action – configuring layers and layer groups for caching   219
Time for action – using tiles with OpenLayers   221
Time for action – seeding a layer   227
Using an external GeoWebCache   231
Summary   233

Chapter 9: Automating Tasks: GeoServer REST Interface   235

Introducing REST   236
Using REST   236
Time for action – installing the Requests library   237
Managing data   238
    Working with workspaces and namespaces   238
Time for action – managing workspaces   239
    Using data stores   246
Time for action – managing data stores   246
    Using feature types   252
Time for action – adding a new shapefile   254
Time for action – adding a PostGIS table   256
Publishing data   260
    Working with styles   260
Time for action – adding a new style   260
    Working with layers   261
Time for action – managing layers   262
Summary   265

Chapter 10: Securing GeoServer Before Production   267
Basic security settings   268
Time for action – enabling strong encryption   269
Time for action – changing the master password   270
Defining users, groups, and roles   271
    User definition   272
    Group definition   272
    User/group services   272
    Roles definition   272
Time for action – creating users and groups   272
Time for action – defining roles   276
Accessing data and services   277
Time for action – securing layers   278
Summary   284

Chapter 11: Tuning GeoServer in a Production Environment   285
Tuning Java   286
Time for action – configuring Java runtime parameters   286
Time for action – installing native JAI   288
Removing unused services   291
Time for action – disabling unused services   291
Setting a proxy   292
Time for action – configuring a proxy   293
Avoiding service faults   295
Time for action – configuring a cluster   297
Summary   303

Chapter 12: Going Further: Getting Help and Troubleshooting   305
Going beyond maps   305
    Delivering vector data   306
Time for action – retrieving vector data   306
    Delivering raster data   310
Time for action – retrieving raster data   310
Getting help   312
Summary   314

Appendix: Pop Quiz Answers   315

Index   319

Preface

Nowadays, web mapping is all over the Internet. User friendly-interfaces and efficiency are mandatory requirements for GIS, as for any other system. If you are going to start a new web mapping application, you will not start from scratch. GeoServer is one of the biggest players in the web mapping field. It has a solid developer community and a high maturity level. Although it's not an easy piece of software to master, the latest releases have greatly improved stability and ease of management.

GeoServer Beginner's Guide offers you a practical introduction to GeoServer. Beginning with the installation and basic usage, you will learn to use the administration interface for adding data, configuring layers, customizing OGC services, and securing your site. You will find included lots of step-by-step examples, covering topics from data store configuration to layer publication and style customization. If all this sounds new and strange to you, don't worry; *GeoServer Beginner's Guide* will introduce you to the fundamentals of GIS and will then clearly explain all the basic tasks performed in order to build maps.

This book is meant to expand your knowledge of web mapping from something you have either heard of or have practised a little, into something you can apply at any level to meet your needs in incorporate maps for a site. I hope you will enjoy reading this book as much as I did writing it.

What this book covers

Chapter 1, GIS Fundamentals, introduces you to GIS concepts. It guides you through spatial data types and maps. You will discover how spatial information is stored and how to set up a map. You may want to skip this chapter if you already have a solid background in GIS.

Chapter 2, Getting Started with GeoServer, guides you in setting up your first GeoServer instance. It shows you, step by step, how to download the most recent version of the software and its requirements, that is, JAVA and a servlet container. For each component, a detailed description about how to install it is included.

Chapter 3, Exploring the Administrative Interface, covers GeoServer's web administration interface. It explains how to log in and access each section. You will familiarize yourself with data configuration following a common workflow that starts by adding data to GeoServer and guides you through to publication. Included in this chapter are screen captures that define the main areas of the program and menu items—all of which is very helpful when accessing the interface for the first time.

Chapter 4, Accessing Layers, guides you through data publication. The chapter covers in detail all output types offered by GeoServer for your data. Raster formats such as JPEG and PNG are discussed for maps, while vector formats such as GeoRSS and GEOJSON are explained for vector output. We will also explore OpenLayers, a JavaScript framework that GeoServer includes in its output format, when you want to serve your data as an application.

Chapter 5, Adding Your Data, demonstrates how you can configure data in GeoServer. The examples included will show you how to add and publish shapefiles and PostGIS tables, two of the most common formats, which are also natively supported by GeoServer. The extensions for Oracle and MySQL are also discussed.

Chapter 6, Styling Your Layers, explains how to apply styles to your layers. Styles let you render your data according to attributes, in order to build pretty maps. SLD's syntax, the standard for data rendering, will be explained in detail, with examples for different geometry types such as point, polyline, and polygons. The chapter also illustrates how to build scale-dependent symbology and how to compose different rendering in a group, to mimic a map in WMS.

Chapter 7, Building a Simple Map for Your Site Using OpenLayers, Google Maps, and Your Geospatial Data, describes how to build client applications with the JavaScript framework. JavaScript is a powerful and widespread language and, unsurprisingly, it is one of the best choices when developing a web application. We will build some sample maps using Google Maps API, OpenLayers, and Leaflet.

Chapter 8, Performance and Caching, covers the use of integrated GeoWebCache. Caching maps is a common strategy with map servers; it allows you to serve pretty complex maps without running out of resources. The GeoServer 2.2 release introduces a great change: you can fully administer the integrated GeoWebCache from the web admin interface. In the examples included, you will configure cache with different strategies, optimizing performance, or disk usage.

Chapter 9, Automating Tasks: GeoServer REST Interface, explains how to control the GeoServer configuration from a remote location through the REST interface. This may prove a great help if you have to administer a GeoServer site without the possibility of using the web admin interface, or if you want to automatize, in an external procedure, some admin tasks. The included examples will let you add data, configure styles and layers, and publish them. All the operations are demonstrated with Python and cURL syntaxes.

Chapter 10, Securing GeoServer Before Production, covers the GeoServer security module. The chapter first discusses general configuration for security, that is, password encryption, and then the security model is explained. A case history shows you how to create a configuration where different users are in charge of administration, editing, and publication tasks.

Chapter 11, Tuning GeoServer in a Production Environment, explains the advanced considerations for running a successful GeoServer site. It covers Java Runtime tuning and data and services optimization. Finally, a high availability configuration is detailed, with instructions for configuring a balanced GeoServer installation.

Chapter 12, Going Further: Getting Help and Troubleshooting, shows you how to access community tools and help for going further than what you will learn from this book. It also covers a concise introduction to other data publication standards implemented in GeoServer, WCS, and WFS. With WCS and WFS, you can serve vector and raster data to clients that not only need to show a map but have to perform some processing on the data.

What you need for this book

Installation and download instructions are described for all the software packages you will need. You just need to have access to a computer with an online connection for downloading packages. The instructions cover both Linux and Windows operating systems, so you may select the one you prefer.

All the software used in this book is freely available, most of the time as an open source project. Hardware requirements for development purposes are not very high. A relatively modern laptop or desktop will be enough for running examples. Source code and data used in this book are freely available on the Packt Publishing site.

Who this book is for

If you are going to use maps on your site, incorporate spatial data in a desktop application, or you are just curious about web mapping, this book offers you a fast-paced and practical introduction.

Particularly if you need to develop a web application supporting maps, you will find that GeoServer is one of the best solutions you can choose.

Analysts will discover how GIS works and how it can be integrated in complex systems. System administrators may also find this book useful for planning installation, tuning, and maintenance.

Conventions

In this book, you will find several headings appearing frequently.

To give clear instructions of how to complete a procedure or task, we use:

Time for action – heading

1. Action 1
2. Action 2
3. Action 3

Instructions often need some extra explanation so that they make sense, so they are followed with:

What just happened?

This heading explains the working of tasks or instructions that you have just completed.

You will also find some other learning aids in the book, including:

Pop quiz – heading

These are short multiple-choice questions intended to help you test your own understanding.

Have a go hero – heading

These practical challenges and give you ideas for experimenting with what you have learned.

You will also find a number of styles of text that distinguish between different kinds of information. Here are some examples of these styles, and an explanation of their meaning.

Code words in text are shown as follows: "Get the `6686_05_mysql_usacounties.sql.zip` file and unzip it. Create a new database in MySQL. Call it `geoserver`."

A block of code is set as follows:

```
_=id:Integer,code:String,name:String,country:Geometry:srid=4326
places.1=1|Rome|Italy|POINT(12.492 41.890)
places.2=2|Grand Canyon|Usa|POINT(-112.122 36.055)
places.3=3|Paris|France|POINT(2.294 48.858)
places.4=4|Iguazu National Park|Argentina|POINT(-54.442 -25.688)
places.5=5|Ayers Rock|Australia|POINT(131.036 -25.345)
```

New terms and **important words** are shown in bold. Words that you see on the screen, in menus or dialog boxes for example, appear in the text like this: "Start Tomcat service and then log in to the GeoServer administration interface. Go to the **Data | Stores** section and click on **Add new store**. You can now see some new options. Select **MySQL**".

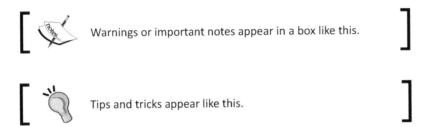

> Warnings or important notes appear in a box like this.

> Tips and tricks appear like this.

Reader feedback

Feedback from our readers is always welcome. Let us know what you think about this book—what you liked or may have disliked. Reader feedback is important for us to develop titles that you really get the most out of.

To send us general feedback, simply send an e-mail to feedback@packtpub.com, and mention the book title through the subject of your message.

If there is a topic that you have expertise in and you are interested in either writing or contributing to a book, see our author guide on www.packtpub.com/authors.

Customer support

Now that you are the proud owner of a Packt book, we have a number of things to help you to get the most from your purchase.

Downloading the example code

You can download the example code files for all Packt books you have purchased from your account at http://www.packtpub.com. If you purchased this book elsewhere, you can visit http://www.packtpub.com/support and register to have the files e-mailed directly to you.

Downloading the color images of this book

We also provide you a PDF file that has color images of the screenshots/diagrams used in this book. The color images will help you better understand the changes in the output. You can download this file from `http://www.packtpub.com/sites/default/files/downloads/6686OS_Graphics.pdf`.

Errata

Although we have taken every care to ensure the accuracy of our content, mistakes do happen. If you find a mistake in one of our books—maybe a mistake in the text or the code—we would be grateful if you would report this to us. By doing so, you can save other readers from frustration and help us improve subsequent versions of this book. If you find any errata, please report them by visiting `http://www.packtpub.com/submit-errata`, selecting your book, clicking on the **errata submission form** link, and entering the details of your errata. Once your errata are verified, your submission will be accepted and the errata will be uploaded to our website, or added to any list of existing errata, under the Errata section of that title.

Piracy

Piracy of copyright material on the Internet is an ongoing problem across all media. At Packt, we take the protection of our copyright and licenses very seriously. If you come across any illegal copies of our works, in any form, on the Internet, please provide us with the location address or website name immediately so that we can pursue a remedy.

Please contact us at `copyright@packtpub.com` with a link to the suspected pirated material.

We appreciate your help in protecting our authors, and our ability to bring you valuable content.

Questions

You can contact us at `questions@packtpub.com` if you are having a problem with any aspect of the book, and we will do our best to address it.

1
GIS Fundamentals

In this chapter, you will learn the foundation of geographical information system and spatial data. Although you do not need to understand these subjects in great depth to take advantage of the features of GeoServer, we will give you the basic information required to understand what you will be doing in the book. You will be introduced to the magic of spatial.

We are going to cover the following topics:

◆ Why is spatial data special?

◆ Spatial data formats.

◆ The magical world of **Spatial Reference System (SRS)**: getting a sphere on a plane.

◆ What is a map and why does it matter?

◆ The art of **Cartography**. Building map types such as Choropleth and Proportional Symbol.

By the end of the chapter, you will have the basic skills to identify which spatial data format best suits your needs.

What is GIS about?

Since you were a kid at school you have been exposed to a lot of maps. Maps of countries, where you spent hours memorizing the boundaries, rivers, and capitals; historical maps, with the rise and fall of ancient empires, where you dreamed of being a great conqueror; economics maps, with the locations and amounts of goods and services. Every day on newspapers, on TV, or in a far more accurate presentation, in books and academic papers you look at data represented on a map. Maps are a spatial representation of data and are often the main output of a GIS.

GIS is an acronym for **Geographical Information System**. Does it sounds too complicated to you? Don't be afraid; it is not so different from many other systems for managing information you probably already know. The main difference is in the spatial piece of information. All the data contained in a GIS has a spatial dimension or a link to another object with spatial attributes.

So what is GIS? In a nutshell, we can define it as a system to acquire and store data, to process data, and to produce data representations, that is, maps. In this book you will learn that working with GeoServer requires you to prepare your data, process it to render in a beautiful map, and build up a set of functions that enable a user to interact with your data. So building up a GeoServer instance may be described as GIS-building.

A detailed comprehension of GIS is far beyond the scope of this book and it is not required for starting with GeoServer. But you need to have some basic skills in spatial data, maps, and spatial reference systems.

Let's go; we are going to turn you into a neo-cartographer!

The foundation of any GIS – spatial data

If you have ever built a simple map to annotate your hiking on mountains or to send driving directions to your girlfriend or boyfriend, you have dealt with spatial data.

Spatial data is the foundation of any GIS. You know that a building is likely to fall down unless it is sitting atop a strong foundation. So you need to understand spatial data or you will be producing poor map output.

But what is spatial data in simple words? From a general point of view you can consider a piece of spatial information. Each description of an object contains a reference to its position on the Earth's surface. Well, that is not a rigorous formal definition as there are a lot of objects below and over the earth's surface, but for now we are fine with this simplistic definition.

Think of some lists of familiar objects:

- A list of bookshops with addresses
- A list of places you visited during your trips
- A list of points of interest, for example, restaurants, museums, and hotels, you collected with your mobile phone
- An aerial photo with a view of a city, where you can recognize notable places

You can say where each element is located in a more or less precise way. They are real objects represented with spatial data. As you may have noted, the spatial information is represented in quite a heterogeneous way. Most people are able to recognize spatial information in any group from the previous list. Unfortunately, GIS software and GeoServer are an exception to this and tend to prefer a strong structured piece of information. If you are going to use your spatial data with GeoServer, you need to organize it more accurately. We will talk specifically about GeoServer's data connectors in *Chapter 5, Adding Your Own DataStore*, but for now it is important that you understand how spatial data is commonly organized and stored. As you keep on making maps, you will deal with lots of different spatial data.

Measuring the world

So spatial data are references for an object's position on the earth's surface. How can you measure and store them in a numeric format? An elementary model of the earth could be a sphere. On a sphere's surface, you can measure positions with angular units called latitude and longitude. **Latitude** (φ) measures the angle between the equatorial plane and a line that passes through that point and is normal to the surface; whereas **longitude** (λ) measures the angle east or west from a reference meridian (for example, that passing through Greenwich observatory) to another meridian that passes through that point. Angular measures can be expressed in digital degrees or in degrees, minutes, and seconds.

If you want to store the location of The Statue of Liberty, you can express it as Lat. 40° 41' 21" N, Long. 74° 2' 40" W with degrees, minutes, and seconds or as 40.689167, -74.044444 using decimal degrees.

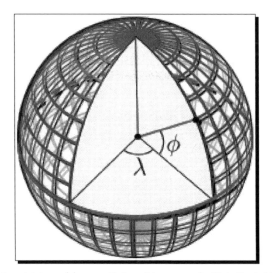

(Image from http://en.wikipedia.org/wiki/Latitude)

We normally think of earth as a sphere but this is not its real shape. Geodesy, the science of studying the earth's shape, defines earth as represented by a **geoid**, an ideal surface defined by the level of sea if oceans would cover the entire earth. For practical purposes, as in projections, geoid is too complicated to use and the earth's shape is defined by an **ellipsoid**. The ellipsoid is described by its semi-major axis (equatorial radius) and flattening.

Have a go hero – move around the planet with decimal degree coordinates

Does it sound a little bit complicated? Don't be afraid and explore locations on earth with Lat. Long. coordinates. In the following table, there are a few famous places with coordinates in decimal degrees. Point your browser to `http://maps.google.com`, insert coordinates in the search textbox, and then press *Enter*. Your map will be panned to the location. Google maps enable you to query for coordinates of any place on earth; find that function and look for some great places.

Rome, Italy	41.890, 12.492
Colorado Grand Canyon, USA	36.055, -112.122
Paris, France	48.858, 2.294
Iguazú National Park, Argentina	-25.688, -54.442
Ayers Rock, Australia	-25.345, 131.036

Projecting a sphere on a plane

Did you ever play with an orange peel? I did it a lot when I was a child, often pressing them in the hope to flatten it almost perfectly. It's a hopeless challenge, but kids are stubborn and ambitious. Many years later I found a similar analogy in a geography book. It was talking about cartographic projection and used an orange as a model of the earth. If you think of the orange's peel as the earth surface, it is suddenly clear why you can't have a planar representation of the earth's surface without a great amount of distortion.

All the maps you will ever find are on a plain paper sheet. Curved digital screens are quite uncommon in GeoGeek's nests. So how do cartographers represent a curved surface on a plain? This is done by means of a mathematical operation called **projection**.

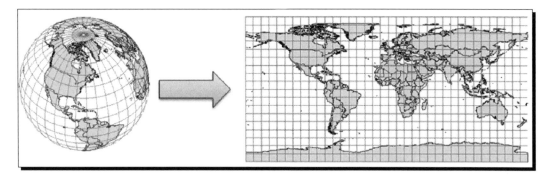

Indeed, there are several different projections developed in the last few centuries by cartographers and mathematicians. There is no mathematical method to transfer a sphere or an ellipsoid to a two-dimensional space without distortion. Hence, projections modify the data and include some deformations about lengths, areas, or shapes you can observe and measure on maps.

We can classify projections according to the geographical features and properties they preserve:

- Conformal projections preserve angles locally. Meridian and parallels intersect at 90-degree angles.

- Equal Area projections preserve proportions between areas. In a map with equal area projections, each part has the same proportional area as the corresponding part of the earth.

- Equidistant projections maintain a scale along one or more lines, or from one or two points to all other points on the map. Lines along which the scale (distance) is correct, are of the same proportional length as the lines they reference on the globe.

It is important that you understand there is no best projection; choosing one for your map is a trade-off. According to the portion of the earth's surface, the map that you are designing will contain and/or use the projections that suit best. Let's explore some widely-used projections.

Understanding coordinate systems

You learned about the earth's shape and about projection. Coordinate systems use these concepts to build a frame of reference to place objects on the earth's surface. There are two types of coordinate systems: projected coordinate systems and geographic coordinate systems.

- **Geographic coordinate systems** use latitude and longitude as angles measured from the earth's centre, as we saw previously. A geographic coordinate system is substantially defined by the ellipsoid used to model the earth, and the position of the ellipsoid positioned relatively to the centre of the earth (called **datum**).

- A **projected coordinate system** is defined on a flat two-dimensional surface. A projected coordinate system is always based on a geographic coordinate system, hence it uses an ellipsoid and a datum. Besides, a projected corporate systems includes a projection method to project coordinates from the earth's spherical surface onto a two-dimensional Cartesian coordinate plane.

Commonly used coordinate systems

Although there are hundreds of different projections, you can limit your knowledge to some which are widely used.

Universal Transverse Mercator system

Commonly known as **UTM**, this is not really a projection. It is a system based on **Transverse Mercator** projection. This projection uses a cylinder tangent to a meridian to unwarp the earth's surface. A maximum of 5° of distortion from the central meridian is acceptable. The UTM splits the world into a series of 6° of longitudinal wide zones. As you may guess, there are 60 zones numbered from Long. 180W towards the east. Please note that you can't have a map representing more than one UTM zone. Indeed, UTM is well suited for big-scale maps.

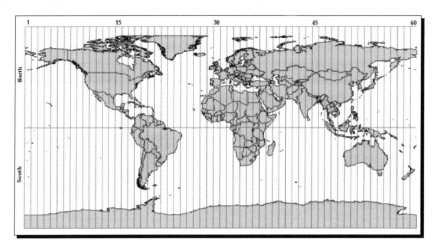

Web Mercator

Web Mercator is a projection derived from Transverse Mercator. It maps ellipsoidal latitude and longitude coordinates onto a plane using spherical Mercator equations. This projection was popularized by **Google** in **Google Maps** and it is now widely used on online mapping systems. It stretches areas in a north-south direction and, unlike the Transverse Mercator, it is not conformal.

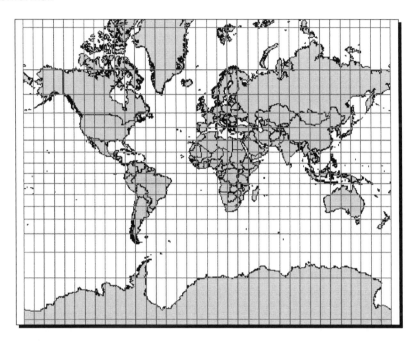

Spatial Reference Identifier (SRID)

A spatial reference system identifier is a code to easily reference a **spatial reference system** (**SRS**). An SRS contains parameters about projection, ellipsoid, and datum. It can be defined using the OGC's **well-known text** (**WKT**) representation. The SRS for the geographic WGS84 reference system is as follows:

```
GEOGCS["WGS 84",
    DATUM["WGS_1984",
        SPHEROID["WGS 84",6378137,298.257223563,
            AUTHORITY["EPSG","7030"]],
        AUTHORITY["EPSG","6326"]],
    PRIMEM["Greenwich",0,
        AUTHORITY["EPSG","8901"]],
    UNIT["degree",0.01745329251994328,
        AUTHORITY["EPSG","9122"]],
    AUTHORITY["EPSG","4326"]]
```

The last line contains the number 4326; this is the SRID uniquely identifying this SRS. The long form should also contain the authority, that is EPSG:4326, but you will often find it indicated only by the number.

 EPSG is the acronym for **European Petroleum Survey Group**. It was founded in 1986 by several European Oil companies to collect and maintain geodetic information. In 2005, EPSG was absorbed by OGP (an international forum of Oil and Gas producers) which formed the OGP Geomatics Committee. The committee maintains the registry and publishes it as a public web interface or a downloadable database.

It is very important that you know which is your data's SRID. Without it you can't represent data on a map without the risk of great errors.

Have a go hero – explore EPSG registry

We described a couple of common and widely used SRSs, but there are a lot of them. There are several archives on the Internet where you can find detailed information about SRSs and their elements, that is ellipsoids, datums, unit of measurements, projected, or geographic reference systems. One of the most authoritative and complete data sets is the EPSG Geodetic Parameter Registry. If you are curious about it, you can open your browser and point it to http://epsg-registry.org. Then try a simple search by inserting a location name in the **Area** textbox:

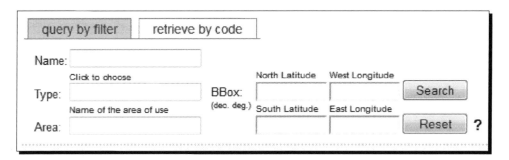

Representing geometrical shapes

You learned how to calculate coordinates on the earth's surface. But how can you represent a real object, for example, a river, in a convenient way for a GIS?

There are two main approaches when building a spatial database, modeling **vector data** or **raster data**. Vector data uses a set of discrete locations to build basic geometrical shapes, such as points, polylines, and polygons.

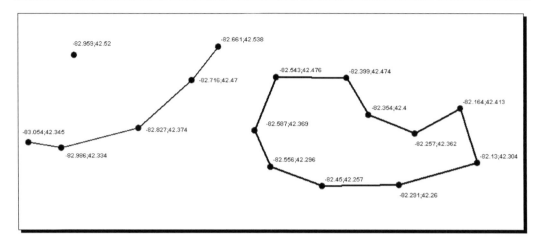

Of course real objects are neither a point, nor a polyline or a polygon. In your model you have to decide which basic shape better suits the real object. For example, a town can be represented as a point if you are going to draw a map of the world with the countries' capitals shown. On the other hand, if you are going to publish a counties map, a polygon will enable you to draw the city boundaries to give a more realistic representation.

The simpler geometric object is a point. Points are defined as single coordinate pairs (x,y) when we work in two-dimensional space or coordinate triplets (x,y,z) if you want to take account of the eight coordinates. In the following examples, we use point features to store the location of active volcanoes:

```
Etna; 37.763; 14.993
Krakatoa; -6.102; 105.423
Aconcagua; -32.653; -70.011
Kilimanjaro; -3.065; 37.358
```

Did you guess the units and projections used? The coordinates are in decimal degrees and SRS is WGS84 geographic, that is EPSG:4326.

Points are simple to understand but don't give you many details about the spatial extent of an object. If you want to store rivers you need more than a coordinate pair. Indeed, you have to memorize an array of coordinate pairs for each feature in a structure called **polyline**:

```
Colorado; (40.472 -105.826, … , 31.901 -114.951)
Nile; (-2.282 29.331, … , 30.167 31.101)
Danube; (48.096 8.155, … ,45.218 29.761)
```

If you need to model an areal feature such as an island, you can extend the polyline object adding the constraint that it must be closed; that is the first and the last coordinate pairs must be coincident:

```
Ellis Island; (-74.043 40.699, -74.041 40.700, -74.040 40.700, -74.040
40.701, -74.037 40.699, -74.038 40.699, -74.038 40.698, -74.039
40.698, -74.041 40.700, -74.042 40.699, -74.040 40.698, -74.042
40.696, -74.044 40.698, -74.043 40.699)
```

> The feature model used in GIS is a little bit more complex than what we have discussed. There are some more constraints regarding vertex ordering, line intersections, and areal shapes with holes. Different GIS specified several different set of rules, often in proprietary formats. **Open Geospatial Consortium (OGC)** defined a standard for simple features, and lately most systems, open source in primis, are compliant with it. If you are curious about it, you can point your browser at http://www.opengeospatial.org/standards/is and look for The OpenGIS® Simple Features Interface Standard.

Modeling the real world with raster data

Raster data uses a regular tessellation, defining cells where one or more values are uniform. Usually the cells are square, although this is not a constraint. Raster data is generally used to represent value continuously changing in the space, that is, a field. You can use a regular tessellation to build a digital elevation model of the earth's surface. In the following figure, each cell has a height and width of 20 meters and the value stored is the height over the sea level in meters:

80	74	62	45	45	34	39	56
80	74	74	62	45	34	39	56
74	74	62	62	45	34	39	39
62	62	45	45	34	34	34	39
45	45	45	34	34	30	34	39

Can you use raster data to model real features like a river? Yes, you can, but there are some drawbacks you have to consider. The following figure shows a linear feature represented as vector data (the red line) and as raster data (the black and white cells). If your purpose is drawing the shapes on a map, raster data is not a good choice as raster graphics are resolution-dependent. They cannot scale up to an arbitrary resolution without the apparent loss of quality.

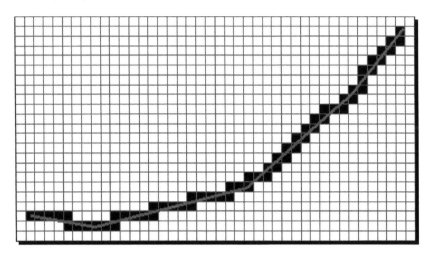

Representing the world

In the previous sections, we explored spatial data and SRS. They are the key elements you need to build your map. Indeed, maps are planar representation of spatial data. You need to collect the appropriate data to represent the real objects you want to include in your map and you need to choose an SRS to organize your data into the map.

Keep in mind that maps are representations, a proposition of yours. They are the way you express your knowledge and your vision of the world. To fully accomplish this, there is a third basic ingredient for your map: symbols.

Symbols enable you to add information to the features shown on a map. For example, colors can be used to indicate a classification of roads. Imagine you need to produce a map of a country with a road network. You have a vector data set containing road polylines. A simple approach is to render all features with the same symbol, as shown in following figure. The map is not really informative unless you are a transportation expert. You won't extract any information from the map and it looks ugly too.

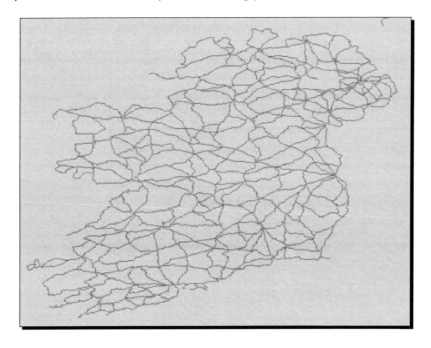

Lets have a look at a similar map produced with **ArcGIS Online** (http://www.esri.com/software/arcgis/arcgisonline).

It contains the road network symbolized with different colors and line widths, labels showing you highway codes, major towns represented with small circles and labels. Besides, there is a background depicting heights with colors and shading. Does it now look more familiar to you?

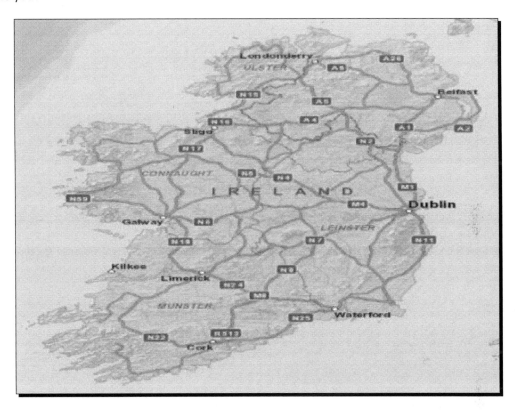

In *Chapter 6*, *Styling Your Layers*, we will learn how to apply symbols in GeoServer to produce maps like the previous one. For now you need to familiarize yourself with simple and thematic maps.

Time for action – exploring OpenStreetMap

Are you ready to explore some nice maps? We are going to navigate through a great bunch of spatial data, **OpenStreetMap**.

1. Open your browser and go to `http://www.openstreetmap.org`.

2. The website offers you a small scale map centered on your actual location, as derived from browser information.

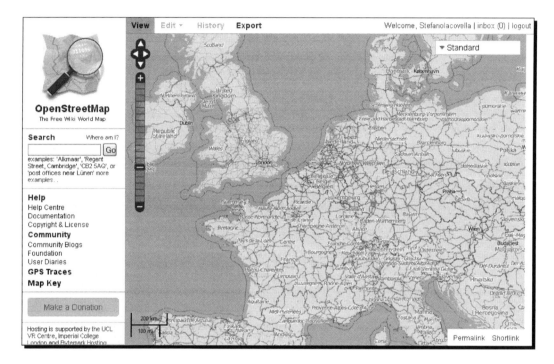

3. Center your map on London, UK and zoom in with the tool shown on the left-hand side. You can see that many more road types and locations are now shown in the map:

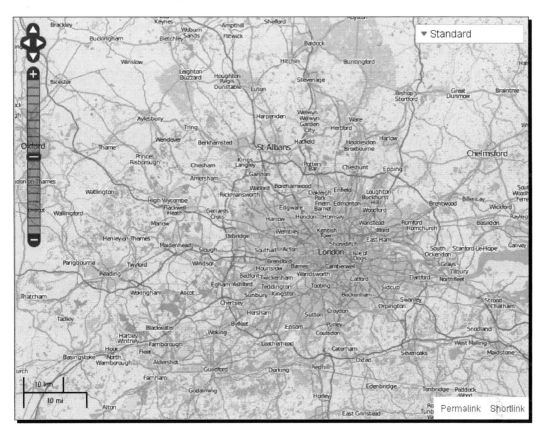

4. Now enter the **Piccadilly Circus, London, UK** address in the **Search** textbox on the left and press the **Go** button. A list of results matching your search is presented on the left side of the map. Pick the first item:

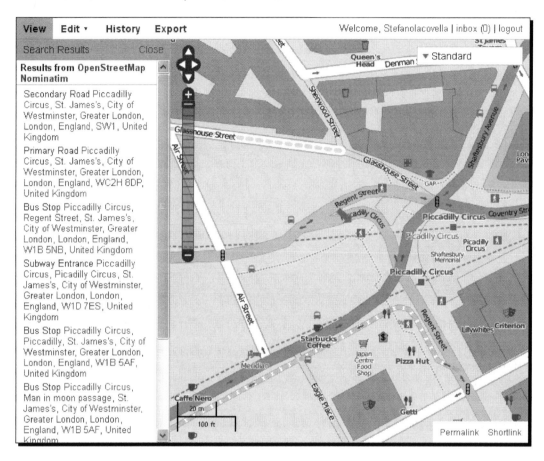

5. The map is now at a great scale (look at the scalebar on the bottom-left angle) and the symbols are changed to show you greater detailed information about roads and locations. You can find street names, directions for car traffic, buildings' footprint, and icons for points of interest. The general look and feel resembles a printed city map you can pick up at tourist offices.

OpenStreetMap does not require you to register for browsing or exporting the data. Anyway, if you are interested in maps and open source data, you may consider getting involved in the project. OSM is a collaborative project to create a free editable map of the world, currently involving over half a million users all around the world. You may add data or find errors on locations you know well.

What just happened?

You explored several maps representing the same data set in quite different ways. Different symbols and hiding subsets of data are powerful tools to produce clear and nice looking maps. You are now ready to discover a different kind of map.

Adding more colors to your maps

The maps we encountered so far are often defined as general maps. General maps focus on the description of the physical, political, and human features on the territory. All this data is portrayed for its own sake. In a nutshell, it can be said that general maps tell you where objects are located in space, while thematic maps talk about things happening in the space. Thematic maps focus on displaying a single topic and portray spatial distribution and variation. You have general data like administrative boundaries or road networks, but this is represented as a base layer for general reference.

Among thematic maps, those using choropleth or dot representations are by far the most common type you will be using GeoServer for.

Choropleth maps

Choropleth maps show statistical data aggregated over predefined regions, such as counties or states, by coloring or shading these regions. You can draw states according to their population, gross domestic product, car owners, and the number of national parks. You are not limited to a single variable; indeed you can merge different values from more than one attribute associated to spatial objects.

The following figure shows a map of European countries colored according to gross domestic product values. **Legend** on the right shows the five classification intervals. Values were normalized to Eu-27 average.

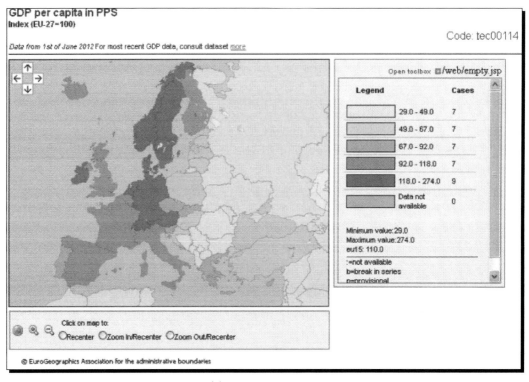

(Courtesy of http://epp.eurostat.ec.europa.eu)

Proportional maps

In proportional maps, symbols of different sizes represent data associated with different areas or locations within the map. As an example, the countries' capitals can be represented with a circle proportional to their population.

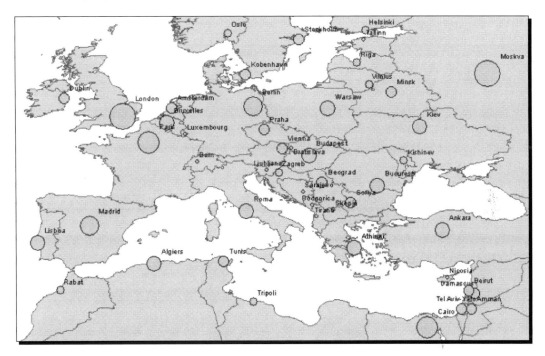

Time for action – making your thematic map

Are you ready for building maps? We can do this without GeoServer; indeed we will install it in the next chapter. For now, you will play with an online map engine and **Google Earth** to try your understanding of thematic maps concepts.

> *1.* Point your browser to `http://thematicmapping.org/engine/`.
>
> *2.* Choose a statistical **Indicator** from the drop-down list, that is, **CO2 emissions**, then select **Year** as **2004**. Leave all other values as the proposed defaults.

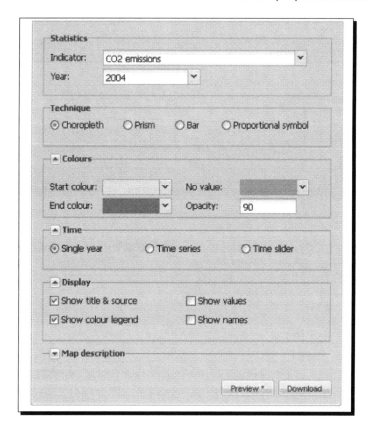

3. Select the **Preview** button; a pop up will show you a **Google earth** plugin with countries rendered in different colors according to CO2 emissions in world countries.

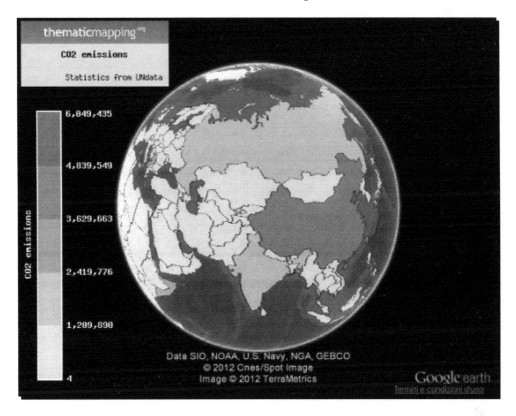

4. Now try a proportional symbol map. Select **Mobile phone subscribers per 100 inhabitants** as **Indicator** and **2006** as **Year**. Choose **Proportional symbol** for **Technique** and **Regular polygon** as **symbol style**. Select **circle** from the drop-down list. Leave the default colors unchanged and select **Equal intervals** for **classification**.

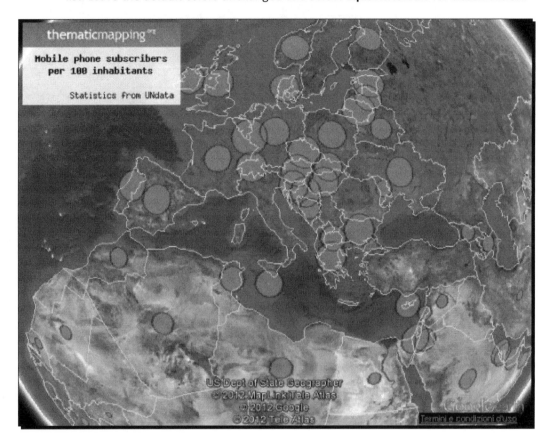

What just happened?

You built a couple of thematic maps selecting data, symbol size, and color. You will need to set exactly these parameters in GeoServer to produce beautiful maps. This time we did it without exploring the technical details behind features rendering. In *Chapter 6, Styling Your Layers*, you will learn how to use **SLD** (**styled layer descriptor**) to make thematic maps.

Summary

We had a brief but complete introduction to spatial data and maps in this chapter. It was somewhat a theoretical chapter, but we promise you it was the first and last of this kind! From now on, we are going to run real stuff with GeoServer.

Specifically, you learned how an object is referenced to its location, which storage models you can use with spatial data (for example, vector versus raster), and eventually you learned to represent spatial features in a map.

We are now ready to pick up GeoServer, unpack, and install it on your computer.

2
Getting Started with GeoServer

Congratulations on your choice to take your data to the world with GeoServer. GeoServer can be installed on many different operating systems, since it's a Java application. You can run it on any kind of operating system for which exists a Java virtual machine. It takes advantage of multi-threaded operations, and supports 64-bit modern operating systems.

This chapter will cover, in detail, the steps that will bring you to a successful installation. Though we will explain the whole process in detail, don't be afraid. As soon as you finish reading it, you will have your running copy of GeoServer. The steps will be illustrated in two scenarios, an Ubuntu 12.04 machine and a Windows 7 machine. We chose these two as they cover the majority of users. Besides Ubuntu being a Debian derivative, the installation process can be easily reproduced on other similar distributions, for example, Debian or Linux Mint.

We'll talk about the advanced settings most useful in taking your configuration to a production environment in *Chapter 10, Securing Your GeoServer Before Production*, and *Chapter 11, GeoServer in a Production Environment*.

In this chapter we're going to cover the following topics:

- ◆ System requirements
- ◆ Obtaining GeoServer (latest 2.2.0)
- ◆ Installation on Ubuntu Linux
- ◆ Installation on Windows 7
- ◆ OS independent installation
- ◆ Basic security measures by changing the default username and password

Installing Java

GeoServer is a Java application. So, we need to ensure that you have it installed and properly working on your machine, but you don't need to know how to write Java™ to install or to get started using GeoServer.

There are two main packages of Java. Depending on what you are planning to do with Java, you may want to install a **JDK (Java Development Kit)** or **JRE (Java Runtime Environment)**. The former enables you to compile Java™ code, while the latter has all you need to run most Java applications.

Starting from release 2.0, GeoServer does not need a full JDK installation and you can go safely with JRE. It works well with Java 6 but as Java 7 is not deeply tested by developers, it should work but you may experience minor issues. Unless you have some strong reasons to use Java 7, you should use JRE 6.

In the 90s, Java development was started by Sun Microsystems. Sun has developed each new release until it merged into Oracle Corporation. While Oracle did not change the Java license to a commercial one, there are some license issues (maybe it would be worthy to add some reference here) preventing Oracle Java™ from being available on an Ubuntu repository.

On Ubuntu current releases, you will find **OpenJDK** already installed in the desktop edition; in the server, you need to choose it at setup. While there are a few users running GeoServer on OpenJDK with no issues, the developers community does not test it intensively and hence you can expect some performance loss.

Oracle Java™ should be your first choice unless you have some specific issues. In the following steps, we will use Oracle Java™ JRE. If your installation machine is a new one, then chances are that there is no Java runtime pre-installed. Let's check.

Time for action – checking the presence of Java on Windows

We will verify the presence of a JRE/JDK installation on Windows, using the following steps:

1. From the **Start** menu, select **Control Panel**.

2. Then select **Programs**. If your system has a JRE/JDK installed, you should see an icon with the **Java** logo as shown in the following screenshot. It is a shortcut to the Java control panel.

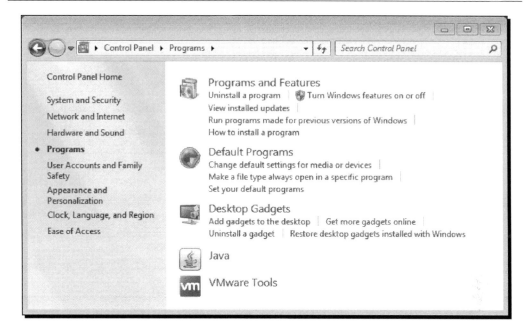

3. Open the Java control panel and select the Java tab. Here you will find settings for JRE. Press the **Show Me** button to visualize the installed release and the installation folder.

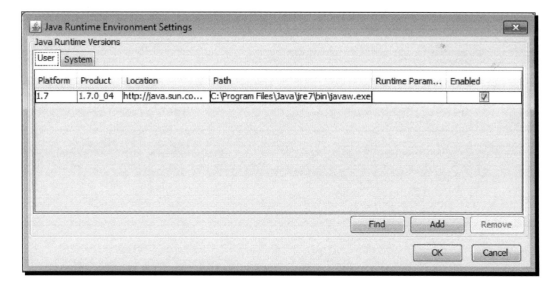

What just happened?

You checked for the presence of Java on your computer. In case you didn't find it, we are going to install it in the next section. (If you did find it, skip to the *Installing Apache Tomcat* section.)

Time for action – checking the presence of Java on Ubuntu

We will check JRE/JDK installation from the command line.

1. Log in to your server and run this command:

   ```
   ~ $ sudo update-alternatives --config java
   ```

2. If there is no Java properly configured you should see an output like the following:

   ```
   update-alternatives: error: no alternatives for java.
   ```

3. In case there is one or more Java installed the output will be similar to:

   ```
   There is only one alternative in link group java: /usr/lib/jvm/
   java-7-openjdk-amd64/jre/bin/java
   Nothing to configure.
   ```

   Or:

   ```
   There are 2 choices for the alternative java (providing /usr/bin/
   java).


   Selection Path Priority Status
   _____

   * 0 /usr/lib/jvm/java-6-openjdk/jre/bin/java 1061 auto mode
   1 /usr/lib/jvm/java-6-openjdk/jre/bin/java 1061 manual mode
   2 /usr/lib/jvm/java-6-sun/jre/bin/java 63 manual mode


   Press enter to keep the current choice[*], or type selection
   number:
   ```

What just happened?

We determined if a Java installation is already present on our machine. This is a basic requirement for our installation. We had the opportunity to check if the installed release, in case we found it, is suitable for running GeoServer.

Now we will go through the installation of JRE.

Time for action – installing JRE on Windows

We will install Oracle JRE 1.6. We are assuming that you didn't find any previous Java installation.

1. Navigate to the **Downloads** tab at `http://www.oracle.com/technetwork/java/javase/downloads/jre6u37-downloads-1859589.html`.

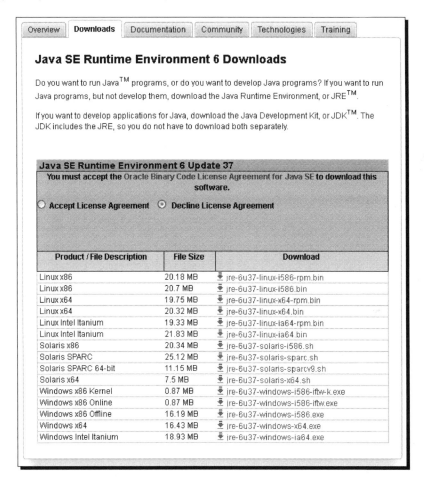

2. Select the installer for Windows 64-bit, that is, **jre-6u37-windows-x64.exe**, and save it in a convenient folder.

3. Select the downloaded file and run it as an administrator; press the **Yes** button when asked from the **User Account** control.

4. Go with the default settings and press the **Install** button.

5. After it has been downloaded, you should see a window informing you about the success of installation.

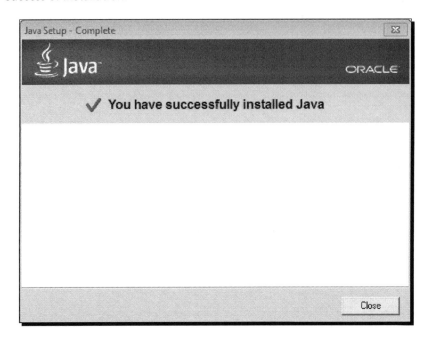

What just happened?

We installed JRE on your Windows computer. The first requirement is now fulfilled and you can go over to the Tomcat installation.

Time for action – installing JRE on Ubuntu

We will install Oracle JRE 1.6. As mentioned previously, there is no Ubuntu package for Java 6; we are going to perform a manual installation.

1. Visit the download area at `http://www.oracle.com/technetwork/java/javase/downloads/jre6u37-downloads-1859589.html`.

2. Download the **tar.gz** archive, choosing the 32-bit or 64-bit archive, depending on the Ubuntu edition you are working with. You must accept the license agreement (reading it might be a nice idea) before you can select one of the **tar.gz** archives (be sure to avoid **rpm** archives as they are not for Debian-based Linux distribution).

3. Save the archive to your home folder and extract it.

```
~ $ chmod a+x jre-6u37-linux-x64.bin
~ $ ./jre-6u37-linux-x64.bin
```

4. The JRE 6 package is extracted into `./jre1.6.0_37` folder. Now move the JRE 6 directory to `/opt` and create a symbolic link to it in the default folder for libraries.

    ```
    ~ $ sudo mv ./jre1.6.0_37* /opt
    ~ $ sudo ln -s /opt/jre1.6.0_37 /usr/lib/jvm/
    ```

5. Let's check the installation:

    ```
    ~ $ /opt/jre1.6.0_37/bin/java -version
    java version "1.6.0_37"
    Java(TM) SE Runtime Environment (build 1.6.0_37-b06)
    Java HotSpot(TM) Client VM (build 20.12-b01, mixed mode)
    ```

6. Although not strictly requested by the GeoServer installation, it is worth configuring the JRE as the primary Java alternative in your system:

    ```
    ~$ sudo update-alternatives --install /usr/bin/java java /usr/lib/jvm/jre1.6.0_37/bin/java 0
    ```

7. Now you need to configure the Oracle JRE as default:

    ```
    ~ $ sudo update-alternatives --config java
    There are 2 choices for the alternative java (providing /usr/bin/java).


    Selection    Path                                         Priority   Status
    ------------------------------------------------------------
    * 0  /usr/lib/jvm/java-6-openjdk-amd64/jre/bin/java 1061   auto mode
      1  /usr/lib/jvm/java-6-openjdk-amd64/jre/bin/java 1061   manual mode
      2  /usr/lib/jvm/jre1.6.0_37/bin/java                  0   manual mode
    Press enter to keep the current choice[*], or type selection number: 2
    update-alternatives: using /usr/lib/jvm/jre1.6.0_37/bin/java to provide /usr/bin/java (java) in manual mode.
    ```

8. Clean your box by deleting the archive:

    ```
    ~$ rm jre-6u37-linux-x64.bin
    ```

What just happened?

We installed JRE. Now we can run a Java application on the JVM contained in the JRE. The JVM supports several different kinds of Java application; for example, a console-only application, an applet running in a browser, or a full desktop application. For GeoServer (a web application), we need another component on top of the JVM, that is, a servlet container.

Installing Apache Tomcat

Having correctly installed the JRE you can now pass on and install the servlet container. Servlet container, or web container, is the component server that interacts with the servlets. It is responsible for managing the lifecycle of servlets, mapping a URL to a particular servlet, and ensuring access security. It should implement Java servlet and JavaServer Pages technologies.

As for JRE, you have a few choices here; a brief list is at `http://en.wikipedia.org/wiki/Web_container`.

Apache Tomcat, GlassFish, and JBoss are most popular and are all available in an open source edition. You may wonder which one is the best choice for running GeoServer. In a production environment, usually the same container is shared among several web applications. You are not going to choose the container; the architects and system administrators made their choices and you have to conform to them. As a beginner, you have the opportunity of selecting it! Apache Tomcat should be your first choice as it is widely adopted in the Geoserver developer's community. If you run into any issues, the answer is probably waiting for you in the mailing list archive.

We are going to install Apache Tomcat. It is an open source project of Apache foundation (`http://tomcat.apache.org`) and there are reasons for installing it such as it is widely used, well-documented, and relatively simple to configure.

So let's start the Apache Tomcat installation.

Time for action – installing Apache Tomcat on Windows

We will install the Apache Tomcat 7.x release.

On Windows, we will use the installer. It will add an item in the service control panel allowing you to set Tomcat for automatic startup.

1. Open your browser and visit the download page for 7.x releases at `http://tomcat.apache.org/download-70.cgi`.

2. Select the **32-bit/64-bit Windows Service Installer** and save the `EXE` file to a folder on your machine.

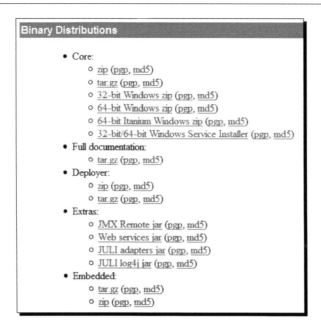

3. Select the downloaded file and run it as the administrator, then press the **Yes** button when asked from the **User Account** control.

4. You need to agree to the license agreement.

5. Leave the default components selection unchanged. We don't need the **Host Manager** nor the web application examples:

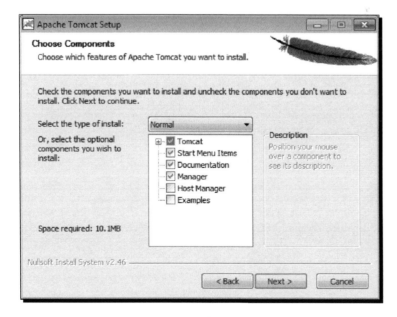

6. Go with the default port number, unless you know there are other services bounded to them. Set the **User Name** and **Password** for web administration (for example, **tomcat**).

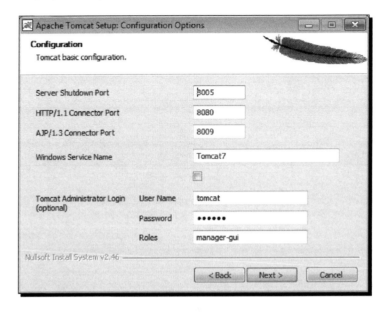

7. If your JRE installation was successful, the installer will prompt you with the right path to it. In case you have more than one JRE/JDK installed, you can choose which one Tomcat will use:

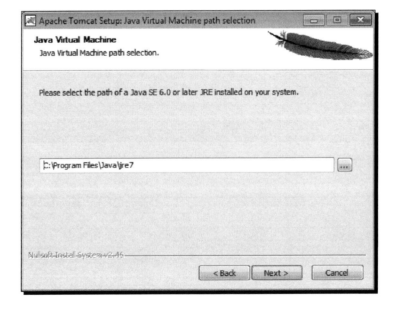

8. Lastly you have to supply the folder where Tomcat will be installed and then press the **Install** button:

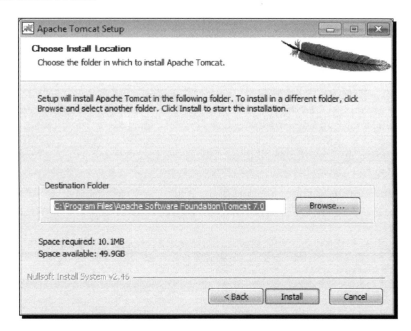

9. The installation process will create a Windows service for you. After the installation, it will try to start the Tomcat 7 service. You will now have a new icon on the system tray. From the pop-up menu, you can control the Tomcat, starting and stopping it or accessing the configuration console:

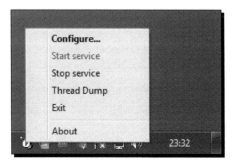

What just happened?

We installed Apache Tomcat as a service on Windows. Your computer is now ready to host the Geoserver web archive.

Time for action – installing Apache Tomcat on Ubuntu

We will install Apache Tomcat 7.x release.

On Ubuntu, you have two alternatives for installing Apache Tomcat. You can use the package manager to get it. At the time of writing, Ubuntu repositories contain the 7.0.26 release of Apache Tomcat for Ubuntu 12.04. I prefer, and we will be following this method in the book, to download the archive and perform a manual installation. You will have full control over the installation and you can choose the appropriate release number. On the other hand, you can't rely on automatic updates for Tomcat.

1. You may want to read the license agreement:
   http://www.apache.org/licenses.

2. Download the archive:
   ```
   ~$ wget http://apache.panu.it/tomcat/tomcat-7/v7.0.27/bin/apache-tomcat-7.0.27.tar.gz
   ```

3. Extract it in a folder for alternate applications, specific to your server; /opt sounds like a good place.
   ```
   ~$ sudo tar xvfz apache-tomcat-7.0.27.tar.gz -C /opt
   ```

4. You need to properly configure Tomcat before you can use it. Go inside the main folder created while extracting the archive; you should see the following structure:
   ```
   ~$ ls -lah /opt/apache-tomcat-7.0.27

   total 120K

   drwxr-xr-x 9 root root 4.0K Jun  6 12:16 .

   drwxr-xr-x 3 root root 4.0K Jun  6 12:16 ..

   drwxr-xr-x 2 root root 4.0K Jun  6 12:16 bin

   drwxr-xr-x 2 root root 4.0K Mar 31 16:45 conf

   drwxr-xr-x 2 root root 4.0K Jun  6 12:16 lib

   -rw-r--r-- 1 root root  56K Mar 31 16:45 LICENSE

   drwxr-xr-x 2 root root 4.0K Mar 31 16:44 logs

   -rw-r--r-- 1 root root 1.2K Mar 31 16:45 NOTICE

   -rw-r--r-- 1 root root 8.7K Mar 31 16:45 RELEASE-NOTES

   -rw-r--r-- 1 root root  11K Mar 31 16:45 RUNNING.txt

   drwxr-xr-x 2 root root 4.0K Jun  6 12:16 temp

   drwxr-xr-x 7 root root 4.0K Mar 31 16:44 webapps

   drwxr-xr-x 2 root root 4.0K Mar 31 16:44 work
   ```

5. The `bin` and `conf` folders contain the configuration files and the `init` script you can edit in order to adjust settings. On a new Unix box, you shouldn't have any issues with the default configuration. If you are installing on a server with other services running, you should check the following points:

1. Default configuration tries to bind the HTTP connector to port 8080. If it is already used for another service, you need to edit the `/opt/apache-tomcat-7.0.27/conf/server.xml` file. Find the following section:

```
<Connector port="8080" protocol="HTTP/1.1"
                connectionTimeout="20000"
                redirectPort="8443" />
```

2. You have to replace 8080 with a port number you know is free to use on your system. Be sure to use a port number higher than 1024. You may guess that changing it to port number 80 is a good idea. On one hand, this will enable you to access your Tomcat installation and web application deployed on it from the browser without having to add the :8080 syntax to your HTTP requests. On the other hand, you have to consider that Apache Tomcat is not developed with strong HTTP security in mind, and this configuration may be unsecure if you expose your container on the Internet. Using a proxy is the correct approach to get the same result while retaining security. Configuring a proxy for Geoserver will be covered in *Chapter 11, GeoServer in a Production Environment*.

3. Also remember you have to restart Tomcat for any change you make to the configuration files.

4. In order to access the web interface for administration tasks you need to edit the security settings. Go into the `conf` folder and edit the `tomcat-users.xml` file. The following file syntax is quite self-explanatory:

```
~$ sudo vi /opt/apache-tomcat-7.0.27/conf/tomcat-users.xml
```

5. Find and uncomment the following section:

```
<!--
  <role rolename="tomcat"/>
  <role rolename="role1"/>
  <user username="tomcat" password="tomcat" roles="tomcat"/>
  <user username="both" password="tomcat"
roles="tomcat,role1"/>
  <user username="role1" password="tomcat" roles="role1"/>
-->
```

6. You also need to add a `"manager-gui"` role and assign it to a user. You may also want to change the `password` value. After the editing, the section should looks as follows:

```
<role rolename="tomcat"/>

<role rolename="role1"/>

<role rolename="manager-gui"/>

<user username="tomcat" password="tomcat"
roles="tomcat,manager-gui"/>

<user username="both" password="tomcat"
roles="tomcat,role1"/>

<user username="role1" password="tomcat" roles="role1"/>
```

7. Start up Tomcat:

```
~$ sudo /opt/apache-tomcat-7.0.27/bin/catalina.sh start

Using CATALINA_BASE:   /opt/apache-tomcat-7.0.27

Using CATALINA_HOME:   /opt/apache-tomcat-7.0.27

Using CATALINA_TMPDIR: /opt/apache-tomcat-7.0.27/temp

Using JRE_HOME:        /usr

Using CLASSPATH:       /opt/apache-tomcat-7.0.27/bin/
bootstrap.jar:/opt/apache-tomcat-7.0.27/bin/tomcat-juli.jar
```

8. You succeeded starting the servlet container and you can now see it among the running processes:

```
~$ ps -ef | grep java

root      1960      1  5 14:06 pts/0    00:00:01 /usr/
bin/java -Djava.util.logging.config.file=/opt/apache-
tomcat-7.0.27/conf/logging.properties -Djava.util.logging.
manager=org.apache.juli.ClassLoaderLogManager -Djava.
endorsed.dirs=/opt/apache-tomcat-7.0.27/endorsed -classpath
/opt/apache-tomcat-7.0.27/bin/bootstrap.jar:/opt/apache-
tomcat-7.0.27/bin/tomcat-juli.jar -Dcatalina.base=/
opt/apache-tomcat-7.0.27 -Dcatalina.home=/opt/apache-
tomcat-7.0.27 -Djava.io.tmpdir=/opt/apache-tomcat-7.0.27/
temp org.apache.catalina.startup.Bootstrap start
```

9. Remove the archive:

```
~$ rm apache-tomcat-7.0.27.tar.gz
```

What just happened?

We installed Apache Tomcat. We are really close to finishing the installation process. You can now run the Java web application on your server.

Time for action – configuring Tomcat as a service on Ubuntu

On Windows we configured Tomcat as a system service, that is, a program running at boot without any user action. Are you wondering why on Ubuntu you have to manually start Tomcat? You don't. Indeed, the operating system can be configured for automatic start of services. In this section, you will create a script and learn how it works.

1. Open your preferred editor and enter the following lines. Be sure to launch the editor with `sudo` as we are going to create a file in a system folder.

```sh
#!/bin/sh
### BEGIN INIT INFO
# Provides:          tomcat
# Required-Start:    $local_fs $remote_fs $network $syslog
# Required-Stop:     $local_fs $remote_fs $network $syslog
# Default-Start:     2 3 4 5
# Default-Stop:      0 1 6
# Short-Description: Start/Stop Tomcat  v7.0.27
### END INIT INFO
#
#  /etc/init.d/tomcat
#
export JAVA_HOME=/usr/lib/jvm/jre1.6.0_37
export PATH=$JAVA_HOME/bin:$PATH
export CATALINA_HOME=/opt/apache-tomcat-7.0.27
export JAVA_OPTS="-Djava.awt.headless=true"

case $1 in
    start)
        sh $CATALINA_HOME/bin/startup.sh
    ;;
    stop)
        sh $CATALINA_HOME/bin/shutdown.sh
    ;;
    restart)
        sh $CATALINA_HOME/bin/shutdown.sh
        sh $CATALINA_HOME/bin/startup.sh
    ;;
    *)
        echo "Usage: /etc/init.d/tomcat {start|stop|restart}"
        exit 1
    ;;
esac

exit 0
```

2. The previous script is simple and contains all of the basic elements you will need to get going. Pay attention to the path; you can adjust your script according to your system settings.

3. Call the new file `tomcat` and save it in the `/etc/init.d` folder.

4. Now, set the permissions for your script to make it executable:

```
~$ sudo chmod a+x /etc/init.d/tomcat
```

5. Let's try to call it and check for any problems:

```
~$ sudo service tomcat
Usage: /etc/init.d/tomcat {start|stop|restart}
```

6. Try starting Tomcat:

```
~$ sudo service tomcat start
```

7. Ok, it is running now:

```
~$ ps -ef | grep java
root      1960     1  5 14:06 pts/0    00:00:01 /usr/bin/
java -Djava.util.logging.config.file=/opt/apache-tomcat-7.0.27/
conf/logging.properties -Djava.util.logging.manager=org.apache.
juli.ClassLoaderLogManager -Djava.endorsed.dirs=/opt/apache-
tomcat-7.0.27/endorsed -classpath /opt/apache-tomcat-7.0.27/
bin/bootstrap.jar:/opt/apache-tomcat-7.0.27/bin/tomcat-juli.jar
-Dcatalina.base=/opt/apache-tomcat-7.0.27 -Dcatalina.home=/opt/
apache-tomcat-7.0.27 -Djava.io.tmpdir=/opt/apache-tomcat-7.0.27/
temp org.apache.catalina.startup.Bootstrap start
```

8. Now stop it:

```
~$ sudo service tomcat stop
```

9. Now that you have a working script, the last step is adding to configured services. We will use `update-rc`:

```
~$ sudo update-rc.d tomcat defaults
 Adding system startup for /etc/init.d/tomcat ...
   /etc/rc0.d/K20tomcat -> ../init.d/tomcat
   /etc/rc1.d/K20tomcat -> ../init.d/tomcat
   /etc/rc6.d/K20tomcat -> ../init.d/tomcat
   /etc/rc2.d/S20tomcat -> ../init.d/tomcat
   /etc/rc3.d/S20tomcat -> ../init.d/tomcat
   /etc/rc4.d/S20tomcat -> ../init.d/tomcat
   /etc/rc5.d/S20tomcat -> ../init.d/tomcat
```

10. Reboot your system and check if Tomcat is already running.

What just happened?

We created a shell script for starting Apache Tomcat. Now as you boot your Ubuntu machine, Tomcat will be initialized and all the web application content will be available for user requests. If you prefer to manually start and stop Tomcat, the script could yet be useful for you. Just create it as described and avoid the last step. You will use the script to start or stop Tomcat from the command line, that is, `sudo tomcat start` or `sudo tomcat stop`.

Have a go hero – exploring the Tomcat web interface

Apache Tomcat ships with a web interface for basic configuration and administration tasks. You are going to use it for installing Geoserver. Open your browser and point to the base main (for example, *http://localhost:8080/*). Do you remember we edited a file about roles, users, and passwords? You will be presented with an HTTP digest authorization form; try to guess which credentials you have to supply. Explore the manager application.

Pop quiz – setting up Java

Q1. You are going to set up a new machine for running GeoServer. The operating system is a 64-bit one; which Java setup you need to download?

1.   A 32-bit JRE

2.   A 64-bit JRE

3.   Both runs fine on a 64-bit OS

Q2. On the same machine where Tomcat is set up, what do you need to install?

1.   A 32-bit Tomcat setup

2.   A 64-bit Tomcat setup

3.   Neither of the above; Tomcat java code runs on 32-bit or 64-bit JVM

Installing GeoServer

We are well on our way! Go to the GeoServer site (`http://geoserver.org/display/ GEOS/Stable`) and review the installation options available. You'll find several versions of GeoServer. We're going to be using the **Web Archive** version.

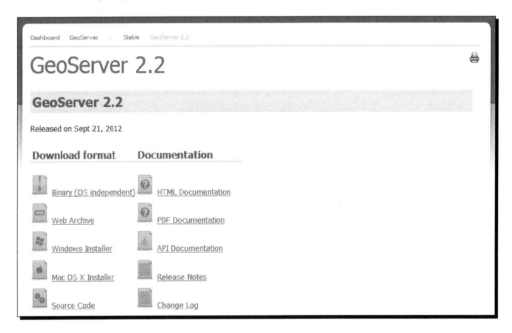

We will deploy the web archive on Apache Tomcat. As you may have guessed, using a Java application server is pretty much the same on any operating system. The next section is common to Linux and Windows and then we will have a little difference in the book, depending on the operating system you are using.

Time for action – deploying GeoServer on Tomcat

With Java installed and working, let's install the GeoServer. The latest version is 2.2.

1. Download the OS-independent version from GeoServer's download page. You can point your browser to the URL or use a command-line tool like `wget`:

```
~$ wget http://downloads.sourceforge.net/geoserver/geoserver-2.2-war.zip
```

2. Unzip the archive file:

```
~$ unzip geoserver-2.2-war.zip
The war file for GeoServer is quite big, actually a little more
than 52 MByte. In Tomcat 7 Manager there is a default limit for
deployable application that is at 50 MByte. You will set it to a
safe size for GeoServer. Open the $CATALINA_HOME/webapps/manager/
WEB-INF/web.xml file and look for this section
    <multipart-config>
      <!-- 50MB max -->
      <max-file-size>52428800</max-file-size>
      <max-request-size>52428800</max-request-size>
      <file-size-threshold>0</file-size-threshold>
    </multipart-config>
```

3. Set the `max-file-size` to `62914560` value both in `max-file-size` and `max-request-size` parameters. Save the file and restart Tomcat.

4. Point your browser to the application manager at *http://localhost:8080/manager/html*.

5. You will be requested to insert a **User Name** and a **Password**, if you follow the instructions on installing Tomcat. Insert **tomcat** as **User Name** and the same as **Password**:

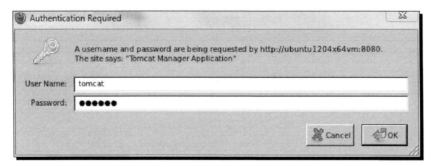

6. Now we are in the application manager, the panel where we control the web application running on our container. Scroll down to the **Deploy** section:

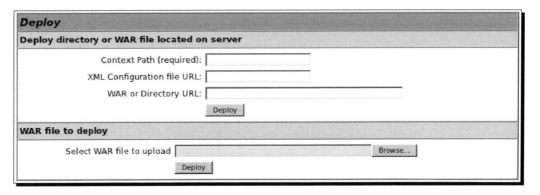

7. Press the **Browse** button in **WAR file to deploy** and select the **geoserver.war** file.

8. Press the **Deploy** button. After a while you will see the **OK** response from the manager. Now **GeoServer** is listed among the web applications deployed in Tomcat.

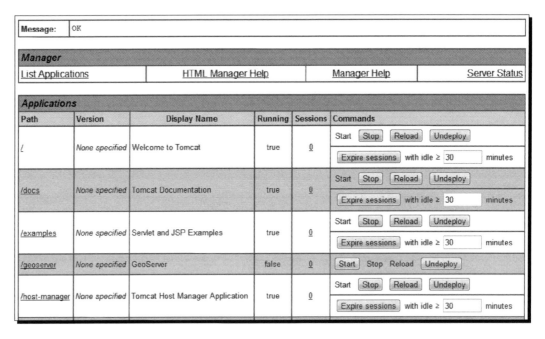

9. Click on the **/geoserver** link shown in the column on the left-hand side of the list. You are now looking at the start page of your brand new GeoServer instance:

What just happened?

We deployed the GeoServer web archive on Tomcat. It unpacked the archive content. If there were no errors in the package, thanks to the great job of GeoServer developers (chances are that you won't find them), then Tomcat automatically starts GeoServer.

Implementing basic security

The web interface shown at *http://localhost:8080/geoserver* requires you to log in. You can use the default values of admin as username and geoserver as password. The new interface will show you some warning about security issues:

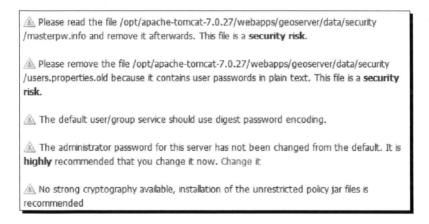

You may ignore the third and fifth warning; we will cover them in detail in *Chapter 10, Securing Your GeoServer Before Production*. It is a good idea to address the others immediately.

Time for action – improving security settings

1. We will start by changing the default password for the administrator. Click on the **Change it** link on the left-hand side of the warning.

2. A new page containing user properties will show up. Insert the new password in the **Password** and **Confirm password** textboxes and click on the **Save** button. You don't need to restart GeoServer or Tomcat; the new password is active now!

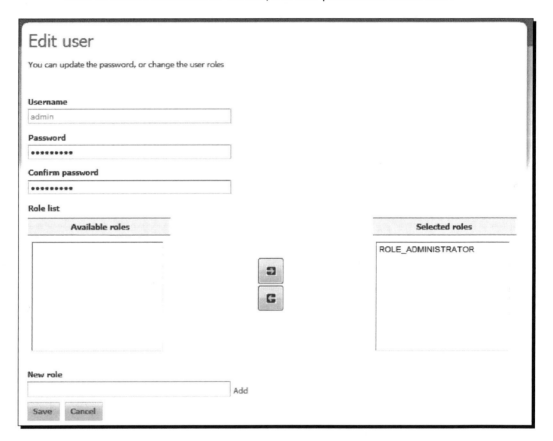

3. The `users.properties.old` file is a security risk because it contains user passwords in plain text. GeoServer does not need it so it's safe to delete it.

```
~$ sudo rm /opt/apache-tomcat-7.0.27/webapps/geoserver/data/
security/users.properties.old
```

4. Now open the `masterpw.info` file. It contains the password generated by GeoServer for the root user. Store it in a secure place and delete the file.

```
~$ sudo rm /opt/apache-tomcat-7.0.27/webapps/geoserver/data/
security/masterpw.info
```

What just happened?

Although you are setting up a development machine, security is always an issue. GeoServer ships with a default administrative password; you logged onto the web interface and changed the default password, then fixed some other issues. You had just a brief taste of the powerful GeoServer's web interface. Be sure we are going to cover it in great detail in the next chapter.

Pop quiz – GeoServer security

Q1. Where can you change the password for accessing GeoServer?

1. In the `CATALINA_HOME\conf\tomcat-users.xml` file
2. In the GeoServer interface
3. In the Windows Control Panel

Q2. Can you run more than one GeoServer on your machine?

1. Yes, but they all share the same administrator password
2. Yes, and each one has an independent administrator account
3. Yes, but you need to use the container administrator account for administering GeoServer
4. No, you can't

Summary

We've laid out a basic foundation to get GeoServer up and running.

In this chapter, you learned how to check whether the Java Runtime Environment (JRE 1.6) is installed and properly working. You also installed Tomcat on Windows and Linux, and configured it to start automatically.

After filling the system requirements, you explored the web archive option to install GeoServer and accessed the administrative interface using a web browser.

The web interface is a very powerful tool and you have to know it well to use all GeoServer's features. In the next chapter, we will explore all the sections, looking in detail at what you can do to configure it, how to add data, and preview maps.

3
Exploring the Administrative Interface

In this hands-on chapter we're going to explore GeoSever 2.2's administrative interface. Big improvements have been made to the interface in the 2.x series. Menu names and icons are consistent across each section. An enhanced interface for the integrated **GeoWebCache** *is available in 2.2; now you can perform almost all caching configurations from the GeoServer interface. Also, the security interface was renewed to keep track of the huge improvements in the GeoServer's security module. The good news is we're going to use the mouse more here than any other chapter, so the keyboard will get a break.*

Let's get right to it. Get logged in.

Understanding the interface

You used the web interface in the previous chapter to change the password for the admin user. Log in again on GeoServer; we will now focus our attention on the layout.

As you can see in the following screenshot, there are three main areas in the GeoServer web interface.

The central area is where information is shown; elements inside it change according to the operation you are performing. Just after you log on, it shows you a briefing of configured data, and warning or errors that you should correct. The release number is shown at the end and there is a link to the administrator mailbox; it defaults to a famous ancient geographer until you insert your data.

On the right-hand side, there is a list showing you GeoServer capabilities. The listed acronyms refer to standard OGC protocols; we will talk about some of them in detail, and each of them has at least one release supported. Those numbers are links to the XML documents that exactly describe which data and operations each protocol supports. They are very valuable resources for clients willing to use your services.

On the left-hand side, there is a table of contents listing the configuration areas. Each area contains links to administrative operations. When you click on one of them, the central area shows you contextual options. We will explore each area in the next paragraphs.

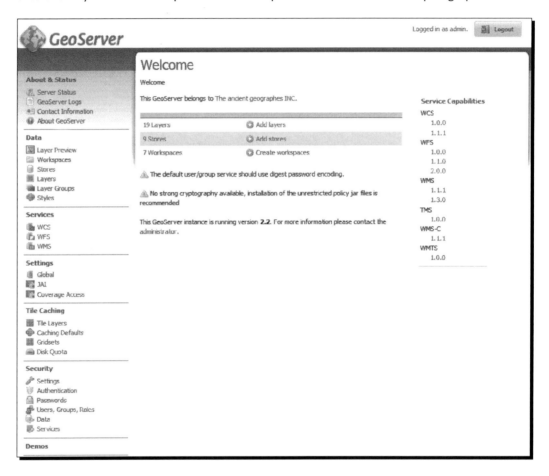

About & Status

This area gives you information about runtime variables and how GeoServer is described to clients that connect to it.

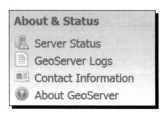

Server Status

Server Status gives you a nice overview of the main configuration parameters and information about the current state of the GeoServer. The information is organized in a table view. Other than being informative, this view lets you perform some maintenance operations. We will describe the main items listed in the following screenshot:

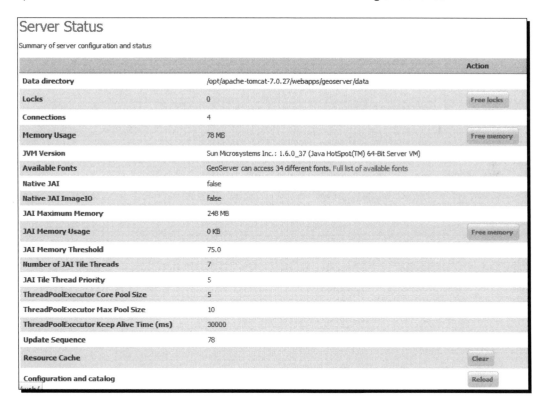

		Action
Data directory	/opt/apache-tomcat-7.0.27/webapps/geoserver/data	
Locks	0	Free locks
Connections	4	
Memory Usage	78 MB	Free memory
JVM Version	Sun Microsystems Inc.: 1.6.0_37 (Java HotSpot(TM) 64-Bit Server VM)	
Available Fonts	GeoServer can access 34 different fonts. Full list of available fonts	
Native JAI	false	
Native JAI ImageIO	false	
JAI Maximum Memory	248 MB	
JAI Memory Usage	0 KB	Free memory
JAI Memory Threshold	75.0	
Number of JAI Tile Threads	7	
JAI Tile Thread Priority	5	
ThreadPoolExecutor Core Pool Size	5	
ThreadPoolExecutor Max Pool Size	10	
ThreadPoolExecutor Keep Alive Time (ms)	30000	
Update Sequence	78	
Resource Cache		Clear
Configuration and catalog		Reload

Locks

Using **Transactional Web Feature Service (WFS-T)** a client may edit the configured feature types. To avoid data corruption, GeoServer locks the data on which a transaction is required until it ends. If the number shown is greater than one, then there are some transactions going on with your data. The **Free Locks** button lets you reset a hung editing session, removing any orphan processes to free locks that might have been abandoned.

Connections

This shows you the number of vector data store connections. Vector data stores are repositories configured for persistence of features.

Memory Usage

This shows you how much memory GeoServer is using. You can manually run the garbage collector by clicking the **Free memory** button. This will destroy the Java objects marked for deletion.

JVM Version and fonts

This is the version of the **Java Virtual Machine (JVM)** that the GeoServer is using. You configured it in *Chapter 2, Getting Started with GeoServer*, in the installation processes. You'll also see a list of the fonts seen by the JVM and GeoServer. Fonts are useful to render labels for spatial features; we will explore this in *Chapter 6, Styling Your Layers*.

JAI usage and configurations

The **Java Advanced Imaging (JAI)** libraries are used for image rendering and allow for better performance when GeoServer manipulates raster data, as with **Web Coverage Service (WCS)** and **Web Map Service (WMS)** requests. We will install native JAI support in *Chapter 11, Tuning GeoServer in a Production Environment*.

Update Sequence

This shows you how many times the server configuration has been updated. It is not that informative as of the time this writing. The developers seem to have plans to use this to let you know that your configuration file has been updated externally from the application. Possibly from a REST call.

Resource Cache

GeoServer caches connections to stores, feature type definitions, external graphics, font definitions, and CRS definitions as well. You can press the **Clear** button to force those GeoServer reopening the stores and rereading image and font information.

Configuration and catalog

This option is very useful to update the configuration without having to restart the service. GeoServer keeps configuration data in memory. If there is an external process updating the files containing the configuration's parameters, you can force GeoServer to reload data from the disk.

GeoServer Logs

From here you can have a preview at the current log file, or you can download the full content from the link on the bottom. It may be useful when you can't access the filesystem where the actual log file is stored.

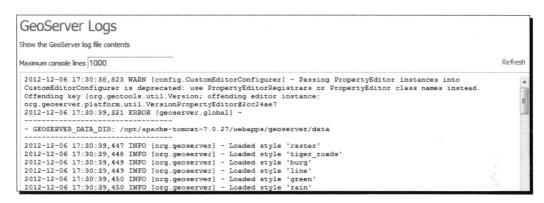

Contact Information

In this panel, you should insert information on the organization and people managing the service. The default configuration pays honor to Claudius Ptolemaeus, an ancient cartographer (http://en.wikipedia.org/wiki/Ptolemy). This information is included in the WMS capabilities and is reference information for your users.

About

Just as it states, this is just a catch-all for build information and where to find GeoServer documentation, bug tracker, and wiki.

About GeoServer

General information about GeoServer

Build Information

Version

2.2

Git Revision

f5b5c35076b52d02eb9cca3fa3232bc17b5f6d80

Build Date

19-Sep-2012 18:33

GeoTools Version

8.2 (rev 704570474295e339c08d1ca140d884f23a8a03a3)

Time for action – manually reloading configuration

We will now perform a simple change on GeoServer's configuration to demonstrate the reload configuration function.

1. Open the `global.xml` file in your preferred editor:

   ```
   -~ $ sudo vi /opt/apache-tomcat-7.0.27/webapps/geoserver/data/
   global.xml
   ```

2. Find the `contact` section and insert your details:

   ```
   <contact>
     <addressCity>Rome</addressCity>
     <addressCountry>Italy</addressCountry>
     <addressType>Work</addressType>
     <contactEmail>Stefano.iacovella@myworkemail</contactEmail>
     <contactOrganization>Packt Publishing</contactOrganization>
     <contactPerson>Stefano Iacovella</contactPerson>
     <contactPosition>Chief geographer</contactPosition>
   </contact>
   ```

3. Now save the file and close it. Then go to the web interface; in the **About and Status** panel, click on the **Server Status** menu link to display the GeoServer status, scroll down, and click on the **Reload** button.

4. Now, go to the **Contact Information** panel. It shows your updated information.

What just happened?

We explored a simple case for using the reload configuration function. This is very useful in case you have to update a remote server with an automatic procedure or you configure more GeoServer instances sharing the same configuration. We will explore such deployment options in *Chapter 11, Tuning GeoServer in a Production Environment*.

Have a go hero – exploring the bug tracker

GeoServer's bug tracker is a great resource to monitor. The link to the bug tracker is located at the end of the **About GeoServer** page. The RSS feed to the activity stream gives you a window into GeoServer development. Put `feed://jira.codehaus.org/plugins/ servlet/streams?key=GEOS` into your feed aggregator and stay in the loop.

Data

Now we're getting into the heart of the GeoServer; the data.

In this area, you can configure the data access. Stores let GeoServer know where your data is and what it is. Layers are about how your data will be published. Jump in and look at the layer previews first. We'll be visiting the **Layer Preview** section many times as we brew up our own layers.

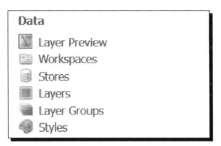

Layer Preview

Layer Preview includes every layer known to GeoServer. You'll find several sample layers already listed. From here you can open an **OpenLayers** sample application to have a look at what your data looks like. There are also several other preview formats; a popular one is the KML format.

Keyhole Markup Language (KML) is used to display data in Google Earth.

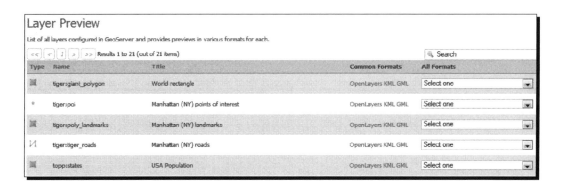

Time for action – OpenLayers preview

Let's try the **OpenLayers** preview. OpenLayers is a powerful JavaScript library that is useful for building web-mapping applications. GeoServer includes a simple template application that lets you look at a map with one layer represented.

1. On the **Layer Preview** page, click the **OpenLayers** link to see the preview.

2. The **OpenLayers** preview opens, showing you the `topp:states` shapefile.

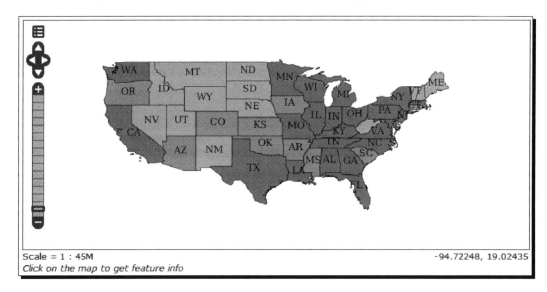

What just happened?

Did you enjoy this first taste of web mapping? OpenLayers is somewhat similar to Google Maps; it allows you to embed your maps into your site.

Time for action – KML preview

Let's try another preview format, KML. This time GeoServer will not open up an application as you select the layer to preview. In fact, KML is a data format and you will need another piece of software to display it on a map.

1. If you haven't already installed Google Earth, you can download it from
   `http://www.google.com/earth/index.html`.

2. Accept the license agreement and save the installation file.

3. On the **Layer Preview** page, scroll to the `topp:states` layer and click the KML link.

4. You are prompted for saving or opening the KMZ output file. Save it on your filesystem.

5. Open the `kmz` file in Google Earth.

What just happened?

Ok, that was pretty cool. We had GeoServer displaying layers in Google Earth. Drop the book and play around with Google Earth. Zoom in and out, and notice how it streams data from GeoServer. Using the drop-down box, you can also preview layers in several other formats. **SVG** is ideal for importing into Adobe illustrator, for example.

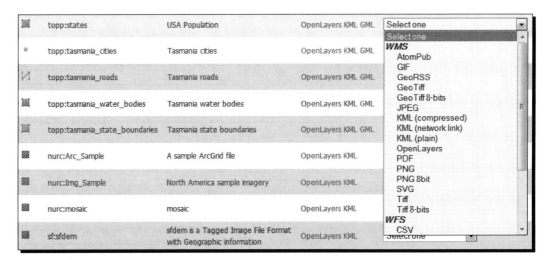

Workspaces

Think of a workspace as your own personal namespace. Workspaces are very useful for organizing your layers. You can associate many layers to one workspace. You are allowed to have several layers with the same name, as long as they're in different workspaces.

You see workspaces and layers referred to each other separated with a colon. For example, when looking at the list of layers in the layer preview, you'll see a number of layer names such as `nurc:Img_Sample`. The workspace name is `nurc` and `Img_Sample` is the layer name.

When you're just getting started with GeoServer, you might not think about organizing with **Workspaces**. As you start to add a number of your own layers, you will soon find that organizing these layers is necessary—think about how easy it will be to sort the layer preview list, for example.

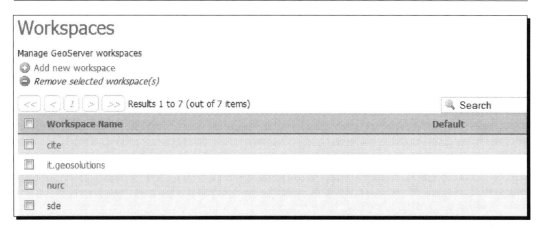

Time for action – creating a workspace

GeoServer has a set of data already configured, and there are a few workspaces to organize them. We will now create a new workspace for the data you will be adding in this book.

1. Select the workspaces list page.

2. Click on **Add new workspace**.

3. In the form, you have to enter a **Name** for your new workspace (in the following screenshot, it is **NaturalEarth**), and **http://www.naturalearthdata.com** as **Namespace URI**. Check **Default Workspace** to assign this as your default:

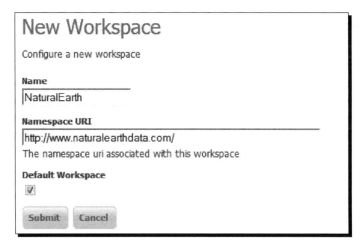

4. Click **Submit** to save your new workspace.

What just happened?

You created a logical category for your data. The default option is useful when you start creating a number of data stores and layers and need to add them to the same workspace, since the default is selected by default. When you start to create layers using the REST interface in a later chapter, you'll quickly find that workspaces are very useful as well.

Stores

Stores connect GeoServer to repositories where your data is located. Each store must be in a workspace, so it's worth setting one up at the beginning instead of sticking stores in one of the defaults. There are a set of stores configured, which are for the namespaces for sample data.

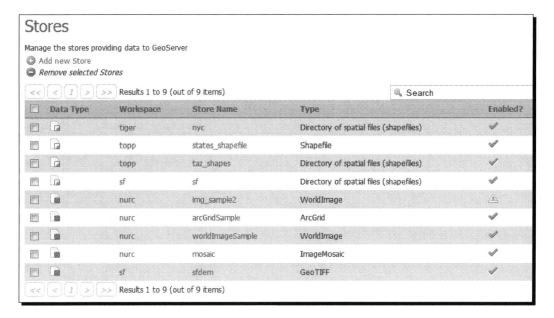

When creating a new data store, you have a few formats available.

New data source

Choose the type of data source you wish to configure

Vector Data Sources

Directory of spatial files (shapefiles) - Takes a directory of shapefiles and exposes it as a data store
PostGIS - PostGIS Database
PostGIS (JNDI) - PostGIS Database (JNDI)
Properties - Allows access to Java Property files containing Feature information
Shapefile - ESRI(tm) Shapefiles (*.shp)
Web Feature Server - The WFSDataStore represents a connection to a Web Feature Server. This connection provides access to the Features published by the server, and the ability to perform transactions on the server (when supported / allowed).

Raster Data Sources

ArcGrid - Arc Grid Coverage Format
GeoTIFF - Tagged Image File Format with Geographic information
Gtopo30 - Gtopo30 Coverage Format
ImageMosaic - Image mosaicking plugin
WorldImage - A raster file accompanied by a spatial data file

Other Data Sources

WMS - Cascades a remote Web Map Service

GeoServer supports several different data formats, but they are classified in two types: **vector** and **raster**. Vector data formats available are as follows:

- **Shapefile**: Both as a single item or as a folder containing several shapefiles. Shapefile is a very common format in GIS and we will use it often in this book.

- **PostGIS**: A famous open source spatial database. You can configure it as a **Java Naming and Directory Interface (JNDI)** resource or with a default connection. In the first case, a `jndi` name has to be configured in the container of GeoServer, for example, Tomcat, with the database connection's parameters.

- **Properties**: This is a connector for a simple, small data set that you can store in a text file. Remember that performances are not optimized with this format; use it only for testing or for very small data sets.

- **WFS**: You can access, and publish, features published by another server. Also, in this case, you can't expect optimal performances, but it may be useful in cascading data.

There are also a set of raster formats. The most used and well-known are the **GeoTIFF** and the **WorldImage**. GeoTIFF is a spatial extension of the `tiff` format; the file header contains georeferencing information so that the map server can properly place the raster on a map. A WorldImage is similar, but georeferencing information is saved in an external text file.

If you are interested in a detailed description of GeoTIFF format, these are two good starting points:

- `http://it.wikipedia.org/wiki/GeoTIFF`
- `http://trac.osgeo.org/geotiff`

GeoServer, after installing optional extensions, supports several other data formats.

Layers

A layer, in GeoServer, holds the metadata information about a feature type. Every time you send some data to GeoServer, a new layer is created for you. By clicking on the link, you can see the list of configured layers.

The list shows you the type of layers in the **Type** column, with a different icon for vector and raster layers, according to the geometry shape. The **Workspace** and **Store** values of each layer are shown. Then there are the **Layer Name** values, which may differ from the file or table name where the data is stored; a tick mark shows if it is enabled, and the last column shows the **Native SRS** values.

From this section, you can view and edit an existing layer, add (register) a new layer, or delete (unregister) a layer.

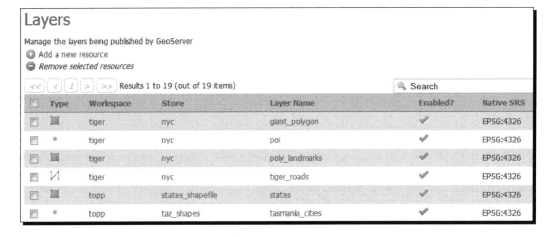

By clicking on a layer name, you open the **Edit Layer** section. You will see there are four tabs in the panel. **Data** contains the feature type's properties, for example, attributes list, and is compiled by GeoServer when adding a new layer. You have to check the values and insert some descriptive information about the feature type.

The **Publishing** tab is for configuring how a layer has to be represented. From here, you can select one or more styles to draw features on a map.

We will add layers, and have a look at each property in *Chapter 5, Adding Your Own DataStore*.

Layer groups

As you build complex layers, you soon discover the need to combine layers together into groups. Layer groups allow you to order your layers to best display your data. For example, if you're creating a map of North America, you might want to show a layer of US states on top of North American coastal lines. Then on top of US states, you might want to show borders for counties of those states. All of those layers can be combined into a layer group.

Styles

Here you can access the style configured in GeoServer. Styles are XML files containing a detailed description of how a feature type has to be drawn on a map.

From here you can access the style editor, a simple, user friendly interface for editing styles. As you may have guessed, building a pretty map is strictly related to styles; we will cover this in detail in *Chapter 6, Styling Your Layers*.

```
⊃ ⊄ ▦ ▤  12pt ▼
1  <?xml version="1.0" encoding="ISO-8859-1"?>
2  <StyledLayerDescriptor version="1.0.0" xmlns="http://www.opengis.net/sld" xmlns:ogc="http://www.opengis.net/ogc"
3    xmlns:xlink="http://www.w3.org/1999/xlink" xmlns:xsi="http://www.w3.org/2001/XMLSchema-instance"
4    xsi:schemaLocation="http://www.opengis.net/sld http://schemas.opengis.net/sld/1.0.0/StyledLayerDescriptor.xsd">
5    <NamedLayer>
6      <Name>redflag</Name>
7      <UserStyle>
8        <Name>burg</Name>
9        <Title>A small red flag</Title>
10       <Abstract>A sample of how to use an SVG based symbolizer</Abstract>
11
12       <FeatureTypeStyle>
13         <Rule>
14           <Title>Red flag</Title>
15           <PointSymbolizer>
16             <Graphic>
17               <ExternalGraphic>
18                 <OnlineResource xlink:type="simple" xlink:href="burg02.svg" />
19                 <Format>image/svg+xml</Format>
20               </ExternalGraphic>
21               <Size>
22                 <ogc:Literal>20</ogc:Literal>
23               </Size>
24             </Graphic>
25           </PointSymbolizer>
26         </Rule>
27
28       </FeatureTypeStyle>
29     </UserStyle>
30   </NamedLayer>
31 </StyledLayerDescriptor>
32
```
SLD file

[　　　　　　　　] [Sfoglia...] Upload ...

[Validate] [Submit] [Cancel]

Services

After you've added some data sources and created layers with those sources, you will want to share these with **Services**. In this section, you can access the general configuration for each service exposed. You can also selectively disable them. By default, all services are enabled.

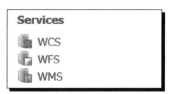

WMS

Web Map Server (**WMS**) is an OGC standard to publish data as maps. The `GetMap` operation as defined by the standard, lets a client request maps as images, for example, a `png` or `jpeg` file.

From this section, you can describe your WMS service, inserting information that will be published by the capabilities of the service. You can also control resource allocation as we have seen in *Chapter 2, Getting Started with GeoServer*, or set the quality parameters for produced pictures.

Time for action – limiting the SRS list from WMS

GeoServer supports a lot of SRSs and can also transform on-the-fly spatial features from one SRS to another. Sometimes this may be not what you want, for example, if you are going to publish data only in a few SRSs and want GeoServer to be heavily loaded from transformation requests. We will now learn how to limit the SRS list.

Do you know an SRS is a spatial reference system? If you are not reading the book from start to end and this acronym sounds confusing, have a look at *Chapter 1, GIS Fundamentals*.

1. On your browser, open the WMS capabilities. This is the standard output for service description. It is an XML file containing data published, operations supported, and other details. Go to the main page of GeoServer's interface and click on the **1.3.0** link:

WMS
   1.1.1
   1.3.0

2. You should get a huge XML file. Scroll down to **All supported EPSG projections**. The following screenshot shows just a few of them; you now have an idea of how many there are!

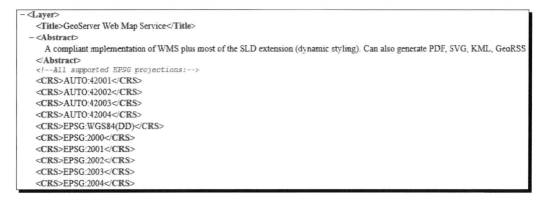

3. Now go to the **service** section and click on **WMS**. Then scroll down and locate the **Limited SRS list** textbox. Insert the SRS code we will use throughout the book: 4326, 3857, 4269. Then press the **Submit** button.

4. Now repeat the capabilities request and search for the CRS section.

What just happened?

We limited the SRS-supported list. This will make the capabilities file clearer and it will also help some clients to deal with it. You can add or remove SRS from the list at any time, according to the data or maps you have to manage.

WFS

Web Feature Server (**WFS**) provides raw vector data from GeoServer layers. This allows you to share your geospatial data in a standard format. Output formats include **GML2**, **GML3**, **ShapeFile**, **JSON**, and **CSV**. As with WMS, from this point on, you can access the general configuration for the service.

WCS

Web Coverage Service (**WCS**) publishes raster-based layers. **Geo ArcGrid** are a couple of geospatial examples of coverages. It's almost like having both WMS and WFS in one service. It allows clients to get raster data along with geospatial data to make more analysis locally.

 Detailed description of WFS and WCS are out of the book's scope; *Chapter 12, Going Further: Getting Help and Troubleshooting*, will give you a brief view of both. You will learn how to perform basic requests.

Settings

This area contains some configuration parameters that cover general GeoServer behavior.

Global

As its name states, here you can find very general parameters.

Verbose Reporting

From here you can enable beautification of XML responses in error messages, by adding line returns. Enabling this option consumes a lot of resources, so only enable this option if you need to. Verbose exceptions will give you multiline error messages.

Enable Global Services

This allows you to enable or disable all services, such as WMS, WFS, and WCS, that are not part of a virtual service. Virtual services are those that are created by workspaces. We'll talk about this in a little more detail in *Chapter 10*, *Securing your GeoServer Before Production*. Also worth noting is that it doesn't affect **GeoWebCache** (**GWC**) or REST-based services.

Proxy Base URL

This is useful if you have GeoServer running behind a proxy, and you want to share the `GetCapabilities` document. The URL embedded in that document needs to display the base URL as seen by the client. We'll dig into this later in future chapters.

Logging Profile

These are the default logging configurations that come with GeoServer. You can add others in the `Log4J` configuration format.

Log to StdOut

This is useful when you are debugging and developing your maps, but you'll find it cleaner to disable and tail the log file instead.

Log location

You may want to keep your logfiles outside of the `data` folder in cases where you want to rotate logs. By default, these are in `$GEOSERVER_HOME/data_dir`, and you might want to keep this folder clean.

Time for action – changing your logging configuration

When testing client-server interaction or exploring new functions, it may be useful to have more information inside the logfile. We will now raise the verbosity of GeoServer.

1. Click on the **Global** link in the **Settings** menu.
2. Scroll down to the logging and profiles section.
3. Now change the **Logging Profile** setting to Verbose logging:

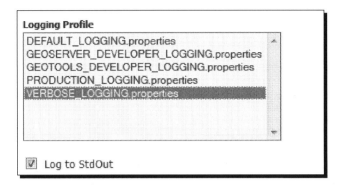

4. Click on GeoServer logs in **About & Status** to review the logs. Optionally, review the log from the filesystem, `/data_dir/logs/geoserver.log`.

What just happened?

You just switched GeoServer to logging in verbose mode. Remember to remove this option when you are no longer testing functionalities, since it stresses the server and requires a lot of space on the log file.

Have a go hero – making your own logging level

Read a little about `log4J` and create your own logging properties configuration. Why wait until the advanced chapter? Duplicate one of the property files in `$GEOSERVER_DATA_DIR/logs`. The filename will be used as the profile name. Check out `http://logging.apache.org/log4j/index.html` to really customize your logging.

JAI

These settings should mostly be overlooked until you take GeoServer into production. The options to change **Memory Capacity**, **Memory Threshold**, **Title Threads**, and **Tile Thread Priority** are best left alone for now. The native acceleration options are checked by default, and will use JAI native acceleration if it's installed for your operating system. We cover the installation in *Chapter 11, Tuning GeoServer in a Production Environment*. If a native version for your OS is not found, it will degrade to the Java implementation.

Tile Caching

This area was greatly improved in Version 2.2 of GeoServer. From here you can control almost all parameters of the integrated GeoWebCache. It is a Java-based application that complements GeoServer. It caches WMS tiles to the filesystem. These images are then used by WMS clients instead of going to GeoServer for each tile request.

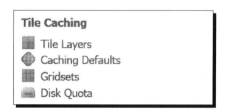

When creating a new layer, you may choose if it has to be cached or not. The **Tile layers** section lists all cached layers and lets you review and modify parameters. It also contains a link to a layer preview very similar to that listed in the data section. The main difference is that this preview uses cached tiles.

GeoWebCache is a companion for GeoServer, and if it is strictly integrated, there are a set of global parameters for configuring it too. Caching defaults is your entry point for them.

The **Gridsets** option lets you create new tiling schemas or modify the existing ones.

All the tiles you are going to create when caching need to be stored on a filesystem. The **Disk Quota** option lets you set predefined amounts of space for each layer.

Caching is a strong ally for your site's performance. In *Chapter 8*, *Performance and Caching*, we will explore in detail how to properly cache data.

Security

Along with caching, security is an area greatly improved in the 2.2 release. Most of the improvements are very advanced topics, such as for integrating security with other external systems, for example, LDAP. In the **Security** panel, you can find links for setting user properties and bind data to security rules, as shown in the following screenshot:

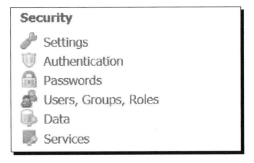

The basic idea is that you create users and roles and combine them with data to enable specific access policies. You can also limit read and write access by role. We will go over these in detail in a later chapter.

Settings

From here you can control the global security settings.

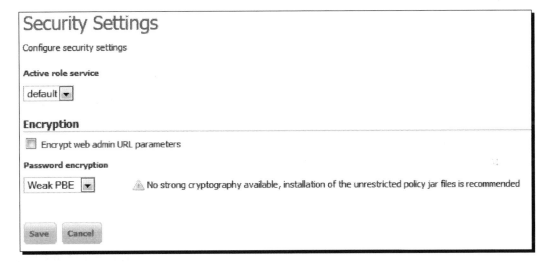

Users, Groups, and Roles

A list of the users, groups, and roles that are configured on GeoServer are shown here. By default, you have one user called **ADMIN**, and one role called **ROLE_ADMINISTRATOR**.

Clicking the username allows you to edit the account password, assign new roles, and add a role.

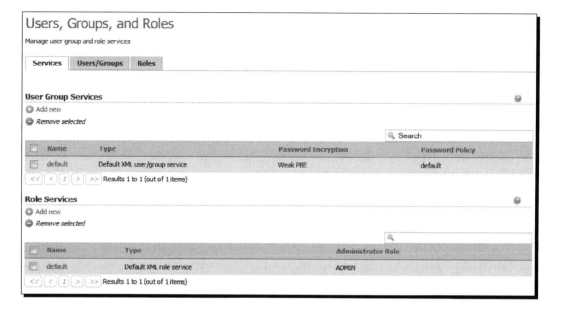

Data

You're able to give access to workspaces and layers in a granular way. So, after you add a number of workspaces, you can assign roles to them here. Be on the lookout for more information on data access rules later on in the book.

Catalog security

These options are pretty well explained here. In a nutshell, you have three modes when a user is challenged for access. I recommend you use **HIDE**, which is the default. It's better to show users only what they have access to, instead of advertising that other services and layers exist.

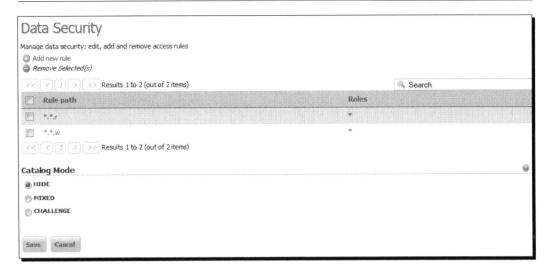

Services security

We went over the various service types (WCS, WFS, WMS) a few pages back. This feature gives you control over read/write access to them. By default, no service-based security is in effect in GeoServer. However, rules can be added, removed, or edited here.

Please note that data security and service security cannot be combined; for example, if you disable a user's access to WMS, he will not see any layer even if you grant him access to that layer.

Demos

A few demo applications are included with GeoServer.

The **WCS request builder** application is pretty handy to piece together a **GetCoverage** request. It's not something you'll likely do as a beginner, but worth remembering that the tool is available.

The **Demo requests** application has a number of example requests to query WCS, WFS, and WMS. Examples to delete, update, and insert records are also included.

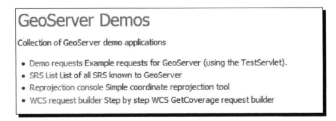

Time for action – exploring Demo requests

You learned that WMS, WFS, and WCS are standards describing the interaction among clients and servers. Each standard defines a set of operations that, from a client's point of view, are requests. On the OGC site, you can download detailed documents describing each admitted request. The demo application is a valuable tool to help you practice with requests. Let's explore some basic operations:

1. Open the **Demo requests** application. The page is similar to the Style Editor. From the drop-down list, you can select a set of prepared requests. They are listed with a syntax declaring the standard as a prefix and the standard's version as a suffix. Choose **WFS_getCapabilities-1.1.xml**.

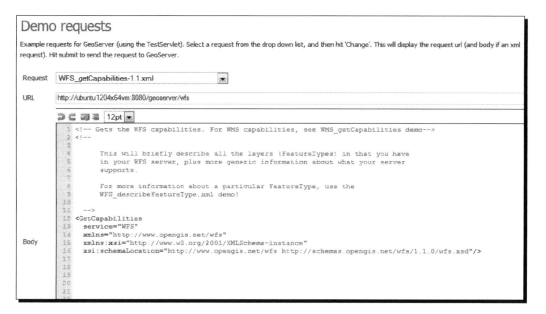

2. Press the **Submit** button. A new panel shows, and after a while it lists the XML response from GeoServer.

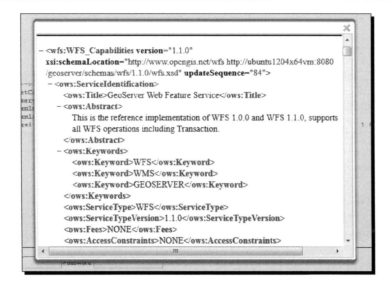

3. Another basic WFS operation is `getFeature`, which will retrieve a feature for you. Select **WFS_getFeature-1.1.xml**. If you look at the XML code, you can see a clear reference to the **topp:states** layer, which is included in the sample set.

| Request | WFS_getFeature-1.1.xml |
| URL | http://ubuntu1204x64vm:8080/geoserver/wfs |

```
1  <!-- Performs a get feature.  Feel free to play with the Filter elements,  -->
2  <!-- to get different results.  No filter will get all features, and you    -->
3  <!-- can do filtering on spatial and non-spatial attributes.  See the ogc   -->
4  <!-- filter specification http://www.opengis.org/docs/02-059.pdf for the     -->
5  <!-- the complete syntax and examples.                                       -->
6  <!--
7      This particular Query will return the topp:states with the FID (unique ID)
8      of 'states:3'. (Thats Delaware)
9
10     You can also try a filter like:
11             <PropertyIsEqualTo>
12                     <PropertyName>STATE_NAME</PropertyName>
13                     <Literal>Delaware</Literal>
14             </PropertyIsEqualTo>
15  -->
16  <wfs:GetFeature service="WFS" version="1.1.0"
17    xmlns:topp="http://www.openplans.org/topp"
18    xmlns:wfs="http://www.opengis.net/wfs"
19    xmlns:ogc="http://www.opengis.net/ogc"
20    xmlns:xsi="http://www.w3.org/2001/XMLSchema-instance"
21    xsi:schemaLocation="http://www.opengis.net/wfs
22                        http://schemas.opengis.net/wfs/1.1.0/wfs.xsd">
23    <wfs:Query typeName="topp:states">
24      <ogc:Filter>
25        <ogc:FeatureId fid="states.3"/>
26      </ogc:Filter>
27      </wfs:Query>
28  </wfs:GetFeature>
29
30
31
```

4. Press the **Submit** button. A new panel shows, and after a while it lists the XML response from GeoServer. The code is a GML representation of the features with `fid = 3`, as requested in the filter.

5. Modify the following code by inserting the `states.23` value:

```
<ogc:Filter>
    <ogc:FeatureId fid="states.23"/>
</ogc:Filter>
```

6. Click on the **Submit** button again; when the panel shows the **gml** code, scroll down until you see the **STATE_NAME** field. Which state did you select?

What just happened?

The **Demo requests** interface lets you select sample requests and modify them to perform testing on GeoServer. When in doubt with a specific operation, this application should be the first point where you go to debug. From here, you can concentrate on the request's syntax, avoiding network issues or other problems that you may have experienced on an external client.

SRS List

This is a list of projections that GeoServer knows about. You can filter it easily using the **Search** field.

Time for action – filtering the projection list

Previously, you filtered the SRS list for WMS. Are you wondering what you will find inside this demo? Let's see.

1. Open the SRS list demo application. Wow, there are **4,956** items in the list! Yes, you just filtered items for WMS; but all supported SRSs are still there.

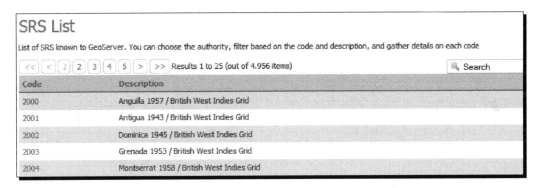

2. In the **Search** textbox, type in the project code for the basic projection, **4326**; then press *Enter*.

3. Click on the projection code to show the projection detail. Along with the Well Known Text description of the SRS, there is also a map showing you the area of validity. For **4326**, it is the planet's surface:

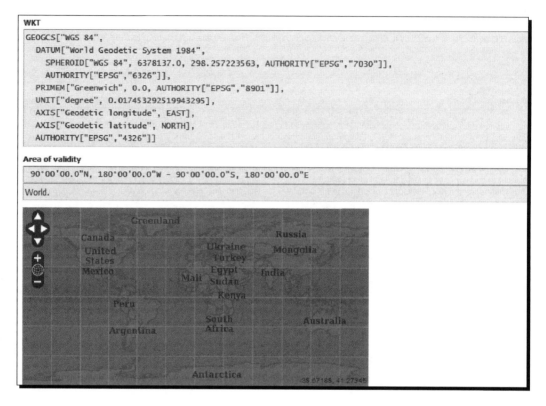

```
WKT
GEOGCS["WGS 84",
  DATUM["World Geodetic System 1984",
    SPHEROID["WGS 84", 6378137.0, 298.257223563, AUTHORITY["EPSG","7030"]],
    AUTHORITY["EPSG","6326"]],
  PRIMEM["Greenwich", 0.0, AUTHORITY["EPSG","8901"]],
  UNIT["degree", 0.017453292519943295],
  AXIS["Geodetic longitude", EAST],
  AXIS["Geodetic latitude", NORTH],
  AUTHORITY["EPSG","4326"]]
```

Area of validity
```
90°00'00.0"N, 180°00'00.0"W - 90°00'00.0"S, 180°00'00.0"E
```
World.

4. Repeat these steps to review 3857, which is the Google Mercator projection.

What just happened?

This gives you an idea of how each projection (4326 and 3857, in this example) is defined. Each projection is defined by several parameters formatted in the WKT format.

If you have custom projections, they'll be included in this list. You can also check your `data_dir/user_projections` folder for a `epsg.properties` file. Any custom projections configured will be here, along with those that are overridden.

Summary

We had a concise introduction to the GeoServer web interface. Hopefully, you are now more confident with every section and you have a good idea of how they work.

Specifically, we covered how you can retrieve information on general configuration, server status, and logs. Next we explored the interface section where you can configure data access, create new layers, and publish them.

We briefly described how you can create workspaces and a data store from the shapefile. In this chapter we also covered service-specific configurations for WFS, WMS, and WCS. GeoServer's developers constantly take great efforts to enforce standards compliance. In this area you can tune the services and discover the vendor options that GeoServer offers you.

Finally we explored two areas greatly improved in the 2.2 release: caching and security configuration.

All of these topics will be further explored in the following chapters.

In the next chapter, we will explore data stores. You will add new data to GeoServer. Not only will you use the `shapefile` and `PostGIS` built-in data formats, you will also download and configure two data extensions, for MySQL and Oracle.

With all these formats, you will be ready to publish 90 percent of the existing vector data.

4
Accessing Layers

One of the main aims of this book is to help you learn how to publish your data. GeoServer lets you create layers, items containing configuration for your data, and the way they are represented on a map. In this chapter we'll go over different vector and raster layer output types and explore ways to use them. We'll discover a hidden gem called the **Reflector**. *For good measure, we'll toss in some other output extensions.*

We will cover the following points in detail:

- ◆ Vector output types including GeoRSS and GEOJSON
- ◆ Raster output types such as JPEG and PNG
- ◆ OpenLayers single tile and tiled output
- ◆ Freemarker temples
- ◆ Using the Reflector
- ◆ Output extensions

Layer types

In the previous chapter, we explored the Layer list interface. All layers, publishing raster or vector data, are listed here. You can use **Web Mapping Service** (**WMS**) to publish them or the **Web Feature Service** (**WFS**) to deliver vector features. Using the **Layers Preview** panel you can easily check how your data looks:

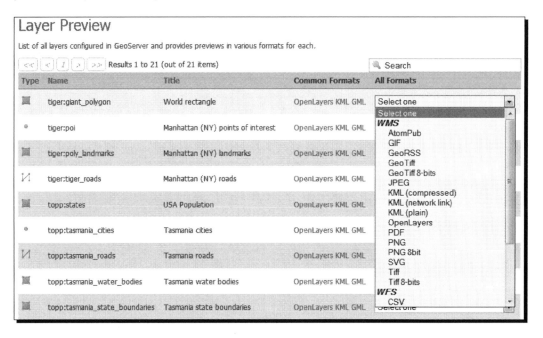

As of GeoServer 2.2, the **All Formats** drop-down box on the **Layer Preview** page will still include options for **WFS** and **WMS**, even when they are not active. Due to security restrictions, when the respective services are disabled or when output formats don't apply, you'll get an error. If your layers seem to output incorrectly and display errors or are not being found, you might need to check your security settings.

OpenLayers

Remember this from *Chapter 3, Exploring the Web Interface and Demos*? Building web-based maps is the inspiration for the book. OpenLayers is an open source JavaScript library to display web-based maps, similar to the mapping client from Google Maps and a growing number of others. OpenLayers is also a project of the **Open Source Geospatial Foundation** (**OSGeo**).

LeafLet (http://leafletjs.com) is a promising mapping client with ties to OpenLayers. Be on the lookout for examples using LeafLet in future chapters.

You'll notice several options at the top of the OpenLayers preview after you click the **Options** icon. Some of these options are specific to GeoServer, and not part of the WMS specification.

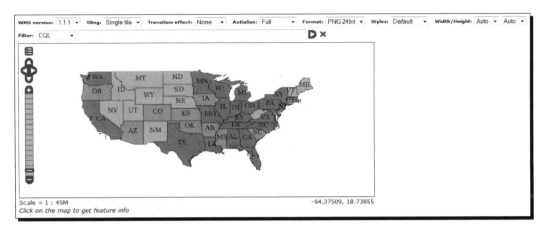

Time for action – exploring OpenLayers options

As the OpenLayers map opens, you will see three icons inside the map. Clicking on the top-left one shows several options to interact with GeoServer WMS. We will now explore some of these options.

1. If you haven't already, select the **OpenLayers output** option for `topp:states`; or use the following URL to open the demo:

```
http://localhost:8080/geoserver/topp/wms?service=WMS&versi
on=1.1.0&request=GetMap&layers=topp:states&styles=&bbox=-
124.73142200000001,24.955967,-66.969849,49.371735&width=780&heig
ht=330&srs=EPSG:4326&format=application/openlayers
```

As you can see, the request itself is a `GetMap` request to the WMS service, so why are you getting a full app and not a plain image? Look at the parameters; there is a `format=application/openlayers` key-value pair. This makes GeoServer deliver you a full JavaScript app.

2. Change the height to `512` and width to `512` in the URL bar:

```
http://localhost:8080/geoserver/topp/wms?service=WMS&versi
on=1.1.0&request=GetMap&layers=topp:states&styles=&bbox=-
124.73142200000001,24.955967,-66.969849,49.371735&width=512&heig
ht=512&srs=EPSG:4326&format=application/openlayers
```

3. After OpenLayers loads, click on the top-left icon. Map options are shown.

4. In the tiling drop-down list, toggle between **Single tile** and **Tiled** as you pan and zoom the map. Notice how the map refreshes for each option.

What just happened?

Single tile loads an image that fills the entire viewable area, and the **Tiled** version gets 256x256 square images and combines them. If you use **Firebug** for **Firefox**, you can see the request sent to GeoServer as `width=256&height=256` for the tiled version, and one request as `width=512&height=512` for the single tile.

Working with tiles

For an OpenLayers map of 512 width and 512 height, you get four images to display the map. Each request to the server is the same, except the `bbox` parameter specifying the area.

 The bounding box parameter is called `bbox`. The value for `bbox` is the latitude and longitude of the area you're calling from GeoServer. The format for this parameter is `bbox=minx,miny,maxx,maxy`.

If your map's height and width are fairly small, using a single tile will likely take less time to render. This depends on your data filter and number of features too, but it is a good rule of thumb. Using a single tile will also be useful if you need to output JPEG or PNG larger than 256x256 for larger display needs. It's the same display, but as a single tile.

Most of your web-based maps (using OpenLayers, for example) will use tiled images. Splitting images into smaller chunks helps them load faster.

Have a go hero – selecting a features subset with filters

Get a jump start on filtering. Enter a filter by using the `FeatureID` parameter from the **Filter** dropdown. Enter `states.17,states.6`. This should show **Colorado** and **Alabama**. We dive deeper into **CQL** (**Contextual Query Language**) filters in later chapters.

Exploring the Web Map Service output formats

Let's look at the URL parameters from the output request to GeoServer's WMS. Consider this output request for the OpenLayers demo. The format parameter is `application/openlayers`. The format parameter is the key to this chapter, but it's worth going over the other parameters while we're here.

```
http://localhost:8080/geoserver/topp/wms?service=WMS&versi
on=1.1.0&request=GetMap&layers=topp:states&styles=&bbox=-
124.73142200000001,24.955967,-66.969849,49.371735&width=780&height=330
&srs=EPSG:4326&format=application/openlayers
```

The first parameter, `service`, explains to GeoServer what kind of request you are sending. The value is `WMS` as we want to retrieve a map.

Several versions exist, so we use the `version` parameter to specify which WMS dialect we are speaking, `1.1.0` in this example.

The specific request is `GetMap`. The `layer` parameter defines which data has to be represented on the map. We can insert a comma-separated list of layers, but in this case we are happy with just `topp:states`.

We go with the default rendering for the `topp:states` layer so the style parameter is empty. `bbox` is the bounding box, or area of the map we want to display. The format of `bbox` is `minx,miny,maxx,maxy`.

The size of the area returned will be `780` wide and `330` high. `srs` or projection will be latitude and longitude, that is, `EPSG:4326`. Finally, the output format will be OpenLayers.

Documentation on GeoServer-specific parameters can be found at the URL `http://docs.geoserver.org/latest/en/user/services/wms/vendor.html`.

AtomPub

The **Atom Publishing Protocol** (**Atom Pub**) format is an XML-based output. Also known as a Vector output type, it is comparable to RSS feeds which are more common. It allows others to subscribe to features published by GeoServer. The output format is specified by `application/atom+xml` as the format parameter value.

GIF

This output format is well-known. **Graphics Interchange Format** (**GIF**) has been around for a long time on the Web. This format only supports 256 colors, so it's rarely used for high quality images. In some cases, it is useful when simple shape outputs are produced. It's not the best for completeness, and you will most likely favor PNG, TIFF, or JPEG instead.

The output format is specified by `image/gif` as the format parameter value.

I have to mention, GIF should be pronounced Jif (peanut butter). CompuServe came up with the format and the Jif pronunciation back in the late 1980s. Check out `http://www.olsenhome.com/gif`.

GeoRSS

This output format is similar to your RSS feeds you'd use for syndicating other content. The noticeable difference is the `georss` tag. Take a look at the `georss` output for the `sf:bugsites` layer; you'll see that the first item has the location using `<georss:point>44.384907731239096 -103.86762869467091</georss:point>` to specify the location of the site. Google and other search engines are indexing this content. Google accepts this output format as a Geo sitemap.

The output format is specified by `application/rss+xml` as the format parameter value.

 For more resources, take a look at the following links:
- `http://en.wikipedia.org/wiki/GeoRSS`
- `http://www.georss.org`

```
<?xml version="1.0" encoding="UTF-8"?><rss xmlns:atom="http://
www.w3.org/2005/Atom" xmlns:georss="http://www.georss.org/georss"
version="2.0">
<channel>
<title>sf:bugsites</title>
<description>Feed auto-generated by GeoServer</description>
..
<item>
<title>bugsites.1</title>
<link><![CDATA[http://192.168.1.112:8080/geoserver/wms/
reflect?format=application/atom+xml&layers=sf:bugsites&featureid=bugsi
tes.1]]></link>
<guid><![CDATA[http://192.168.1.112:8080/geoserver/wms/
reflect?format=application/atom+xml&layers=sf:bugsites&featureid=bugsi
tes.1]]></guid>
<description>
<![CDATA[<h4>bugsites</h4>
<ul class="textattributes">

  <li><strong><span class="atr-name">cat</span>:</strong> <span
class="atr-value">1</span></li>
  <li><strong><span class="atr-name">str1</span>:</strong> <span
class="atr-value">Beetle site</span></li>
```

```
</ul>
]]>
</description>
<georss:point>44.384907731239096 -103.86762869467091</georss:point>
</item>
..
</channel></rss>
```

 Check out more on GeoRSS in the documentation at
`http://docs.geoserver.org/stable/en/user/`
`tutorials/georss/georss.html`

JPEG

There is not much to say about this output format. Since PNG is more widely used these days, it seems that this output is not often called from GeoServer. You may want to use this format when static images of areas of maps are needed though. You can call these URLs with wget or CURL to manually cache the output.

You can do this with GeoWebCache, but this method is quick and easy.

The output format is specified by image/jpeg as the format parameter value.

KML (Plain)

We talked about this a little bit in *Chapter 3, Exploring the Administrative Interface*. The *Time for action* section installed Google Earth and viewed the topp:state layer. You can also use this format directly with Google Maps. You can type the URL directly into the Google Map search field. Obviously, your GeoServer needs to be accessible from the Internet.

Google accepts this output format as a Geo sitemap. Google is sensitive to the mime-type for KMZ and KML outputs for Sitemaps. GeoServer meets these requirements.

The output format is specified by application/vnd.google-earth.kml.xml as the format parameter value.

KMZ (Compressed)

This is a Keyhole compressed formatted file. In a nutshell, it's a ZIP file of KML. Google accepts this output format as a Geo sitemap as well.

The output format is specified by application/vnd.google-earth.kmz+xml as the format parameter value.

If you're proxying a request to/from GeoServer, you'll want to ensure its setting is the mime-type. For Apache, use `AddType` in your `httpd.conf`.

```
AddType application/vnd.google-earth.kmz .kmz
```

PDF

This output format is ideal for sharing maps. For example, you might want to display a map using OpenLayers and provide a link to export the visible map to PDF.

The output format is specified by `application/pdf` as the format parameter value.

PNG

This is the format you'll be using more often for your maps, although each image will be 255 pixels wide and 255 pixels in height, otherwise known as tiles. We'll go over that further in *Chapter 8, Performance and Caching*. In the output example delivered by clicking on the output dropdown, it gives you a single tile of the entire bounding box of the data you have.

The output format is specified by `image/png` as the format parameter value.

SVG

This format can be used with **Adobe Illustrator** or **Inkscape** – you need to export and further style your maps outside of GeoServer. This format seems to be the most popular vector format.

The output format is specified by `image/svg+xml` as the format parameter value.

From the Inkscape FAQ:

> *Inkscape is an open-source vector graphics editor similar to Adobe Illustrator, Corel Draw, Freehand, or Xara X. What sets Inkscape apart is its use of Scalable Vector Graphics (SVG), an open XML-based W3C standard, as the native format.*

Check out their website: `http://inkscape.org`.

TIFF

You'll have several versions of TIFF available. By default, you'll have TIFF and TIFF-8. As of this writing, using GeoServer 2.2, GeoTIFF is included in the drop-down list for **All Formats**.

The GeoTIFF output is the same as a normal TIFF, but includes metadata for describing geospatial data.

The output format is specified by `image/tiff`, `image/tiff8`, or `image/geotiff8` as the format parameter value.

 There's more information in the GeoServer documentation:

- `http://docs.geoserver.org/stable/en/user/services/wms/outputformats.html`
- `http://trac.osgeo.org/geotiff`

Web Feature Service

Although the result looks completely different, sending requests to WFS works pretty much the same as the WMS output options, except for the URL format. There are a few big differences here; notice that the format parameter name changes to `outputFormat`:

```
http://localhost:8080/geoserver/topp/ows?
service=WFS&
version=1.0.0&
request=GetFeature&
typeName=topp:states&
maxFeatures=50&
outputFormat=csv
```

CSV

This is the most common form of data exchange, but not likely the one you'd want to use unless you're planning to import into a spreadsheet (that is, Microsoft Excel) or for importing into an external database where other layer output formats don't apply.

The output format is specified by `csv` as the `outputFormat` parameter value.

GML (plain text)

This format seems to be overshadowed by the more popular KML format from Google. The KML format is somewhat based on GML; a GML output file can be converted to KML, but it's always the other way around. Both formats are XML-based. The most visible reason is that GML handles basic vector shapes, and KML on the other hand, supports 3D shapes.

The output format is specified by `GML2`, `GML/3.1.1`, or `GML/3.2` as the `outputFormat` parameter value.

GML2 (compressed GZIP)

This is the same as GML plain, except as the name implies, it's compressed. This format might be favored over plain GML outputs where bandwidth is an issue, and data sets are large.

The output format is specified by `GML-GZIP` as the `outputFormat` parameter value.

 Wikipedia has a good overall history of GML and its usage (`http://en.wikipedia.org/wiki/Geography_Markup_Language`).

GeoJSON

This format is a highly-desirable output from GeoServer. **GeoJSON** is just a JSON-formatted string, with additional keys for the geospatial data. For example, jQuery has a method called `getJSON` to get (local or remote file) parse JSON strings. Let's take a look at that now. The output format is specified by `json` as the `outputFormat` parameter value.

Time for action – parsing GeoJSON

You might want to query GeoServer and parse features in jQuery. We're just parsing a JSON string.

1. Go to the **Layer Preview** screen and click on the dropdown for **All Formats** for the `topp:states` layer.

2. Select the **GeoJSON** option or get the output directly using the following URL. Note that to limit the results, we are using the `featureid` parameter. We'll talk about filters in another chapter.

    ```
    http://localhost:8080/geoserver/topp/ows?service=WFS&version=1.0.0
    &request=GetFeature&typeName=topp:states&featureid=states.1,states
    .2,states.3&maxFeatures=50&outputFormat=json
    ```

3. Save this output in a text file called `states.json`.

4. Parse with jQuery. The following is a snippet of the code example included in this chapter:

    ```
    <script>
    $.getJSON('states.json', function(data) { $.each(data.features,
    function(key, val) { $('body').append('properties.STATE_NAME
    ' + val.properties.STATE_NAME + 'geometry.coordinates ' + val.
    geometry.coordinates); }); });
    });
    </script>
    ```

Shapefile

This seems to be the most common output format for GIS data exchange, but it's not so useful for building web-based maps. If you need to exchange large static data sets with someone else, then this might be a good option. The output file is a ZIP file containing the details for the layer. For example, consider this unzipped file for the `topp:states` layer.

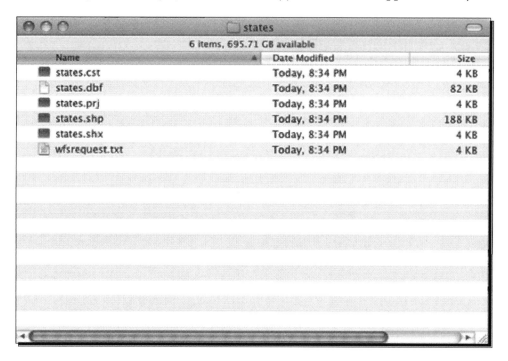

The output format is specified by `SHAPE-ZIP` as the `outputFormat` parameter value.

```
http://localhost:8080/geoserver/topp/ows?service=WFS&version=1.0.0&re
quest=GetFeature&typeName=topp:states&maxFeatures=50&outputFormat=SHA
PE-ZIP
```

Extra output options

The GeoServer gives you the ability to extend the output options for your data using extensions. Most of those extensions require additional setup; outside of dropping a `JAR` into `WEB-INF`. Let's look at a few that you might consider.

GDAL and OGR output

This is based on the GDAL library, and used for WFS output raster graphics. Using the `ogr2ogr` command, you can convert to several output formats. With OGR, you can convert from one vector format to another. We'll get into examples in future chapters.

> Take a look at the following links for more information on GDAL:
>
> ◆ http://docs.geoserver.org/latest/en/user/data/gdal.html
>
> ◆ http://docs.geoserver.org/stable/en/user/extensions/ogr.html
>
> ◆ http://www.gdal.org/ogr/ogr_formats.html

TEXT/HTML

One of the ways you can get information from GeoServer about features you click on is by querying WMS with a point, and getting a list of surrounding features.

The `outputFormat` format can be anything. The `INFO_FORMAT` should be `text/html`.

Time for action – using the GetFeatureInfo freemarker template

1. Go to the OpenLayers demo for `topp:states`.

2. After the map loads, click on a state. The layer information about that state loads under the map. Consider the following example for clicking on **Alabama**:

fid	STATE_NAME	STATE_FIPS	SUB_REGION	STATE_ABBR	LAND_KM	WATER_KM	PERSONS
states.17	Alabama	01	E S Cen	AL	131443.119	4332.268	4040587.0

3. Now examine the URL that was called. The `INFO_FORMAT=text/html` outputs features as a HTML string by default:

    ```
    http://localhost:8080/geoserver/topp/wms?REQUEST=GetFeatureInfo&E
    XCEPTIONS=application/vnd.ogc.se_xml&BBOX=-139.848709,18.549282,-
    51.852562,55.77842&SERVICE=WMS&INFO_FORMAT=text/html&QUERY_
    LAYERS=topp:states&FEATURE_COUNT=50&Layers=topp:states&WIDTH=780&H
    EIGHT=330&format=image/png&styles=&srs=EPSG:4326&version=1.1.1&x=4
    71&y=201
    ```

4. Create new files in `$GEOSERVER_DATA/workspaces/topp/states_shapefile/states` called `content.ftl`, `footer.ftl`, and `header.ftl`.

5. Place the following text in the `header.ftl` file:

```
<?xml version='1.0' encoding='utf-8'?>
<states>
```

6. In the `content.ftl` file, place the text:

```
<#list features as feature>
  <state>
    <STATE_ABBR>${feature.STATE_ABBR.value}</STATE_ABBR>
    <STATE_NAME>${feature.STATE_NAME.value}</STATE_NAME>
    <SUB_REGION>${feature.SUB_REGION.value}</SUB_REGION>
  </state>
</#list>
```

7. For the `footer.flt` file, the text would be simpler:

```
</states>
```

8. Go to **Server Status | Configuration and catalog** and click the **Reload** button:

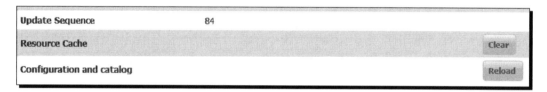

9. Click on a state, Alabama for example. The new state information will be shown below the map.

What just happened?

We changed the default template for the `topp:states` feature by creating three new files and added them to `workspaces/topp/state_shapefiles/states`. We then reloaded the GeoServer configuration by using the **Reload** feature in **Server Status**, or optionally by restarting GeoServer.

Since GeoServer is setting the output as `text/html`, you will need to treat the returned string as text, and then parse to XML before using it in JavaScript.

For more resources, take a look at http://docs.geoserver.org/
latest/en/user/tutorials/GetFeatureInfo/index.html.

Have a go hero – changing another layer

Find another layer and create a new template. Explore ways to format this data using the documentation.

ImageMap

Everyone remembers the days when ImageMaps were commonly used. The idea of using an image map to describe POIs on your maps seems like a good one.

One of the extensions you can install by just dropping a JAR into `$GEOSERVER_HOME/WEB-INF/lib` is ImageMap. The only challenge with this output option is that PointSymbolizer is represented as circles only, and in most cases you will have icons for features that aren't circles. The image maps don't always match.

> For more information, take a look at `http://docs.geoserver.org/latest/en/user/extensions/imagemap.html`.

Using WMS Reflector

This is a great way to preview options in GeoServer without coding a long URL. The reflector will output PNG (the default), JPEG, PNG8, and GIF. Also, in cases where you don't want to use GeoWebCache, this is quite useful.

The URL passes a number of parameters to specify what output you want. Most of these will not be changed. Reflector uses default values for missing parameters. The only parameter you need to provide is the `layers` parameter by default. Check out the GeoServer documentation for more information on these values. There's no need to rehash them here.

> For more information, take a look at `http://docs.geoserver.org/stable/en/user/tutorials/wmsreflector.html`.

Time for action – using WMS Reflector

1. Let's use the `topp:states` layer preview for this example. Enter the following URL into your browser, or select the **JPEG** output option from the **All Formats** drop-down list on the **Layer Preview** page. The layer preview URL is quite long:

   ```
   http://localhost:8080/geoserver/topp/wms?service=WMS&versi
   on=1.1.0&request=GetMap&layers=topp:states&styles=&bbox=-
   124.73142200000001,24.955967,-66.969849,49.371735&width=780&heig
   ht=330&srs=EPSG:4326&format=image/png
   ```

2. Now open a new window, or browser tab, and use the Reflector to get the same results. Just type the following URL in the address bar and then press *Enter*:

   ```
   http://localhost:8080/geoserver/wms/reflect?layers=topp:states
   ```

3. Now add a new projection from the native EPSG: 4326 to Google Mercator. EPSG:900913. You will see the image flatten out:

   ```
   http://localhost:8080/geoserver/wms/reflect?layers=topp:states&srs
   =EPSG:900913
   ```

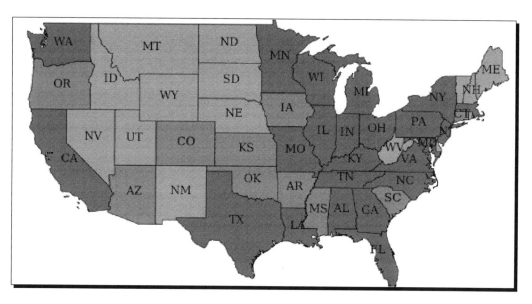

What just happened?

We just saved some considerable time for sure. All we needed to provide was the `layers` parameter, since that's the minimum, and the Reflector will default to a PNG for its output.

Then we changed the projection to Google Mercator EPSG: 900913. The Reflector does some heavy lifting for you.

Have a go hero – exploring the pdf Reflect option

To output `pdf`, you'll want to add the format parameter `application/pdf`, as shown in the following URL. Want to reproject? Add the `srs` parameter, most commonly Google Mercator EPSG:900913:

```
http://localhost:8080/geoserver/wms/reflect?layers=topp:states&format=
application/pdf&srs=EPSG:900913
```

Pop quiz – accessing data

Q1. Which output format lets you use your data in the Google Earth interface?

1. The TIFF format, which you can wrap on the globe.

2. The GeoRSS; you can show the data as a pinpoint in Google Earth.

3. The KML, KMZ; you can export your data in the native format of Google Earth.

Q2. Can you have more than an output format for WFS?

1. No, with WFS you can only publish data in the OGC standard, that is, GML.

2. Yes, you can publish the data in different GML releases.

3. Yes, you can publish the data in GML, shapefile, GeoJSON, and CSV.

Summary

That was a quick overview of output options GeoServer offers you.

We talked about the vector outputs such as GeoRSS and GeoJSON. We also talked about raster outputs formats, such as JPEG and PNG. One of the coolest things we talked a little about was the Reflector.

In the next chapter, we'll go over some data store options, exposing your geospatial data to Geoserver, and creating layers.

5
Adding Your Data

In this chapter, we'll take a look at the types of data you can use with GeoServer. We will have a quick overview of the formats supported, both built-in and via extensions, and how to add them to your configuration. More specifically, we will load data from a shapefile, MySQL table, PostGIS table, and an Oracle table using US census data.

In this chapter, we will cover the following points:

◆ Vector data sources

◆ Connecting to a MySQL database

◆ Connecting to a PostGIS database

◆ Connecting to an Oracle database

◆ Raster data sources

◆ Data source extensions

We're adding data now. Buckle up!

Configuring your data

In *Chapter 3, Exploring the Administrative Interface*, we covered the administration interface. Specific to data configuration, we explored workspaces, data sources, and layers. In this chapter, you will use them to publish new data sets.

Do you remember we already added a shapefile? We are now going to add some more data using different formats. GeoServer could access some data formats by default, while others require optional extensions and libraries. The following screenshot shows the default format GeoServer is shipped with.

According to the types of spatial data we defined in *Chapter 1, GIS Fundamentals*, you'll have two types of data sources in GeoServer: **vector** and **raster**.

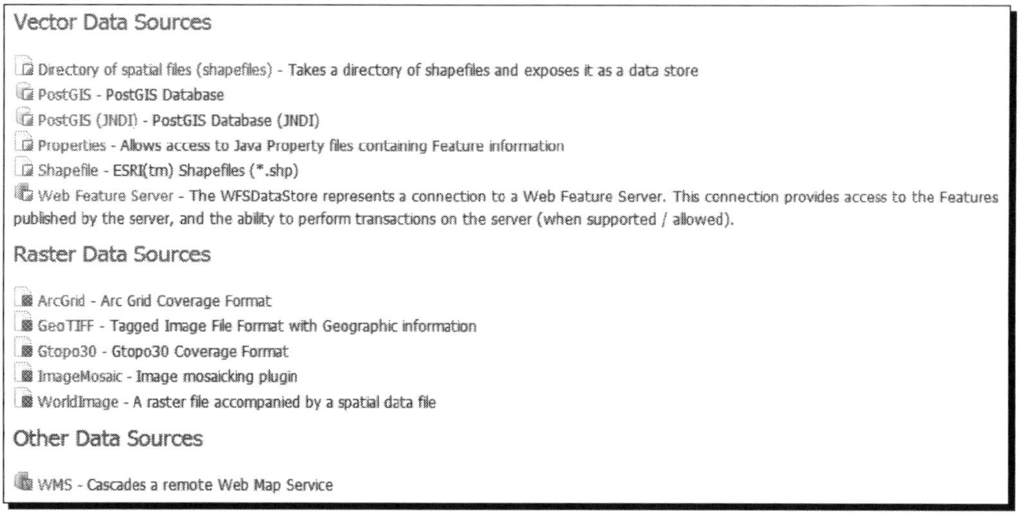

Vector Data Sources

Directory of spatial files (shapefiles) - Takes a directory of shapefiles and exposes it as a data store
PostGIS - PostGIS Database
PostGIS (JNDI) - PostGIS Database (JNDI)
Properties - Allows access to Java Property files containing Feature information
Shapefile - ESRI(tm) Shapefiles (*.shp)
Web Feature Server - The WFSDataStore represents a connection to a Web Feature Server. This connection provides access to the Features published by the server, and the ability to perform transactions on the server (when supported / allowed).

Raster Data Sources

ArcGrid - Arc Grid Coverage Format
GeoTIFF - Tagged Image File Format with Geographic information
Gtopo30 - Gtopo30 Coverage Format
ImageMosaic - Image mosaicking plugin
WorldImage - A raster file accompanied by a spatial data file

Other Data Sources

WMS - Cascades a remote Web Map Service

Configuring vector data sources

GeoServer has several built-in vector data sources. Shapefiles and PostGIS are great formats to store your spatial data.

Adding a properties file

You can store your data in Java properties files. This is a great option if you only have a handful of features (under 25, for example), and creating a real data store would be overkill. You can also add features at runtime without the need to recreate or reconfigure the data store. A properties file is a text file containing a header and a row for each record with KEY=VALUE pairs. Do you remember the places list in *Chapter 1, GIS Fundamentals*? You can publish it in GeoServer with this properties file:

```
_=id:Integer,code:String,name:String,country:Geometry:srid=4326
places.1=1|Rome|Italy|POINT(12.492 41.890)
places.2=2|Grand Canyon|Usa|POINT(-112.122 36.055)
places.3=3|Paris|France|POINT(2.294 48.858)
places.4=4|Iguazu National Park|Argentina|POINT(-54.442 -25.688)
places.5=5|Ayers Rock|Australia|POINT(131.036 -25.345)
```

Configuring an external Web Feature Service

This data source enables you to add an external WFS server as a data provider. Layers published by the remote server can be added to your GeoServer and published as WFS or WMS in a cascading style.

 For Drupal developers, you might consider checking out the WFS Drupal project. It works pretty well for a small number of features. For big data sets, you should point GeoServer to your relational geospatial database. For most Drupal developers that would be **MySQL**. (http://drupal.org/project/wfs)

Adding shapefiles

You can add shapefiles to GeoServer with two data sources. With the first you configure a folder containing a set of shapefiles and you can also add new ones after the data source is created. The other data source works the same way as the shapefile directory store, except you provide a path to just one shapefile.

Time for action – adding shapefiles

You'll notice a lot of results from doing a Google search for shapefiles. This is the most common format to exchange GIS data sets. Let's download one of those and publish it as a layer.

1. Download Tiger 2011 county census data as a shapefile and place it in an appropriate folder:

    ```
    ~/shapes$ wget http://www2.census.gov/geo/tiger/TIGER2011/COUNTY/
    tl_2011_us_county.zip
    ```

2. Unzip the archive:

    ```
    ~/shapes$ unzip tl_2011_us_county.zip
    Archive:  tl_2011_us_county.zip
      inflating: tl_2011_us_county.dbf
      inflating: tl_2011_us_county.prj
      inflating: tl_2011_us_county.shp
      inflating: tl_2011_us_county.shp.xml
      inflating: tl_2011_us_county.shx
    ```

In fact a shapefile is not a single file. According to specifications (`http://www.esri.com/library/whitepapers/pdfs/shapefile.pdf`), you need at least three files with `shp`, `dbf`, and `shx` extensions. Although not strictly required, it is really worthwhile to also have the `.prj` file. It contains the SRS definition for the data contained in the shapefile.

3. If you are unsure about SRS of data, have a look at the `.prj` file. The census data are in geographic coordinates, the EPSG code is 4269:

```
~/shapes$ cat tl_2011_us_county.prj
GEOGCS["GCS_North_American_1983",DATUM["D_North_American_1983",SPH
EROID["GRS_1980",6378137,298.257222101]],PRIMEM["Greenwich",0],UNI
T["Degree",0.017453292519943295]]
```

Do you feel confused with this syntax? If you didn't go through the *Have a go hero* section in *Chapter 1, GIS Fundamentals*, it could be the right moment to have a look at `http://epsg-registry.org`.

4. Now open the administration interface, go to the **Data | Stores** section and click on **Add new Store | Shapefile**.

5. **Workspace** is **tiger**. **Data Source Name** is **tiger_counties**. **Description** is **tiger counties**. For **Connection Parameters**, click on **Browse** and select the directory where you downloaded and unzipped the shapefile:

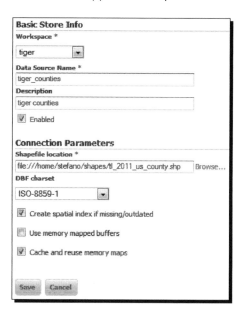

6. Click on **Save**.

7. On the next screen, click on **Publish** to start the process of creating a layer:

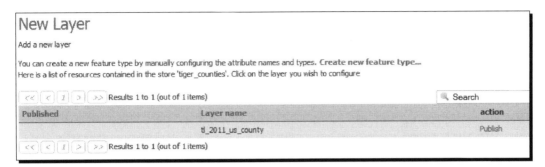

8. You have to complete some information in the form. Scroll down to the **Coordinate Reference Systems** and insert the **Declared SRS** option as **EPSG:4269**. Click on **Compute from data** and **Compute from native bounds** in the **Bounding Boxes** section:

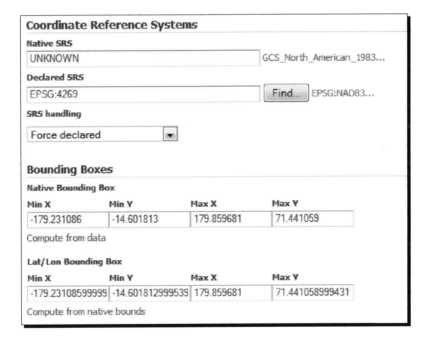

9. Click on **Save**.

10. Left navigation to **Layer Preview | OpenLayers** next to `tiger:tl_2011_us_county`.

What just happened?

We downloaded county borders from the US census and unzipped it into the folder called `shapes` – our workspace name for the book. We then walked through the steps to create a new vector data store for shapefile and publish it. With a little effort, the data are now accessible from a client making a WMS or WFS request. Publishing data in GeoServer is really straightforward, isn't it?

Using PostGIS

This is the most popular and most capable of all open source relational databases with spatial capabilities, and its features are constantly increasing. It leverages on PostgreSQL, a well-known and powerful RDBMS challenging top commercial products such as Oracle. The current release for PostGIS is 2.0.1 and for PostgreSQL is 9.1.4.

Both have an equally bad reputation of being a hard horse to ride. While fully understanding all possibilities or dealing with fine tuning may be complicated, using PostGIS as a repository for your data is not rocket science. Are you wondering where PostGIS is located in the GeoServer installation? It is not there, but we are just making sure you install it in a few steps and load some data to play with GeoServer.

If you are eager to learn more than the simple steps we will perform, then there are two wonderful references to read. Project sites for PostgreSQL and PostGIS contain a lot of pages ranging from basic to complex topics:

- `http://www.postgis.org/documentation/manual-2.0/`
- `http://www.postgresql.org/docs/9.1/static/index.html`

Time for action – installing PostgreSQL and PostGIS

We are going to transform the census data from shapefile to a PostGIS table. Unless you already have a PostGIS installation, we will first need to build it up. You can install PostGIS in several ways, and official and user documentation on customized installation is widely available. In order to get you started, we will use nice packages freely distributed from EnterpriseDB™. Apart from choosing the proper binary package, installation runs the same way on Linux or Windows.

1. The entry point for download is located at `http://enterprisedb.com/downloads/postgres-postgresql-downloads`. The PostgreSQL column contains links to the binary packages for Windows and Linux; choose one and download it.

Current Releases		
	Postgres Plus Advanced Server 9.1	**PostgreSQL 9.1**
Release Notes	Download	
Windows	Win32 Win64	Win32 Win64
Linux x86-32	Download	Download
Linux x86-64	Download	Download
Mac		Download
Solaris SPARC	Download	
Solaris x86-64	Download	
HP-UX	Download	

2. Run the installer.

3. You can go with the default **Installation Directory**:

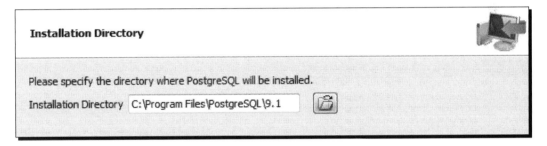

4. Go with the default **Data Directory** too:

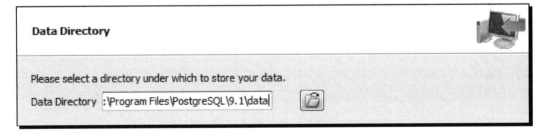

5. You can keep things simple on your development box; set **postgres** as your **Password**:

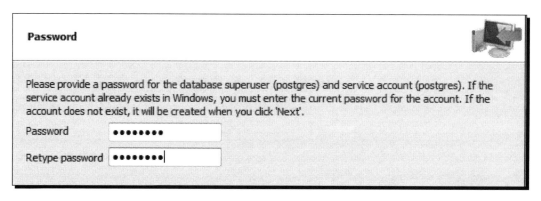

6. Don't change the default listening port unless you know it is already binded to another service:

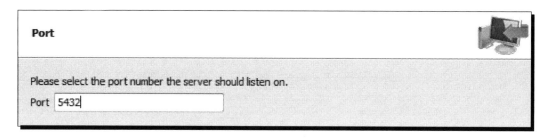

7. Leave the **Locale** for DB to **Default**:

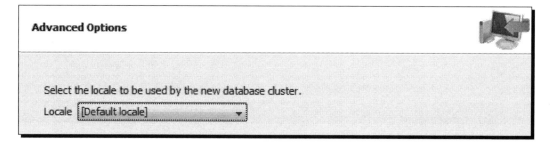

8. And at last we are really starting the installation process. Click on **Next** and wait until it completes.

9. We have now completed PostgreSQL installation; leave the Stack Builder running option flagged and click on **Finish**. Stack Builder is a great option to customize your PostgreSQL installation. We will use it to add PostGIS:

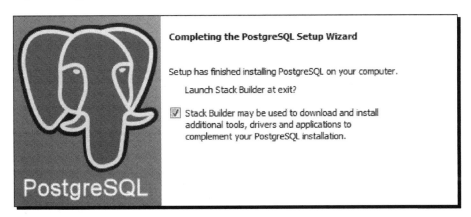

10. Select your local instance of PostgreSQL and click on **Next**:

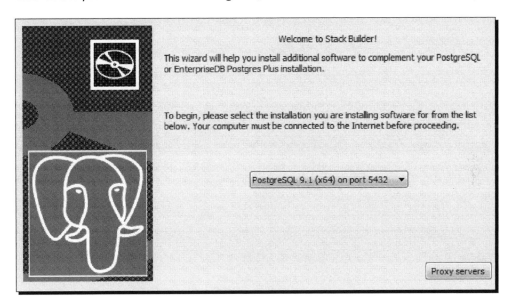

11. Select **PostGIS 2.0**, or newer, from the available applications in the catalog tree:

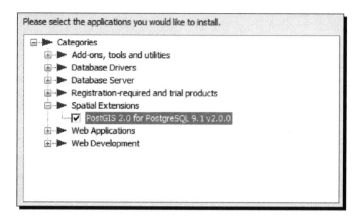

12. Stack Builder will now download the PostGIS installer and launch it.

13. After you accept the license agreement, you will be prompted to select components to be installed. It is a good idea to have the installer create a spatial database for you:

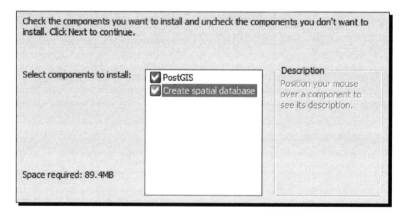

14. PostGIS installer will find your PostgreSQL location; as you have only one, there is no need to make any changes here.

15. Insert the password for the **postgres** user you selected previously, and leave the default listening port:

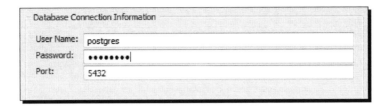

16. Leave the default name for the spatial database and click on **Install**:

17. PostGIS is now installed. When prompted for **GDAL_DATA** settings you should answer **Yes**. PostGIS needs data contained in that folder to perform data reprojection (that is, transforming coordinates from a SRS to another). If you already have a GDAL installation, you may want to say **No** here and perform manual configuration later:

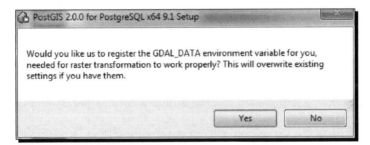

18. Click on **Close** to dismiss the PostGIS installer and then click on **Finish** to close Stack Builder.

What just happened?

We installed PostgreSQL and PostGIS. With these tools you can build a full repository for your spatial data. We are going to lay the first brick of your geodatabase in the next section. Let's use PostGIS!

Time for action – loading data in PostGIS and publishing them in GeoServer

Now that you have a functioning instance of PostGIS, it's time to load some data. We will keep the same census data used for shapefiles and turn them into a PostGIS spatial table.

1. Start the PostGIS Shapefile Import/Export Manager, an easy tool installed along with PostGIS. Click on the **View Connection details** button and insert the parameters needed to connect to PostGIS:

2. Now, click on the **Add File** button and browse to the shapefile containing Tiger 2011 county census data. The tool doesn't recognize the SRS contained in the `prj` file. Set the value of the field to **4269**:

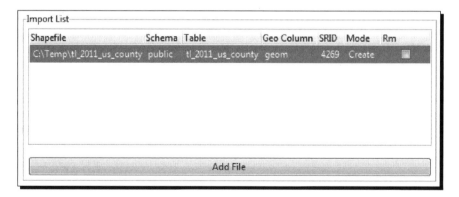

3. Click on the **Import** button and set the encoding to **LATIN1** as **DBF file character encoding**:

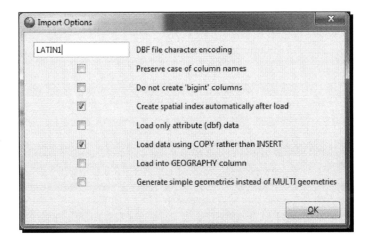

4. Wait while the loader transforms your data and inserts them into a new PostGIS table. Eventually, you should see a success message in the log textbox. Click on **Cancel** to dismiss the loader utility:

```
===============================
Importing with configuration: tl_2011_us_county, public, geom, C:\Temp\tl_2011_us_county,
mode=c, dump=1, simple=0, geography=0, index=1, shape=1, srid=4269
Shapefile type: Polygon
PostGIS type: MULTIPOLYGON[2]
Shapefile import completed.
```

5. Now open the administration interface, go to the **Data | Stores** section, and click on **Add new store | PostGIS**.

6. Select **tiger** for **Workspace**. Set **Data Source Name** and **Description** as **myPostGIS**. For **Connection Parameters**, you need to insert the same values you used with the loader. For your simple database, you don't need to play with the other settings; go with default values and click on **Save**:

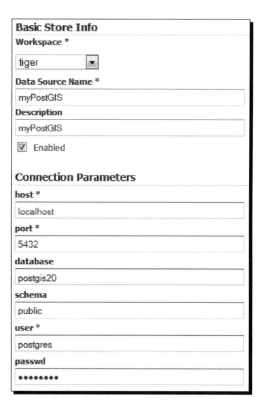

7. GeoServer will connect to PostGIS and present you a list with all tables containing spatial features. Click on the **Publish** link to the right of the **tl_2001_us_county** table.

Are you wondering who created the two tables called **raster_columns** and **raster_overviews**? They are system tables, used by PostGIS to store metadata for rasters loaded in the database. Apart from really esoteric configurations, you won't publish them in GeoServer.

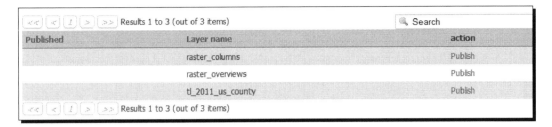

8. You now have the same publishing form we used for the shapefile. Note that this time GeoServer recognizes the native SRID for data. Click on **Compute from data** and **Compute from native bounds** in the **Bounding Boxes** section.

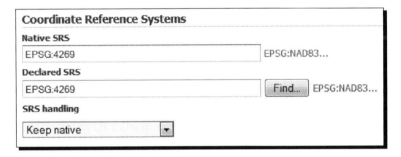

9. Click on **Save** and your data is published. You can now see a preview on **Layer Preview | OpenLayers** next to **tiger:tl_2011_us_county_PG**.

What just happened?

We installed PostgreSQL/PostGIS, then loaded the counties data set and published it in GeoServer. Did you notice that the layer's publishing runs almost the same, whatever the format of the data is? GeoServer architecture relieves you from details of different data sources; as long as you have a driver for a specific RDBMS or binary format you can add data in GeoServer, simply ignoring the actual format.

GUI loader is a great tool, but you may need to load shapefiles on a remote server, probably with only a remote shell session. Don't be afraid! **shp2pgsql** is there to help you. It is a command-line tool, available both on Windows and Linux editions of PostGIS. In fact, shapefiles are not really loaded by shp2pgsql but they are translated in a form that **psql** can keep and load for you. So you just have to pipe the output to psql:

```
$ shp2pgsql -s 4269 -g geom -I ~/data/tl_2011_us_
county.shp public.tl_2011_us_county | psql -h localhost
-p 5432 -d postgisDB -U gisuser
```

The basic set of parameters required are -s to set the spatial reference system, -g to name the geometric column (useful when appending data), and -I to create a spatial index. There are quite a few of other parameters that make it a flexible tool; as usual, -? is your friend if you need to execute a less trivial data loading. Apart from creating a new table—default option—you can append data to an existing table, drop it, and recreate or just create an empty table modeling its structure according to the shapefile data.

Have a go hero – filtering data

PostGIS gives you greater usage flexibility with data. You can process and reuse the data to produce new data sets. A simple processing is filtering data to show a subset. Let's say you want to publish a new map of counties, but limited to the state of California. You can accomplish this in PostGIS with a view. Open **PgAdmin**, connect to PostGIS, create the view, and publish it.

Configuring raster data sources

Raster data sources are commonly used to read satellite imagery, scanned maps, and **digital elevation model (DEM)**. You can add this data as a base layer for your maps.

ArcGrid

This is a proprietary binary format created by Esri and used with ArcGIS. A sample is included with GeoServer. Check out the `arcGridSample` data store and the `nurc:Arc_Sample` layer.

GeoTiff

A `TIFF` file is commonly used as the storage format for an aerial picture. A `GeoTiff` (`http://trac.osgeo.org/geotiff/`) is an extension of the TIFF format. It includes geoSpatial data in the header, an SRS, and the bounding box. Check out the sample data store called `sf:sfdem`.

Gtopo30

This is a format for DEM developed by the **United States Geological Survey** (**USGS**). The 30 in the name stands for 30 arc seconds, which is the fixed cell size for this format.

ImageMosaic

This data store allows creating a mosaic form of a set of georeferenced images, for example, a folder of geotiff files. It is commonly used when you want to combine several images together to create a continuous flowing coverage. This is a pretty advanced topic. Check out the GeoServer online reference to learn more: `http://docs.geoserver.org/stable/en/user/data/imagemosaic.html`.

WorldImage

This is another format originally developed by ESRI. It's a plain ASCII-formatted file coupled with a raster image. The text file describes how the image is to be used. These are easily spotted by the `tfw` (`tiff`) or `jpw` (`jpeg`) file extensions. Some samples are included with GeoServer. You'll see a data store called `worldImageSample` and a layer called `nurc:Img_Sample`.

Configuring an external Web Map Service

If you know of a remote WMS server that you want to use, this is a good option. You can also ask the GeoServer to pass this data off to GeoWebCache to get a bump in performance.

Pop quiz – adding data to GeoServer

Q1. Can you add different data formats to GeoServer?

1. No you have to choose a data format and get stick to it.
2. Yes but you can only have vector data or raster data.
3. Yes you can add data for any format available in GeoServer.

Q2. How can you add a set of adjacent raster files?

1. Add a data source for each image and then mash them up in the client.
2. Create a shapefile index and use it as a ImageMosaic data source.
3. Create a shapefile index and add it as a vector data source.

Exploring additional data sources

Several optional formats are supported by GeoServer beyond the built-in data sources. In the remaining part of this chapter, we will explore a couple of RDBMS quite popular and supporting spatial data: **Oracle** and **MySQL**.

Using Oracle

Oracle is probably the most widely-used commercial RDBMS. It has support for spatial since release 7, back in 1980's. The current release, 11.2, comes with two flavors of spatial data extensions, **Oracle Spatial** and **Oracle Locator**. They share the same geometry type and basic set of operators and functions. Oracle Spatial incorporates a richer set of functions for spatial analysis. Oracle is not free open source software like GeoServer or PostGIS and it has a quite complicated and expensive license model. We won't cover installation here; as long as you are going to use Oracle, you should have expertise and/or a proper budget to have it up and running.

Time for action – adding Oracle support in GeoServer

So you managed to get an Oracle service with spatial data loaded? Well, you are now just two steps away from victory. We will add the Oracle data source and configure it properly.

1. To add Oracle support, we need to download an extension. Point your browser to `http://geoserver.org/display/GEOS/Stable`, locate the **Extensions** section, and click on the **Oracle** link to download the ZIP file.

> When adding extensions to GeoServer, pay attention at the release. You should always match GeoServer and an extension's releases.

2. Stop Tomcat service. Extract the ZIP file, select the two `.jar` files and move them to the `webapps/geoserver/WEB-INF/lib` folder under the Tomcat installation folder.

3. Start Tomcat service and then log in to the GeoServer administration interface. Go to the **Data | Stores** section and click on **Add new store**. You can now see some new options. Select **Oracle NG**:

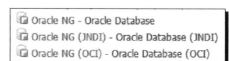

4. You have to insert the hostname for the Oracle server, the port on which the Oracle listener is waiting for connection requests (this is **1521** by default but ask your DBA for exact value). The **database** is the Oracle instance name, and finally insert a username and password. **schema** is an optional parameter; it tells GeoServer where it should look for spatial data. Click on Save:

5. GeoServer will connect to Oracle and present you a list with all tables containing spatial features. Clicking on the **Publish** link to the right of a table will bring you to the same publication form you used for shapefiles and PostGIS tables.

What just happened?

You added Oracle support to GeoServer. To do this, you copied a couple of JAR files in the Geoserver installation. The `ojdbc14.jar` file contains base classes for Oracle communication and usage and `gt-jdbc-oracle-2.7.5.jar` is the GeoTools library for spatial data management.

Using MySQL

You'll find that MySQL is the least popular of the relational databases offering spatial abilities. Indeed it has only limited support for spatial data. We are going to cover it here as it is very popular among web developers. Be aware that, unless for PostGIS or Oracle, the MySQL extension is unmaintained and unsupported. If you encounter bugs, you should be prepared to fix them yourself or provide funding to do that.

Time for action – adding MySQL data source

As for Oracle, we are assuming here that you already have a MySQL database available.

1. Before we add our MySQL data store, let's get some geospatial data inserted into MySQL. Get the `6686_05_mysql_usacounties.sql.zip` file and unzip it. Create a new database in MySQL. Call it `geoserver`.

2. Import `6686_04_mysql_usacounties.sql` into MySQL:

   ```
   mysql --connect_timeout=60 --max_allowed_packet=32MB -u root -p
   geoserver < 6686_04_mysql_usacounties.sql
   ```

3. To add MySQL support, we need to download an extension. Point your browser to `http://geoserver.org/display/GEOS/Stable`, locate the **Extensions** section, and click on the **MySQL** link to download the ZIP file.

4. Stop Tomcat service. Extract the ZIP file, select the two `.jar` files, and move them to the `webapps/geoserver/WEB-INF/lib` folder under the Tomcat installation folder.

5. Start Tomcat service and then log in to the GeoServer administration interface. Go to the **Data | Stores** section and click on **Add new store**. You can now see some new options. Select **MySQL**:

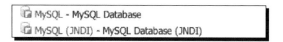

6. Now insert the **host** name, **port** for your MySQL server, **user**, and **password**. Click on **Save**:

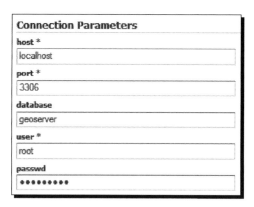

7. If it was able to connect to MySQL, you should see a list of tables visible to GeoServer:

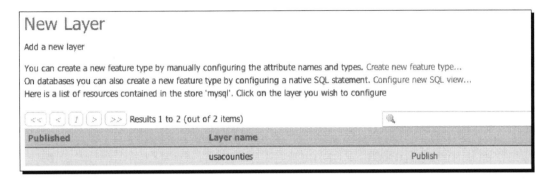

8. Clicking on the **Publish** link to the right of the **usacounties** table will bring you to the same publication form you used for shapefiles and PostGIS tables.

What just happened?

We imported a MySQL version of the county data. Then, we created a MySQL data store with this table. GeoServer discovered this table; we created a layer using the default polygon style and accepted the other default settings. We viewed the new layer using **Layer Preview**.

Pop quiz – adding data

Q1. Do I need to purchase an optional plugin to access data inside an RDBMS?

1. Yes, commercial vendor sell data options for GeoServer.
2. No, but you can only use open source RDBMS.
3. No, GeoServer supports most used commercial and open source RDBMS.

Q2. Is the publishing process dependent on the data format?

1. No, GeoServer/GeoTools abstraction layer relieves you from the internal structure of data.
2. No, but GeoServer can understand only a basic subset of data details.
3. Yes, you need to configure specific parameters for layers build on different data formats.

Summary

In this chapter we added some data sets to GeoServer. We used different formats for vector data. It should be now clear to you that as far as there is a data source available, you can manage different binary formats in GeoServer and mix them together in a map.

Specifically, we covered how to publish shapefiles and PostGIS tables. We then explored additional extensions and added Oracle and MySQL support to GeoServer.

In the next chapter, we will go forward with data publication. We will cover in detail how to use styles for rendering spatial features. You will learn how to set proper rules for different shapes, for example, point or polygon, and how to create styles with symbols reflecting the attributes' values of each feature.

Let's move on to ways to change the style of the maps using SLD defined styles.

6
Styling Your Layers

In the previous chapters, you learned how to add some data to GeoServer and you worked with maps by exploring Layer Preview. Also, with really simple maps, a fundamental process that GeoServer performs is the rendering of features. This involves assigning a symbol to each feature and applying a set of rules about how features have to be drawn. Choosing a symbol and how it has to be applied is the styling process. Styling is really important in web mapping. A map cannot be rendered without a style associated to the data. When you configured layers, you were using styles bundled with the GeoServer. In this chapter, we will explore what the style documents are and how you can create styles to produce beautiful maps.

We will cover the following points in detail:

- What style contains
- What symbol can be used in GeoServer
- How you can set rendering rules
- How to edit your styles with the GeoServer web interface and external tools

By the end of this chapter, you'll be able to style layers and also use style rules.

Understanding Styled Layer Descriptor

A map is generally composed of a set of layers. Each layer contains features of a determined type. When you ask GeoServer for a map, it has to extract features from the repository (for example, from a shapefile) and draw them according to some rules. Of course, it needs a repository for storing those rules and hence GeoServer developers need to decide a format for the storage medium containing rules.

Map rendering is not just a GeoServer problem; not surprisingly, it is common to all software-producing maps. Hence, it is not surprising that someone has defined a standard approach to styling layers. Indeed, GeoServer doesn't use a custom format for styles; instead it leverages on an OGC standard.

The standard describes the structure of the documents and which rules can be used. A document containing symbols' definitions and drawing rules is called a **Styled Layer Descriptor** (SLD) style and it is a text/XML file (its extension in GeoServer is `.sld`). SLD is an XML-based markup language and attached to the standard is an XSD schema that defines SLD syntax.

 If you are curious about the standard, you can find official papers for SLD at `http://portal.opengeospatial.org/files/?artifact_ id=22364` and XSD schemas at `http://schemas.opengis.net/sld/`.

Editing styles

Being an XML file, you can use different editing tools to edit a style. The first choice should be your preferred text editor, for example, **vi**, **emacs**, or **notepad++**. Consider that as you add rules and symbols, things may become fairly complicated. A tool that has highlight syntax for XML may greatly help you in debugging your styles. Of course, if you are trained to use it, a specialized XML editor that has support for XSD validation may help further, but usually I find it overkill.

Talking about editing styles, we shouldn't forget to mention the GeoServer administration interface. Indeed, GeoServer includes a simple GUI to view and edit XML files containing style rules. It contains a rich editor and a SLD validator; you got a first look at it in *Chapter 3, Exploring the Administrative Interface*.

Apart from XML/text editors, you can also consider a GUI tool to create styles; some open source Desktop GIS may produce SLD files. For example, **QGIS** may translate a layer legend in an XML file. QGIS supports shapefiles, Oracle, and PostGIS layers. After you add them to a map, you can use a GUI to set color, line width, and other drawing properties. You can then export your layer symbology in an SLD file.

Have a look at the QGIS project site at `http://qgis.osgeo.org/`.

Exploring the standard structure of a style

If you are going to create your styles with a graphical program hiding the complexity of your XML code, it is worthwhile to understand the basic syntax and structure of your documents. You may need to modify the styles after creation and the features you need to add may not be supported from the program, or simply you are on a server where the only way to edit is by using a text editor. Besides, you will write XML code in the examples in this chapter.

The first part of a style is always as in the following code fragment:

```
<?xml version="1.0" encoding="ISO-8859-1"?>
<StyledLayerDescriptor version="1.0.0"
    xsi:schemaLocation="http://www.opengis.net/sld
StyledLayerDescriptor.xsd"
    xmlns="http://www.opengis.net/sld"
    xmlns:ogc="http://www.opengis.net/ogc"
    xmlns:xlink="http://www.w3.org/1999/xlink"
    xmlns:xsi="http://www.w3.org/2001/XMLSchema-instance">
```

The first line is the XML declaration, and then we have the root element of every SLD file `<StyledLayerDescriptor/>`. It contains an attribute declaring the version of the standard it is using (GeoServer can use 1.0 and 1.1.0 SLD documents), followed by the namespaces and schema declarations. In the remainder of the chapter, we will omit this part from our example, for the sake of brevity; but keep in mind it is absolutely mandatory for the files you are writing.

`<StyledLayerDescriptor/>` contains a collection of the `<NamedLayer/>` or `<UserLayer/>` elements. Each defines drawing rules for a single layer. Indeed, they contain a collection of the `<UserStyle/>` elements.

A `<UserStyle/>` element contains `<FeatureTypeStyle/>` if the layer is a vector one, or `<CoverageStyle/>` if we are writing rules for a raster.

Both `<FeatureTypeStyle/>` and `<CoverageStyle/>`, contain a collection of the `<rule/>` element. This is the element where we will define how to draw features and we will look at its syntax in detail.

Time for action – viewing GeoServer bundled styles

Before we start to write rules specific to feature types, let's have a look at styles bundled with GeoServer. You already used them when you added data in the previous chapters. Let's have a look at those documents and search for the elements we know:

1. Open your GeoServer administration interface at `http://localhost:8080/geoserver/web/` and log in. Then select the **Data | Styles** item from the left menu:

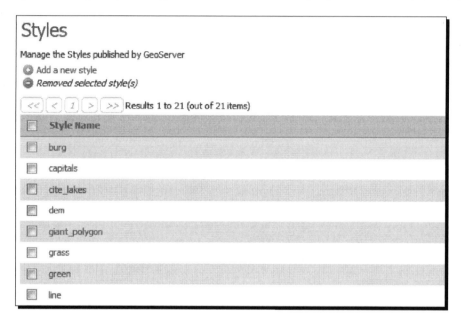

2. Select the **capitals** style. The **Style Editor** window will open up and load the XML code:

3. **capitals** is a fairly simple example. You can see the mandatory elements required for a style. There is **UserStyle** with a single rule defining a **circle** symbol with a red fill and a black stroke.

4. Now try to add something wrong. Insert the following code after the `<Rule>` element at line 11:

```
<Title>This is a clever rule</Title>
```

5. Click on the **Validate** button. GeoServer checks your file and reports an error occurring where you inserted your code. It complains about line 13 because you can't have two instances of **Name** inside a rule:

```
org.xml.sax.SAXParseException; lineNumber: 13; columnNumber: 18;
cvc-complex-type.2.4.a: Invalid content was found starting with
element 'Title'. One of '{"http://www.opengis.net/sld":Abstract,
"http://www.opengis.net/sld":LegendGraphic, "http://www.opengis.
net/ogc":Filter, "http://www.opengis.net/sld":ElseFilter,
"http://www.opengis.net/sld":MinScaleDenominator, "http://www.
opengis.net/sld":MaxScaleDenominator, "http://www.opengis.net/
sld":Symbolizer}' is expected.
```

6. Remove the line you inserted and click on the **Validate** button again. Now GeoServer shows the following message:

```
No validation errors.
```

7. Load some other style and have a look at the syntax. You don't need to fully understand them; we will cover it in the remaining part of the chapter.

What just happened?

We had a brief look at the GeoServer style editor and the styles bundled. A very important feature of the style editor is the **Validate** button. You can compose your styles with an external tool and have them validated before starting to use them.

Pop quiz – SLD basic elements

Q1. Can you have more than one `<StyledLayerDescriptor>` element in a style?

1. No, it is the root element and it must be the first one in each style and only one occurrence can be included.
2. Yes, but only if you are creating a multilayer style.
3. No, it is the child of the root element and can be included only once.

Q2. Can you have more than one `<Title>` element in a style?

1. No, it defines the title of the style and it can appear only once as child of the root element.
2. Yes, for example, you can have one as child of both the `<UserStyle>` and `<Rule>` elements.
3. No, it isn't an SLD element; you must use `<Name>` for descriptive strings.

Loading data for styling

We need some data to compose pretty maps. We are going to use the freely available Natural Earth data set.

Natural Earth provides several data sets in the shapefile format, packaged in three different reference scales. In the styles examples of this chapter we will use a subset; you need to download the following data sets:

◆ `http://www.naturalearthdata.com/http//www.naturalearthdata.com/download/50m/cultural/ne_50m_populated_places.zip`

◆ `http://www.naturalearthdata.com/http//www.naturalearthdata.com/download/50m/physical/ne_50m_rivers_lake_centerlines.zip`

◆ `http://www.naturalearthdata.com/http//www.naturalearthdata.com/download/10m/cultural/ne_10m_roads.zip`

◆ `http://www.naturalearthdata.com/http//www.naturalearthdata.com/download/10m/cultural/ne_10m_railroads.zip`

◆ `http://www.naturalearthdata.com/http//www.naturalearthdata.com/download/50m/cultural/ne_50m_admin_0_countries.zip`

Save all of them in the same folder and add it as a new data store to your GeoServer configuration. Refer to *Chapter 5*, *Adding Your Data*, for details about data store configuration. You don't need to publish the shapefiles; if you want to have a first look at the data, use the default styles. All the data is in geographic coordinates, WGS84. The SRID is ESPG:4326.

Apart from this data, you may find some resources in the code files accompanying this book that you can download from the Packt website. Code files contain XML files for all the styles we will write in this chapter, but I would suggest you take them just as a reference and a graphic resource used in styling.

Working with point symbols

We will start our exploration from styles for point features. The `Populated places` shapefile perfectly fits our purposes. If you added it with default values, you should see it rendered with a small red square as shown in the following screenshot:

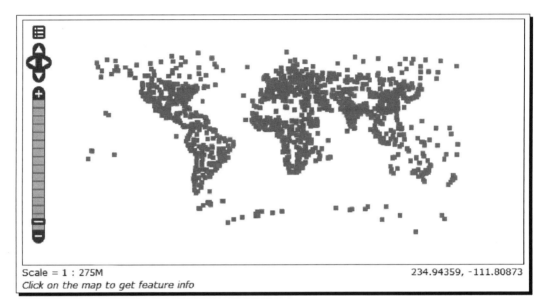

Scale = 1 : 275M

234.94359, -111.80873

Click on the map to get feature info

To modify the map, you need to add a new style and associate it to the layer. For setting point symbol properties, you have to use the `<PointSymbolizer>` element and its children.

Time for action – creating a simple point style

To familiarize you with SLD files creation, we will compose a simple style for using a small red circle applied to all the point features:

1. Open your favorite text editor. As mentioned previously, we will consider you have already inserted the XML declaration and the `StyledLayerDescriptor` part of the code. So start inserting a `NamedLayer` element. Then add a `Name` element and inside it write the name you want for your layer:

```
<NamedLayer>
  <Name>PopulatedPlaces</Name>
</NamedLayer>
```

2. Now you need to define at least one style for the layer. We use the `Title` element to assign a descriptive name to the style:

```
<NamedLayer>
  <Name> PopulatedPlaces </Name>
  <UserStyle>
    <Title>Geoserver Beginners Guide: Populated Places simple
mark</Title>
  </UserStyle>
</NamedLayer>
```

3. The data you want to apply the styles to are points, hence its vector data. You need to insert a `FeatureTypeStyle` element and a `Rule` for a `PointSymbolizer` element that is a style for point data:

```
<NamedLayer>
  <Name> PopulatedPlaces </Name>
  <UserStyle>
    <Title>Geoserver Beginners Guide: Populated Places simple
mark</Title>
    <FeatureTypeStyle>
      <Rule>
        <PointSymbolizer>
        </PointSymbolizer>
      </Rule>
    </FeatureTypeStyle>
  </UserStyle>
</NamedLayer>
```

4. You have now arrived at the core of our style. The elements you are going to add define the symbol used to draw the point features. You use a predefined graphic with the `WellKnownName` element (options are circle, square, triangle, star, cross, and x). A `Fill` element defines the point color with the `CssParameter` element. The color is in the form #RRGGBB. Finally, you define how many pixels the circle should be with the `Size` element:

```
<NamedLayer>
  <Name> PopulatedPlaces </Name>
  <UserStyle>
    <Title>Geoserver Beginners Guide: Populated Places simple
mark</Title>
    <FeatureTypeStyle>
      <Rule>
        <PointSymbolizer>
          <Graphic>
            <Mark>
              <WellKnownName>circle</WellKnownName>
```

```
            <Fill>
              <CssParameter name="fill">#FF0000</CssParameter>
            </Fill>
          </Mark>
          <Size>5</Size>
        </Graphic>
      </PointSymbolizer>
    </Rule>
  </FeatureTypeStyle>
</UserStyle>
</NamedLayer>
```

5. Now save your document as `PopulatedPlaces.xml` and open Style Editor in GeoServer.

6. Click on the **Add a new style** link to open the editor form:

7. Click on the **Browse** button and go to the folder containing your file and select it.

8. Click on the **Upload** link next to the **Browse** button; your file is loaded in the editor form.

9. Click on **Validate** to check if you misspelled something. When it returns no errors, click on the **Submit** button.

10. Now go to the **Data | Layers** section and click on **ne_50m_populated_places** to open the layer's properties form. Switch to the **Publishing** tab:

11. Go to the **Style** section and set **PopulatedPlaces** as **Default Style**. Click on the **Save** button:

12. Go to the **Layer Preview** section and open up OpenLayers preview for the **PopulatedPlaces** layer. Your map should now look as shown in the following screenshot:

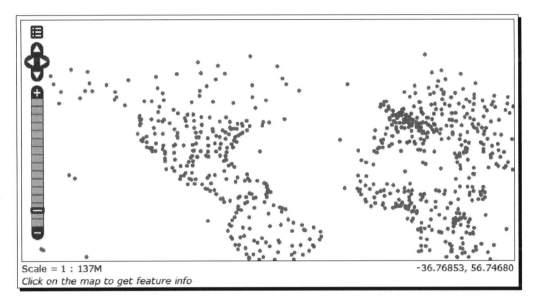

What just happened?

We created a new style for a simple point symbol and assigned it as default to a layer. We have just started creating custom maps, where you decide how and what has to be drawn.

Time for action – adding a stroke value

Now we will continue exploring point symbology by changing the shape and adding a stroke value:

1. Take the `PopulatedPlaces.xml` file, make a copy of it, and name it as `PopulatedPlacesStroke.xml`. Edit the new file in your text editor:

2. Go to line 9 and replace the text inside the `Name` element with the following:

```
<Name>PopulatedPlacesStroke</Name>
```

3. Go to line 11 and replace the text inside the `Title` element with the following:

```
<Title>Geoserver Beginners Guide: Populated Places square mark
with stroke</Title>
```

4. Now we will change the shape form used to represent points on map. Go to line 17 and replace the text inside the `WellKnownName` element with the following:

```
<WellKnownName>square</WellKnownName>
```

5. To add a stroke to your shape, you have to add a `Stroke` element just after the `Fill` element. Insert the following code inside the `CssParameter` element to set the color and width of the stroke:

```
<Stroke>
  <CssParameter name="stroke">#000000</CssParameter>
  <CssParameter name="stroke-width">1</CssParameter>
</Stroke>
```

6. Now save your document and upload it to the Style Editor in GeoServer.

7. Click on **Validate** to check if you misspelled something. When it returns no errors, click on the **Submit** button.

8. Now go to the **Data | Layers** section and click on **ne_50m_populated_places** to open the layer's properties form. Switch to the **Publishing** tab.

9. Go to the **Style** section and add **PopulatedPlacesStroke** to the **Selected Styles** list. Click on **Save**:

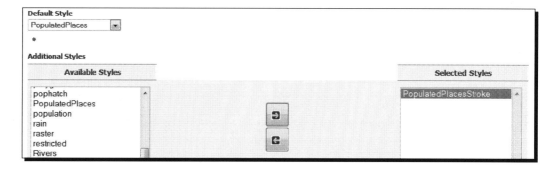

10. Open the **Layer Preview** map. Your map is still presenting the simple marker, indeed you didn't change the default style. Click the button on the top-left of the map to show the options toolbar:

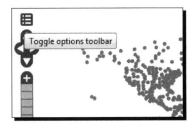

11. From the **Styles** drop-down list, select **PopulatedPlacesStrokes**. Your map will suddenly be updated with the new point symbol. If you zoom to North America, it should look as shown in the following screenshot:

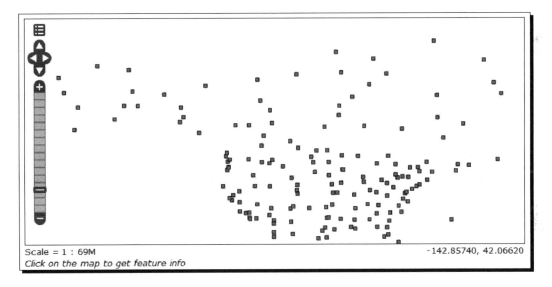

What just happened?

We modified a simple style by adding a stroke. You also learnt that a layer may be associated to more than one style and you can decide which one to use to render maps.

Time for action – dealing with angles and transparency

When representing a point marker, you can add a rotation angle to those shapes where it makes sense to. You can also set opacity to make the fill, stroke, or both more or less transparent. Let's create a new style experimenting with these features:

1. Take the `PopulatedPlacesStrokes.xml` file, make a copy of it, and name it as `PopulatedRotateTransparent.xml`. Edit the new file in your text editor.

2. Go to line 9 and replace the text inside the `Name` element with the following:

   ```
   <Name>PopulatedRotateTransparent</Name>
   ```

3. Go to line 11 and replace the text inside the `Title` element with the following:

   ```
   <Title>Geoserver Beginners Guide: Populated Places rotated
   mark with transparency</Title>
   ```

4. Now we will change the size for marker. Go to line 26 and replace the text inside the `Size` element with the following:

   ```
   <Size>9</Size>
   ```

5. To rotate the marker, add a line after the `Size` element setting an angle of `45` degrees:

   ```
   <Rotation>45</Rotation>
   ```

6. After the `CssParameter` element's `fill` color setting, add the following line to set transparency:

   ```
   <CssParameter name="fill-opacity">0.35</CssParameter>
   ```

7. Save your document and upload it to the Style Editor in GeoServer.

8. Click on **Validate** to check if you misspelled something. When it returns no errors, click on the **Submit** button.

9. Now go to the **Data | Layers** section and click on **ne_50m_populated_places** to open the layer properties form. Switch to the **Publishing** tab.

10. Go to the **Style** section and add **PopulatedRotateTransparent** to the **Selected Styles** list. Click on **Save**.

11. Open the **Layer Preview** map, and change the style used to **PopulatedRotateTransparent** as you did in the previous section.
    Your map now shows the rotated square marker with a transparent fill.

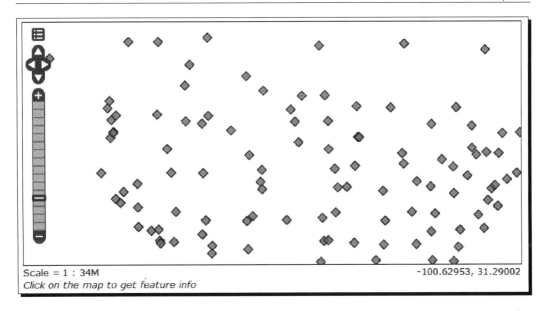

Scale = 1 : 34M
Click on the map to get feature info
-100.62953, 31.29002

What just happened?

You learned how to set a rotating angle to markers and set transparency. Step-by-step, you are discovering how flexible SLD is and how many different symbols you can create from quite simple shapes. Are you wondering if you can mix them? You can, let's jump to next section.

Time for action – composing simple shapes

You know you can specify `WellKnownName` as a marker, but if you need something more complex you can always merge two or more basic shapes to create a new marker. In the following steps you will see how to do so:

1. Take the `PopulatedPlacesStrokes.xml` file, make a copy, and name it as `PopulatedPlacesComplex.xml`. Edit the new file in your text editor.

2. Go to line 9 and replace the text inside the `Name` element with the following:

    ```
    <Name>PopulatedPlacesComplex</Name>
    ```

3. Go to line 11 and replace the text inside the `Title` element with the following:

    ```
    <Title>Geoserver Beginners Guide: mark composed of three basic
    shapes</Title>
    ```

4. Now we will change the size for the square marker. Go to line 26 and replace the text inside the `Size` element with the following:

```
<Size>10</Size>
```

5. To compose a complex marker, you need to add other markers as in a pile. Keep in mind that GeoServer will draw the markers in the inverse order; hence the first marker you insert in the rule will be at the bottom of others in the map. We want to have a green circle with a black stroke containing the square marker. Insert a new `PointSymbolizer` after the `Rule` element at line 13:

```
<PointSymbolizer>
  <Graphic>
    <Mark>
      <WellKnownName>circle</WellKnownName>
      <Fill>
        <CssParameter name="fill">#00FF00</CssParameter>
      </Fill>
      <Stroke>
        <CssParameter name="stroke">#000000</CssParameter>
        <CssParameter name="stroke-width">1</CssParameter>
      </Stroke>
    </Mark>
    <Size>16</Size>
  </Graphic>
</PointSymbolizer>
```

6. Now we want to have a small black circle inside the square. After the closure of the `PointSymbolizer` element, at line 43, add a new `PointSymbolizer` section:

```
<PointSymbolizer>
  <Graphic>
    <Mark>
      <WellKnownName>circle</WellKnownName>
      <Fill>
        <CssParameter name="fill">#000000</CssParameter>
      </Fill>
    </Mark>
    <Size>5</Size>
  </Graphic>
</PointSymbolizer>
```

7. Save your document and upload it in the Style Editor in GeoServer.

8. Click on **Validate** to check if you misspelled something. When it returns no errors, click on the **Submit** button.

9. Now go to the **Data | Layers** section and click on **ne_50m_populated_places** to open the layer properties form. Switch to the **Publishing** tab.

10. Go to the **Style** section and add **PopulatedPlacesComplex** to the **Selected Styles** list. Click on the **Save** button.

11. Open the **Layer Preview** map and select the **PopulatedPlacesComplex** style from the drop-down list. The symbol is quite large, so you may have to zoom out a little to have a look at it without overlapping.

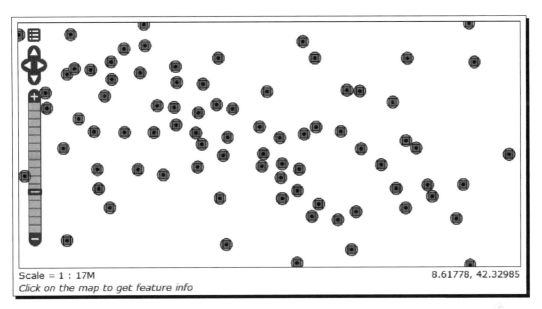

What just happened?

We created a complex symbol merging three basic markers. Playing with size, colors, and positions you may think of quite a few possibilities with this technique. But eventually you will find something too hard to mimic with the markers. Then what do you do? It's time to use external graphics. Go ahead to the next section.

Time for action – using external graphics

When merging markers and setting colors and transparency can't help you to realize the symbol you need, it's time to use external graphics. External graphics are vector or raster files containing a complex image. The supported formats are the common graphic files you use in web application such as PNG, JPG, and SVG. The resources are referred to by a URL so you can store it in your GeoServer `data` folder, as in this example, or get it from an online resource:

1. Take the `town.svg` file from the source code and copy it to the `<GEOSERVER_HOME>/data/styles` folder.

2. Take the `PopulatedPlacesStrokes.xml` file, make a copy, and name it as `PopulatedPlacesGraphics.xml`. Edit the new file in your text editor.

3. Go to line 9 and replace the text inside the `Name` element with the following:

   ```
   <Name>PopulatedPlacesGraphic</Name>
   ```

4. Go to line 11 and replace the text inside the `Title` element with the following:

   ```
   <Title>Geoserver Beginners Guide: Populated Places with
   external graphics</Title>
   ```

5. Remove the `Mark` section (from lines 16 to 25) and insert an `ExternalGraphic` element:

   ```
   <ExternalGraphic>
     <OnlineResource
       xlink:type="simple"
       xlink:href="town.svg" />
     <Format>image/svg+xml</Format>
   </ExternalGraphic>
   ```

6. Change the size to `20`:

   ```
   <Size>20</Size>
   ```

7. Save your document and upload it to the Style Editor in GeoServer.

8. Click on **Validate** to check if you misspelled something. When it returns no errors, click on the **Submit** button.

9. Now go to the **Data | Layers** section and click on **ne_50m_populated_places** to open the layer properties form. Switch to the **Publishing** tab.

10. Go to the **Style** section and add **PopulatedPlacesGraphic** to the **Selected Styles** list. Click on **Save**.

11. Open the **Layer Preview** map and select the **PopulatedPlacesGraphic** style from the drop-down list. As in the previous section the symbol is quite large; zoom in a little on a populated area on earth and your map will look as shown in the following screenshot:

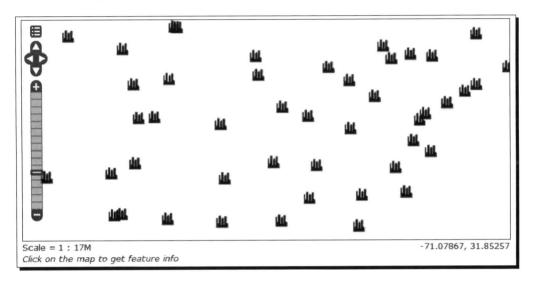

What just happened?

We used a small vector file to add a complex symbol on a map. Using external graphics will open your map to an infinite variety of symbols. You can draw your own or search for a resource file on the Internet, minding the copyright obviously.

After exploring what SLD offers to render point features, you are ready to jump to line features. Before we continue, it is worthwhile to stop and review what you have learned with a couple of tests.

Pop quiz – styling points

Q1. Is there a way to modify basic point symbols?

1. No, you may only use external resources.

2. Yes, but only regarding to drawing properties, such as color, size, and tilting.

3. Yes, you can insert code to reshape a basic marker.

Q2. Can you have more than a symbol inside a rule?

1. No, you may have only a `PointSymbolizer` element for each rule

2. Yes, for example, you can merge two `PointSymbolizer` elements to compose a symbol

3. Yes, but only if you add a query to filter features for each `PointSymbolizer`

Have a go hero – composing your symbol

Did you like the possibility to add external graphics to your map? You can compose them on your own. A great open source tool for creating/modifying graphic files is **Inkscape**. It is available in binary packages for Linux and Windows and it has an excellent set of tools for working with vector graphics. You can save your creations in SVG, an XML-based specification from W3C for vector graphics. Are you ready to use your creative side? Then go to `http://inkscape.org/` and give it a try.

Linestring symbols

Lines are other simple features you can draw on your map. Inside a rule for lines, you have the `<LineSymbolizer>` element where you define color, thickness, and also the type of line to draw (for example, a continuous or a dashed line). As for points, we will start with a simple symbol and then move to more complex examples.

Time for action – creating a simple line style

We will use a rivers and lake centerlines shapefile from Natural Earth to create a map of the rivers of the world with a light sky blue color:

1. Take the `PopulatedPlaces.xml` file, make a copy to `Rivers.xml`, and then edit the new file in your text editor.

2. Go to line 9 and replace the text inside the `Name` element with the following:
   ```
   <Name>Rivers</Name>
   ```

3. Go to line 11 and replace the text inside the `Title` element with the following:
   ```
   <Title> Geoserver Beginners Guide: Rivers simple stroke </Title>
   ```

4. Now, replace the `FeatureTypeStyle` code (from line 13 to 25) with the following code. We are using a continuous line, which is the default, setting a width of 2 pixels and a color:

```
<Rule>
  <LineSymbolizer>
    <Stroke>
      <CssParameter name="stroke">#82CAFA</CssParameter>
      <CssParameter name="stroke-width">2</CssParameter>
    </Stroke>
  </LineSymbolizer>
</Rule>
```

5. Now save your document and upload it to the Style Editor in GeoServer.

6. Click on **Validate** to check if you misspelled something. When it returns no errors, click on the **Submit** button.

7. Now apply the new style to the `50m-rivers-lake-centerlines` layer.

8. Open the **Layer Preview** map. When you zoom to North America, it should look as shown in the following screenshot:

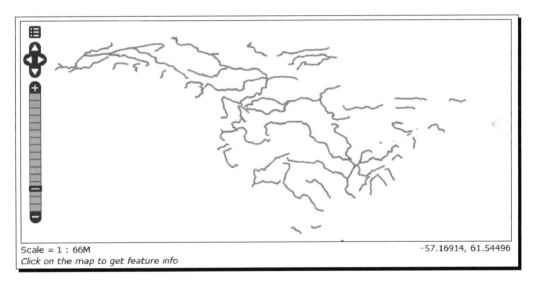

What just happened?

We created a new style for a simple line symbol to draw rivers. As for points, there are several options to draw something prettier than a colored line. As you may have guessed, you can apply the merging technique that we used for points for lines too.

Time for action – adding a border and a centerline

On maps, major roads, such as highways, are often represented with a more complex symbol than a continuous colored line. You are going to use three line symbols to build a representation of highways:

1. Take the `Rivers.xml` file, make a copy to `Roads.xml`, and then edit the new file in your text editor.

2. Go to line 9 and replace the text inside the `Name` element with the following:

   ```
   <Name>Roads</Name>
   ```

3. Go to line 11 and replace the text inside the `Title` element with the following:

   ```
   <Title>Geoserver Beginners Guide: Roads complex symbol</Title>
   ```

4. At line 16, set the color to red:

   ```
   <CssParameter name="stroke">#FF0000</CssParameter>
   ```

5. At line 17, set the width to `5`:

   ```
   <CssParameter name="stroke-width">5</CssParameter>
   ```

6. After line 13, insert a new `LineSymbolizer` section as in the following code fragment. Use a width of `7` and set the color to black. The black line will result as a border on both sides of the line feature.

   ```
   <LineSymbolizer>
     <Stroke>
       <CssParameter name="stroke">#000000</CssParameter>
       <CssParameter name="stroke-width">7</CssParameter>
     </Stroke>
   </LineSymbolizer>
   ```

7. After line 25, insert a new `LineSymbolizer` section. Use a width of `1` and set the color to black. A black line will appear in the center of the line feature.

   ```
   <LineSymbolizer>
     <Stroke>
       <CssParameter name="stroke">#000000</CssParameter>
       <CssParameter name="stroke-width">1</CssParameter>
     </Stroke>
   </LineSymbolizer>
   ```

8. Now save your document and upload it to the Style Editor in GeoServer.

9. Click on **Validate** to check if you misspelled something. When it returns no errors, click on the **Submit** button.

10. Now apply the new style to the `10m_roads_north_america` layer.

11. Open the **Layer Preview** map. The shapefile contains a lot of features and the symbol is too big for a full zoom map. Zoom into a small area, for example, the Los Angeles area as shown in the following screenshot:

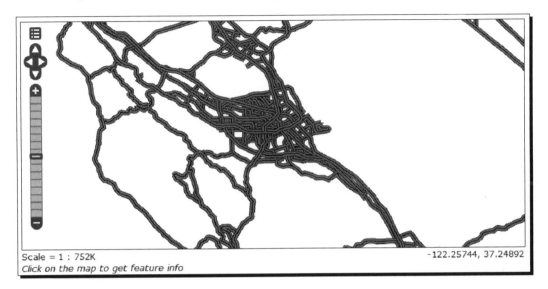

Scale = 1 : 752K -122.25744, 37.24892
Click on the map to get feature info

What just happened?

You learned to create complex line symbols. By merging lines of different sizes and colors, you can create symbols to represent almost all type of roads you would find on a Rand McNally© Atlas. But what if you are going to leave for a trip on a railroad?

Time for action – using hatching

Until now we have used standard SLD syntax; you may take the styles and use them on another map server and it will produce the same maps. But this book is focused on a specific map server and we can use a vendor option, a small trick that is only available on GeoServer, to create a symbol that resembles railroads:

1. Take the `Rivers.xml` file, make a copy to `RailRoads.xml`, and then edit the new file in your text editor.

2. Go to line 9 and replace the text inside the `Name` element with the following:

```
<Name>RailRoads</Name>
```

3. Go to line 11 and replace the text inside the `Title` element with the following:

```
<Title>Geoserver Beginners Guide: RailRoads with hatching</
Title>
```

4. Go to line 16 and change the color to black:

```
<CssParameter name="stroke">#000000</CssParameter>
```

5. Go to line 20 and after the end of the `Rule` element, add another `Rule` for a `LineSymbolizer` element:

```
<Rule>
  <LineSymbolizer>
    <Stroke>
    </Stroke>
  </LineSymbolizer>
</Rule>
```

6. The rule you added is for the hatching; you need to specify how the hatch line has to be drawn. Insert the following code fragment inside the `stroke` element. In the fourth line, you specify a `WellKnownName` element to inform GeoServer that the line has to be drawn perpendicular to the geometric feature. In the 6th and 7th lines, you set the color to black and width of the hatching line to `1`. Finally at line 10, you set the length of the hatching line.

```
<GraphicStroke>
  <Graphic>
    <Mark>
      <WellKnownName>shape://vertline</WellKnownName>
      <Stroke>
        <CssParameter name="stroke">#000000</CssParameter>
        <CssParameter name="stroke-width">1</CssParameter>
      </Stroke>
    </Mark>
    <Size>8</Size>
  </Graphic>
</GraphicStroke>
```

7. Now save your document and upload it to the Style Editor in GeoServer.

8. Click on **Validate** to check if you misspelled something. When it returns no errors, click on the **Submit** button.

9. Now apply the new style to the `10m_railroads` layer.

10. Open the **Layer Preview** map. Zoom to a small area and look at the result.

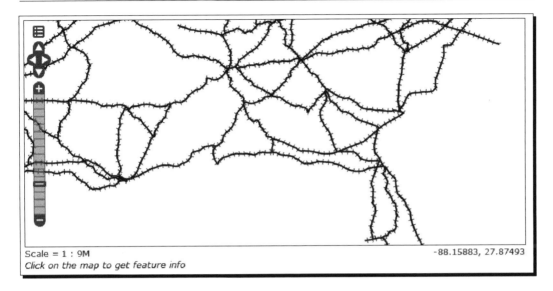

Scale = 1 : 9M   -88.15883, 27.87493
Click on the map to get feature info

What just happened?

You used a vendor option to enable hatching lines. Although this way of styling feature is not portable, it helps you greatly in composing pretty maps. Let's see another variation for lines in next section.

Time for action – using dashed lines

On many paper maps, a common symbol for representing roads under construction or planned is a couple of parallel dashed lines. Can you imagine how to do it with SLD? It requires a couple of lines merged together with a new SLD element. We will see that element in this section:

1. Take the `Roads.xml` file and make a copy to `DashedRoads.xml`, then edit the new file in your text editor.

2. Go to line 9 and replace the text inside the `Name` element with the following code:

   ```
   <Name>DashedRoads</Name>
   ```

3. Go to line 11 and replace the text inside the `Title` element with the following code:

   ```
   <Title>Geoserver Beginners Guide: Roads under construction
   with dashing</Title>
   ```

4. Go to line 17 and change the width of the symbol to `5`:

   ```
   <CssParameter name="stroke-width">5</CssParameter>
   ```

5. Add a line just after the previous line to set dashing for the black lines:

```
<CssParameter name="stroke-dasharray">15 10</CssParameter>
```

6. Go to lines 22-23 and change the color to black and width to `3`:

```
<CssParameter name="stroke">#FFFFFF</CssParameter>
<CssParameter name="stroke-width">3</CssParameter>
```

7. Add a line just after the previous one to set dashing for the black lines:

```
<CssParameter name="stroke-dasharray">15 10</CssParameter>
```

8. Remove the last `LineSymbolizer` code, from lines 28 to 33. The third line is no longer needed to represent roads with parallel dashed lines.

9. Now save your document and upload it to the Style Editor in GeoServer.

10. Click on **Validate** to check if you misspelled something. When it returns no errors, click on the **Submit** button.

11. Now go to the **Data | Layers** section and click on `10m_roads_north_ america` to open the layer properties form. Switch to the **Publishing** tab.

12. Go to the **Style** section and add **DashedRoads** to the **Selected Styles** list. Click on **Save**.

13. Open the **Layer Preview** map and select the **DashedRoads** style from the drop-down list. As this is a complex symbol, you have to zoom in to a small area to have a clear view of how the symbol looks:

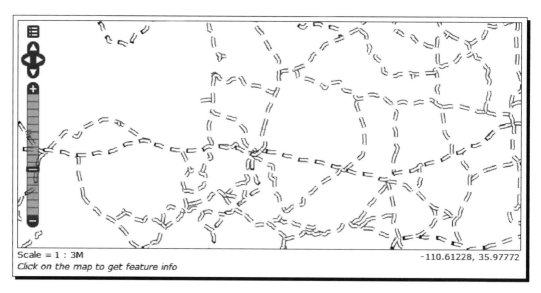

What just happened?

You built a dashing symbol by merging two lines. But there is more that can be done with merging; you can mix dashing lines and marker symbols.

Time for action – mixing dashing lines and markers

Natural Earth does not provide a data set for aqueducts, but you might wonder how you can create an appropriate symbol for representing them. Aqueducts are usually represented in maps with a dashed line alternated with small circle, all colored light blue:

1. Take the `DashedRoads.xml` file, make a copy to `DashingAndMarkers.xml`, and then edit the new file in your text editor.

2. Go to line 9 and replace the text inside the `Name` element as:

```
<Name>DashingAndMarkers</Name>
```

3. Go to line 11 and replace the text inside the `Title` element as:

```
<Title>Geoserver Beginners Guide: Aqueducts with dashing and
circle</Title>
```

4. Go to line 16 and change the setting of the `LineSymbolizer` element we will use to represent the dashing line. Set the color to hexadecimal value for light blue, set a width of 2, and a `dasharray` of 10 10 to have regularly-spaced dashing:

```
<CssParameter name="stroke">#ADD8E6</CssParameter>
<CssParameter name="stroke-width">2</CssParameter>
<CssParameter name="stroke-dasharray">10 10</CssParameter>
```

5. Now delete all the code from line 21 to line 27. We need a totally different symbolizer, something similar to what we used for hatching.

6. Go to line 23 and insert the following code fragment. You can see that in the 6th line, we add a `WellKnownName` element and set it to a `circle`. Then we set its color to light blue and `width` to 1. The circle width is set to 5 to make it larger than the dashed line:

```
<LineSymbolizer>
  <Stroke>
    <GraphicStroke>
      <Graphic>
        <Mark>
          <WellKnownName>circle</WellKnownName>
          <Stroke>
            <CssParameter name="stroke">#ADD8E6</CssParameter>
            <CssParameter name="stroke-width">1</CssParameter>
```

```
            </Stroke>
          </Mark>
          <Size>5</Size>
        </Graphic>
      </GraphicStroke>
      <CssParameter name="stroke-dasharray">5 15</CssParameter>
      <CssParameter name="stroke-dashoffset">7.5</CssParameter>
    </Stroke>
  </LineSymbolizer>
```

7. Now save your document and upload it to the Style Editor in GeoServer.

8. Click on **Validate** to check if you misspelled something. When it returns no errors, click on the **Submit** button.

9. Now go to the **Data | Layers** section and click on **50m-rivers-lake-centerlines** to open the layer properties form. We don't really have a layer containing aqueducts features; we will transform rivers to pipelines! Switch to the **Publishing** tab.

10. Go to the **Style** section and add **DashingAndMarkers** to the **Selected Styles** list. Click on **Save**.

11. Open the **Layer Preview** map and select **DashingAndMarkers** style from the drop-down list. Zoom to North America and check if your map looks as shown in the following screenshot. Do you see that big aqueduct that covers all the Middle West lands?

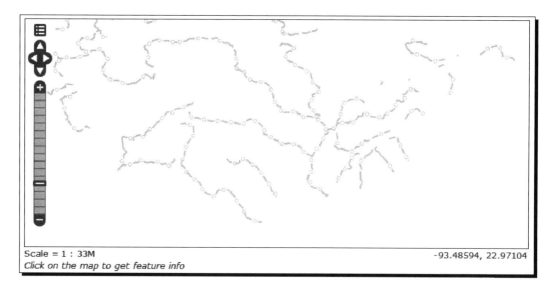

Scale = 1 : 33M   -93.48594, 22.97104
Click on the map to get feature info

What just happened?

We have merged markers, that you learned using point features and lines. It's now time to switch to the last type of shapes: polygons.

Working with polygon symbols

Polygons are defined by a set of rings, closed linestring, so it is not surprising that you have the possibility of setting the stroke color and width. By defining a closed area, you may also set how this area has to be filled. The key element is `<PolygonSymbolizer>`; include it inside any rule you are defining for polygons. We will start with a fairly simple example.

Time for action – creating a simple polygon style

Since you were a kid you have been familiarized with the political maps of the world. Countries were rendered with brown boundaries and there were different colors for each country. Isn't this a wonderful example for your first polygon styling? We will create a map with all features rendered with the same color and outline, to start with a simple example, but we will return to this style in the thematic mapping section:

> You may wonder how many different colors you need to build a map where each adjacent country doesn't share the same color. The answer is not really trivial, indeed it is a surprisingly little number. Four different colors are enough for a map with any number of polygonal features. Take a look at http://en.wikipedia.org/wiki/Four_color_theorem for more information.

1. Take the `Rivers.xml` file, make a copy to `Countries.xml`, and then edit the new file in your text editor.

2. Go to line 9 and replace the text inside the `Name` element witht the following:

   ```
   <Name>Countries</Name>
   ```

3. Go to line 11 and replace the text inside the `Title` element witht the following:

   ```
   <Title> Geoserver Beginners Guide: Countries with outline and
   fill</Title>
   ```

4. As we are using polygons, you need to change lines 14 and 19 and replace `LineSymbolizer` with `PolygonSymbolizer`:

   ```
   <PolygonSymbolizer>
   </PolygonSymbolizer>
   ```

5. Set the outline color to brown and the width to 2:

```
<CssParameter name="stroke">#A52A2A</CssParameter>
<CssParameter name="stroke-width">2</CssParameter>
```

6. Lines are rendered with stroke but polygons may have a fill defined too. Insert the following three lines at line 14, after the PolygonSymbolizer starts. This will set the fill color to a complementary color for brown:

```
<Fill>
  <CssParameter name="fill">#29A6A6</CssParameter>
</Fill>
```

7. Now save your document and upload it to the Style Editor in GeoServer.

8. Click on **Validate** to check if you misspelled something. When it returns no errors, click on the **Submit** button.

9. Now apply the new style to the ne_50m_admin_0_countries layer.

10. Open the **Layer Preview** map and zoom to Europe. Your map should look as shown in the following screenshot:

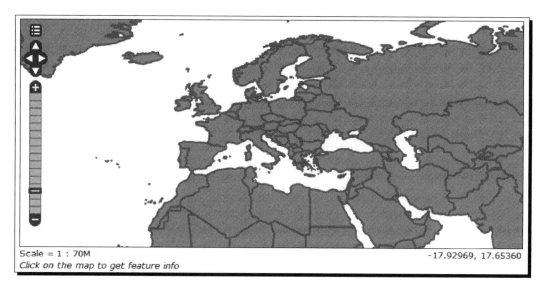

Scale = 1 : 70M
Click on the map to get feature info
-17.92969, 17.65360

What just happened?

You built a basic polygon symbol. You may work with outlines much the same way as with linestrings, applying dashing, transparency, and different colors and widths. We will explore the different ways of filling polygons in the next section.

Time for action – using a graphic filling

Colors may help you in pointing out some areas, but you may need something different. If you want to represent wooded areas in topographic maps, you can insert many little markers, each one representing a circle. Patterns of markers are widely used in mapping. As we did with points and lines, the solution is using an external graphic resource. A bitmap or a vector, for example, an SVG file, can be used to fill a polygon:

1. Take the `Countries.xml` file, make a copy to `CountriesGraphics.xml`, and then edit the new file in your text editor.

2. Go to line 9 and replace the text inside the `Name` element with the following:

```
<Name>CountriesGraphics</Name>
```

3. Go to line 11 and replace the text inside the `Title` element with the following:

```
<Title>Geoserver Beginners Guide: Countries with graphics
filling</Title>
```

4. Take the `fill.svg` file and copy it to the `<GEOSERVER_HOME>/data/styles` folder.

5. Now you need to add a `Fill` section just inside `PolygonSymbolizer`, at line 14:

```
<Fill>
  <GraphicFill>
    <Graphic>
      <ExternalGraphic>
        <OnlineResource
          xlink:type="simple"
          xlink:href="fill.svg" />
        <Format>image/svg+xml</Format>
      </ExternalGraphic>
    </Graphic>
  </GraphicFill>
</Fill>
```

6. Now save your document and upload it to the Style Editor in GeoServer.

7. Click on **Validate** to check if you misspelled something. When it returns no errors, click on the **Submit** button.

8. Now go to the **Data | Layers** section and click on **ne_50m_admin_0_ countries** layer to open the layer properties form.

9. Go to the **Style** section and add **CountriesGraphics** to the **Selected Styles** list. Click on the **Save** button.

10. Open the **Layer Preview** map and select **CountriesGraphics** style from the drop-down list. Zoom to North America and check if your map looks as shown in the following screenshot:

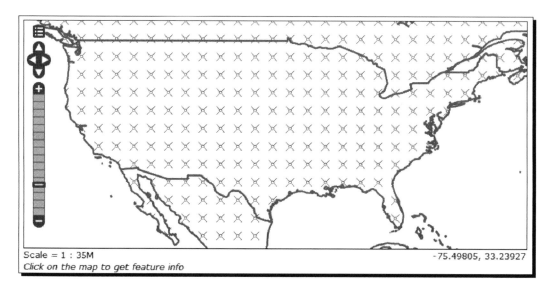

Scale = 1 : 35M

-75.49805, 33.23927

Click on the map to get feature info

What just happened?

Working with external graphic lets you build any pattern you may need, but GeoServer offers you yet another possibility. Go to the next section and see.

Time for action – using hatching with polygons

Hatching a polygon is a different way to produce maps similar to those seen in the previous example. The pros are that you don't need to search for or build a graphical resource; you have a set of hatching patterns ready for you. It is also faster for GeoServer to render a map without using external graphic resources. When it is feasible to achieve the same results with internal resources, stick to hatching!

1. Take the `CountriesGraphics.xml` file, make a copy to `CountriesHatching.xml`, and then edit the new file in your text editor.

2. Go to line 9 and replace the text inside the `Name` element with the following:

```
<Name>CountriesHatching</Name>
```

3. Go to line 11 and replace the text inside the `Title` element with the following:

```
<Title>Geoserver Beginners Guide: Countries with hatching</Title>
```

4. To add code for hatching you need to replace the code of the `Graphic` element, from lines 17 to 24. Insert a `Mark` element where you set the shape to use with a `WellKnownName` element (remember that the `shape://` notation is only supported in GeoServer).

```
<Graphic>
  <Mark>
    <WellKnownName>shape://dot</WellKnownName>
    <Stroke>
      <CssParameter name="stroke">#29A6A6</CssParameter>
      <CssParameter name="stroke-width">3</CssParameter>
    </Stroke>
  </Mark>
  <Size>16</Size>
</Graphic>
```

5. Now save your document and upload it to the Style Editor in GeoServer.

6. Click on **Validate** to check if you misspelled something. When it returns no errors, click on the **Submit** button.

7. Now go to the **Data | Layers** section and click on the **ne_50m_admin_0_ countries** layer to open the layer properties form.

8. Go to the **Style** section and add **CountriesHatching** to the **Selected Styles** list. Click on **Save**.

9. Open the **Layer Preview** map and select the **CountriesHatching** style from the drop-down list, then zoom to Australia. Can you see how similar hatching is to using an external graphic resource?

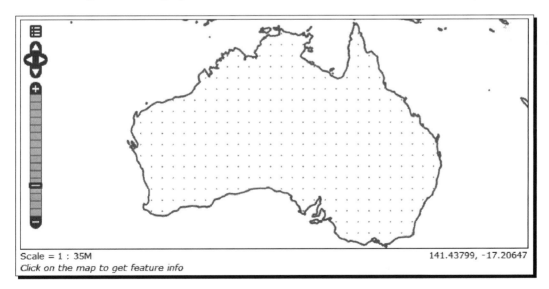

Scale = 1 : 35M
Click on the map to get feature info
141.43799, -17.20647

What just happened?

We used point markers to fill an area enclosed in a polygon. Thanks to the GeoServer extension, this can be done not only with a limited set of point markers supported by standard SLD, but also by using the following markers:

- `shape://vertline`: A vertical line
- `shape://horline`: A horizontal line
- `shape://slash`: A diagonal line leaning forwards like the slash (/) keyboard symbol
- `shape://backslash`: Same as previous, but oriented in the opposite direction (\)
- `shape://dot`: A very small circle with space around it
- `shape://plus`: A + symbol, without space around it
- `shape://times`: An X symbol, without space around it
- `shape://oarrow`: An open arrow symbol
- `shape://carrow`: A closed arrow symbol

Pop quiz – styling lines and polygons

Q1. Can you define an outline for lines?

1. No, lines only have the `stroke` property; you can't have a different form of outline.
2. Yes, you have to define a fill color different from the stroke color.
3. No, lines only have the `stroke` property, but you can mimic a fill superimposing another line with a smaller width.

Q2. How can you fill a polygon?

1. You can leave the internal area transparent or fill it with a color.
2. You can use colors and external graphic resources.
3. You can only define a color.

Adding labels

We had a full exploration of styling for geometry features, but how can you represent textual attributes on maps? As in paper maps, you need a labeling engine and GeoServer provides you with the right tool. You can add labels to any kind of feature; let's start with points.

Time for action – labeling points

You are probably a geography geek and you know what a place name is at the first look at the map. But maps are not always so expressive and common people tend to get confused without some reference text. Do you remember the pretty maps you styled with the `Populated Places` layer? They would look much better with some labels next to markers:

1. Take the `PopulatedPlacesStroke.xml` file, make a copy to `PopulatedPlacesLabeled.xml`, and then edit the new file in your text editor.

2. Go to line 9 and replace the text inside the `Name` element with the following:

   ```
   <Name>PopulatedPlacesLabeled</Name>
   ```

3. Go to line 11 and replace the text inside the `Title` element with the following:

   ```
   <Title>Geoserver Beginners Guide: Populated Places with styled labels</Title>
   ```

4. Go to line 17 and change the marker to a `circle`:

   ```
   <WellKnownName>circle</WellKnownName>
   ```

5. Go to line 26 and set the size to `8`:

   ```
   <Size>8</Size>
   ```

6. After `PointSymbolizer`, add a new `TextSymbolizer` element. Inside it you have to specify which field of the layer attributes will be used for extracting text strings (be aware that the attribute's name is case sensitive). This is done with the `Label` element. Then add a `Font` element to specify which font family GeoServer will use to draw labels and text properties:

   ```
   <TextSymbolizer>
     <Label>
       <ogc:PropertyName>NAME</ogc:PropertyName>
     </Label>
     <Font>
       <CssParameter name="font-family">Arial</CssParameter>
       <CssParameter name="font-size">12</CssParameter>
       <CssParameter name="font-style">normal</CssParameter>
       <CssParameter name="font-weight">italyc</CssParameter>
     </Font>
   </TextSymbolizer>
   ```

7. Now you have to set the position of labels. The position is relative to the point feature, you add a `LabelPlacement` element for this. We want to have a label relative to points on the top-right, so we use an `AnchorPoint` element, setting it to `0` and a `Displacement` element, setting it to `2` pixels along the x axis and `5` pixels along the y axis:

```
<LabelPlacement>
  <PointPlacement>
    <AnchorPoint>
      <AnchorPointX>0</AnchorPointX>
      <AnchorPointY>0</AnchorPointY>
    </AnchorPoint>
    <Displacement>
      <DisplacementX>2</DisplacementX>
      <DisplacementY>5</DisplacementY>
    </Displacement>
  </PointPlacement>
</LabelPlacement>
```

8. Eventually you need to set a color for your label. Use a `Fill` element and set it to black. Include the following code just after the `LabelPlacement` section:

```
<Fill>
  <CssParameter name="fill">#000000</CssParameter>
</Fill>
```

9. Now save your document and upload it to the Style Editor in GeoServer.

10. Click on **Validate** to check if you misspelled something. When it returns no errors, click on the **Submit** button.

11. Now go to the **Data | Layers** section and click on the **ne_50m_populated_places** layer to open the layer properties form.

12. Go to the **Style** section and add **PopulatedPlacesLabeled** to the **Selected Styles** list. Click on **Save**.

13. Open the **Layer Preview** map and select the **PopulatedPlacesLabeled** style from the drop-down list, then zoom in to get a better preview of labels.

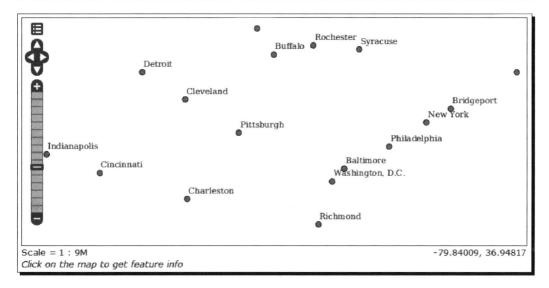

Scale = 1 : 9M   -79.84009, 36.94817
Click on the map to get feature info

What just happened?

We added pretty labels using the font (be aware that fonts must be available on the server side), and placement properties.

Time for action – labeling lines

Place names are useful but a road map without a road name, or at least road codes, is almost useless. You need to get back to the roads style and add code to enable road labeling:

1. Take the `Roads.xml` file, make a copy to `RoadsLabeled.xml`, and then edit the new file in your text editor.

2. Go to line 9 and replace the text inside the `Name` element with the following code snippet:

```
<Name>RoadsLabeled</Name>
```

3. Go to line 11 and replace the text inside the `Title` element with the following code snippet:

```
<Title>Geoserver Beginners Guide: Roads with labels along the
line</Title>
```

4. Remove the last `LineSymbolizer`, from line 26 to 31. We need a simpler symbol to have a pretty map.

5. Set the width of black line to `4`:

```
<CssParameter name="stroke-width">4</CssParameter>
```

6. Set the width of red line to `2`:

```
<CssParameter name="stroke-width">4</CssParameter>
```

7. After the last `LineSymbolizer`, add a new `TextSymbolizer` element. Inside it, you have to specify which field of the layer attributes will be used for extracting text string. (Unfortunately, the Natural Earth road data set does not include road names so we have to use the state name.) This is done with the `Label` element. Then add a `LabelPlacement` element to specify where the label has to be placed, relative to the line:

```
<TextSymbolizer>
  <Label>
    <ogc:PropertyName>NAME</ogc:PropertyName>
  </Label>
  <LabelPlacement>
    <LinePlacement>
      <PerpendicularOffset>10</PerpendicularOffset>
    </LinePlacement>
  </LabelPlacement>
</TextSymbolizer>
```

8. Add a `Fill` element just after the `LabelPlacement` section. Set the label color to black:

```
<Fill>
  <CssParameter name="fill">#000000</CssParameter>
</Fill>
```

9. Now save your document and upload it to the Style Editor in GeoServer.

10. Click on **Validate** to check if you misspelled something. When it returns no errors, click on the **Submit** button.

11. Now go to the **Data | Layers** section and click on **10m_roads_north_america** layer to open the layer properties form.

12. Go to the **Style** section and add **RoadsLabeled** to the **Selected Styles** list. Click on the **Save** button.

13. Open the **Layer Preview** map and zoom to a very little area. Open the controls and select the **RoadsLabeled** style from the drop-down list. Yes, you are in Virginia!

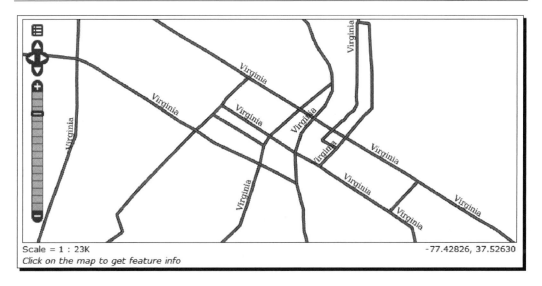

14. Now add some GeoServer extensions. After the `Fill` element, add an option to have labels following bending roads and set a maximum angle value for bending. The maximum displacement of the label sets how many pixels the GeoServer label engine may shift text to avoid overlapping. The last parameter makes GeoServer repeat labels every 300 pixels for long roads.

```
<VendorOption name="followLine">true</VendorOption>
<VendorOption name="maxAngleDelta">90</VendorOption>
<VendorOption name="maxDisplacement">400</VendorOption>
<VendorOption name="repeat">300</VendorOption>
```

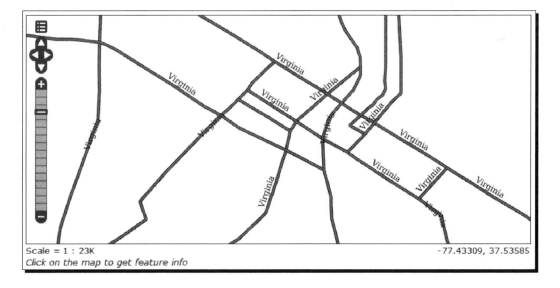

What just happened?

You placed labels upon roads with your style. By merging SLD features and options only available in GeoServer, you can create pretty labels and place them in a well-readable form.

Have a go hero – styling labels for lines

We didn't set a font to road labels, nor did we set any text properties like we did for points. Can you modify the last style applying text styling? Try on your own and have a look at the `RoadsLabeledStyled.xml` file included in the resources of this chapter, if you need any help.

Time for action – labeling polygons

We will now come back to our countries data set to add labeling to the countries style. While most of the properties are what we already saw in the labeling of points and lines, we will add code to make halos around our labels. Halos could enhance readability of labels:

1. Take the `Countries.xml` file, make a copy to `CountriesLabeled.xml`, and then edit the new file in your text editor.

2. Go to line 9 and replace the text inside the `Name` element with the following code snippet:

   ```
   <Name>CountriesLabeled</Name>
   ```

3. Go to line 11 and replace the text inside the `Title` element with the following code snippet:

   ```
   <Title>Geoserver Beginners Guide: Countries with labels</Title>
   ```

4. Add a `TextSymbolizer` element just after the `PolygonSymbolizer`. Inside it, define the feature field containing the text and the font name and style to draw the label:

   ```
   <TextSymbolizer>
     <Label>
       <ogc:PropertyName>NAME</ogc:PropertyName>
     </Label>
     <Font>
       <CssParameter name="font-family">Arial</CssParameter>
       <CssParameter name="font-size">11</CssParameter>
       <CssParameter name="font-style">normal</CssParameter>
       <CssParameter name="font-weight">bold</CssParameter>
     </Font>
   <TextSymbolizer>
   ```

5. The placement of polygon labels is very similar to points. After the `Font` section, add `LabelPlacement` and set the `AnchorPoint`:

```
<LabelPlacement>
  <PointPlacement>
    <AnchorPoint>
      <AnchorPointX>0.5</AnchorPointX>
      <AnchorPointY>0.5</AnchorPointY>
    </AnchorPoint>
  </PointPlacement>
</LabelPlacement>
```

6. Set the text color to black by adding a `Fill` section:

```
<Fill>
  <CssParameter name="fill">#000000</CssParameter>
</Fill>
```

7. After this add a couple of vendor options. The first line ensures that long labels are split across multiple lines by setting line wrapping on the labels to 50 pixels, and the second sets 150 pixels as the maximum displacement for places where labels crowd:

```
<VendorOption name="autoWrap">50</VendorOption>
<VendorOption name="maxDisplacement">150</VendorOption>
```

8. Lastly add the code for halos. We will use a white halo, for maximizing contrast, with a 3 pixel width around the text:

```
<Halo>
  <Radius>3</Radius>
  <Fill>
    <CssParameter name="fill">#FFFFFF</CssParameter>
  </Fill>
</Halo>
```

9. Now save your document and upload it to the Style Editor in GeoServer.

10. Click on **Validate** to check if you misspelled something. When it returns no errors, click on the **Submit** button.

11. Now go to the **Data | Layers** section and click on the **ne_50m_admin_0_ countries** layer to open the layer properties form.

12. Go to the **Style** section and add **CountriesLabeled** to the **Selected Styles** list. Click on **Save**.

13. Open the **Layer Preview** map and zoom to Europe. Open the controls and select the **CountriesLabeled** style from the drop-down list.

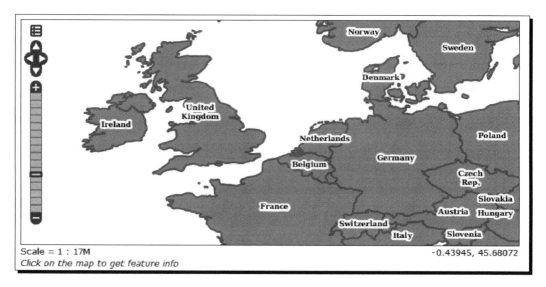

Scale = 1 : 17M   -0.43945, 45.68072
Click on the map to get feature info

What just happened?

We used standard SLD elements and GeoServer extensions to build pretty labels for the polygon feature. You may have noticed that, apart from labels, all the styles we created use the same symbol for all features. It is now time to explore thematic mapping.

Thematic mapping

Very simple maps may be well defined with just one symbol per layer, but this is not the case for the vast majority of maps you can find, nor for what you will create with your GeoServer. To fully express the meaning of features, you need to apply a symbology that can make it easy to recognize different real features on a map. Think of the road layer containing North America's roads, a map where interstates have a different symbol than is state or federal road is much more readable. Countries symbolized according to their GDP can be mapped as the richest area of the world.

There are many different kinds of thematic maps. One of the most common is the choropleth map; we talked about it in *Chapter 1, GIS Fundamentals*.

Of course SLD can be used to build choropleth maps; you just have to define a classification rule and a symbol for each class.

Time for action – classifying roads

The roads data set provided by Natural Earth has some attributes that can be used to classify roads. You may use the CLASS field for thematic mapping, assigning a different symbol to each class:

1. Take the Roads.xml file, make a copy to RoadsThematic.xml, and then edit the new file in your text editor.

2. Go to line 9 and replace the text inside the Name element with the following code snippet:

```
<Name>RoadsThematic</Name>
```

3. Go to line 11 and replace the text inside the Title element with the following code snippet:

```
<Title>Geoserver Beginners Guide: Roads thematic map</Title>
```

4. The CLASS field contains six different values: Interstate, Federal, State, Other, Closed, and U/C. We will re-use the symbol for the first value, Interstate. You need to add a filter inside the rule, so that the symbol will be applied only to features with the Interstate value in the CLASS field. Add a Name element inside the Rule element and set it to Interstate:

```
<Name>Interstate</Name>
```

5. Now add a Filter element and use PropertyIsEqualTo to set the filter operator. PropertyName sets which field to search for and Literal sets the value to be searched:

```
<ogc:Filter>
  <ogc:PropertyIsEqualTo>
    <ogc:PropertyName>CLASS</ogc:PropertyName>
    <ogc:Literal>Interstate</ogc:Literal>
  </ogc:PropertyIsEqualTo>
</ogc:Filter>
```

6. Now create a new FeatureTypeStyle element and set its Filter for Federal roads:

```
<FeatureTypeStyle>
  <Rule>
    <Name>Federal</Name>
    <ogc:Filter>
      <ogc:PropertyIsEqualTo>
        <ogc:PropertyName>CLASS</ogc:PropertyName>
```

```
          <ogc:Literal>Federal</ogc:Literal>
        </ogc:PropertyIsEqualTo>
      </ogc:Filter>
    </Rule>
  </FeatureTypeStyle>
```

7. For `Federal` roads, use an orange line with black borders:

```
<LineSymbolizer>
  <Stroke>
    <CssParameter name="stroke">#000000</CssParameter>
    <CssParameter name="stroke-width">4</CssParameter>
  </Stroke>
</LineSymbolizer>
<LineSymbolizer>
  <Stroke>
    <CssParameter name="stroke">#FF7F00</CssParameter>
    <CssParameter name="stroke-width">2</CssParameter>
  </Stroke>
</LineSymbolizer>
```

8. Now add a `Rule` for `State` roads; use a symbol yellow with black borders:

```
<FeatureTypeStyle>
  <Rule>
    <Name>State</Name>
    <ogc:Filter>
      <ogc:PropertyIsEqualTo>
        <ogc:PropertyName>CLASS</ogc:PropertyName>
        <ogc:Literal>State</ogc:Literal>
      </ogc:PropertyIsEqualTo>
    </ogc:Filter>
    <LineSymbolizer>
      <Stroke>
        <CssParameter name="stroke">#000000</CssParameter>
        <CssParameter name="stroke-width">4</CssParameter>
      </Stroke>
    </LineSymbolizer>
    <LineSymbolizer>
      <Stroke>
        <CssParameter name="stroke">#FFFF00</CssParameter>
        <CssParameter name="stroke-width">2</CssParameter>
      </Stroke>
    </LineSymbolizer>
  </Rule>
</FeatureTypeStyle>
```

9. To remember the old times when paper maps were all you could count on when driving around the country, we will add a rule for `Other` roads using a blue symbol with gray borders:

```
<FeatureTypeStyle>
  <Rule>
    <Name>Other</Name>
    <ogc:Filter>
      <ogc:PropertyIsEqualTo>
        <ogc:PropertyName>CLASS</ogc:PropertyName>
        <ogc:Literal>Other</ogc:Literal>
      </ogc:PropertyIsEqualTo>
    </ogc:Filter>
    <LineSymbolizer>
      <Stroke>
        <CssParameter name="stroke">#808080</CssParameter>
        <CssParameter name="stroke-width">4</CssParameter>
      </Stroke>
    </LineSymbolizer>
    <LineSymbolizer>
      <Stroke>
        <CssParameter name="stroke">#0000FF</CssParameter>
        <CssParameter name="stroke-width">2</CssParameter>
      </Stroke>
    </LineSymbolizer>
  </Rule>
</FeatureTypeStyle>
```

10. We are not interested in closed roads, so you don't add a rule for them. Add a rule for `U/C`, that is, under construction roads, and use a grey dashed line:

```
<FeatureTypeStyle>
  <Rule>
    <Name>Under Construction</Name>
    <ogc:Filter>
      <ogc:PropertyIsEqualTo>
        <ogc:PropertyName>CLASS</ogc:PropertyName>
        <ogc:Literal>U/C</ogc:Literal>
      </ogc:PropertyIsEqualTo>
    </ogc:Filter>
    <LineSymbolizer>
      <Stroke>
        <CssParameter name="stroke-dasharray">15 10</
CssParameter>
        <CssParameter name="stroke">#808080</CssParameter>
        <CssParameter name="stroke-width">4</CssParameter>
```

```
            </Stroke>
          </LineSymbolizer>
        </Rule>
     </FeatureTypeStyle>
```

11. You are done! Save your document and upload it to the Style Editor in GeoServer.

12. Click on **Validate** to check if you misspelled something. When it returns no errors, click on the **Submit** button.

13. Now go to the **Data | Layers** section and click on the **10m_roads_north_america** layer to open the layer properties form.

14. Go to the **Style** section and add **RoadsThematic** to the **Selected Styles** list. Click on **Save**.

15. Open the **Layer Preview** map and zoom to Houston, Texas. Open the controls and select the **RoadsLabeled** style from the drop-down list. It seems like there are some big plans for new roads around the town!

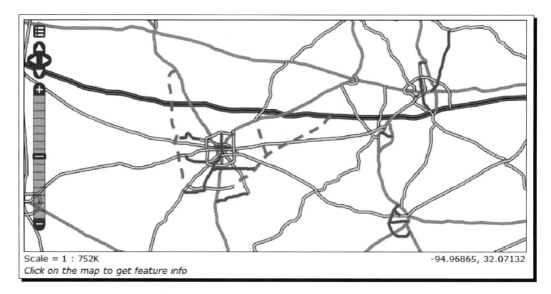

Scale = 1 : 752K   -94.96865, 32.07132
Click on the map to get feature info

What just happened?

We made a choropleth road map. It wasn't more difficult than doing a single symbol map, just a bit longer. Using the `Filter` element, you can classify your feature and group them in homogenous sets to which you can apply a single symbol.

Have a go hero – styling labels for lines

We didn't set road labels. You can find the road number by clicking on it, but it may be useful to have labels. I'm sure you can modify the last style by applying what you learned before about line labeling. If you have any issues, take a look the at `RoadsThematicLabeled.xml` file included in the resources of this chapter.

Setting visibility

When you look at Google maps or another web-mapping application, you can see that the map changes its style according to the zoom level. When you are looking at an entire continent, symbols are simple and there are a few features drawn on the map. As you get closer you can see more labels, major roads change their symbols, and minor roads appear.

This approach permits us to insert a large quantity of information on a web map while avoiding producing an almost unreadable crowd of labels and symbols. As an example, you can think of a cadastral map containing all USA parcels with a label showing owners. When you are looking at the entire country, it is impossible to show all this information without owning a several thousand inches wide display! A good approach would be to just show the country's boundaries and major roads and places on smaller scales and avoid showing parcels until you are not so close to see just a county.

The way to build such a map with SLD is by using filters. We will try them out in the following section.

Time for action – enhancing thematic roads map

In the previous section, we styled a thematic roads map. It is a pretty map, but it lacks something to be ready for publication. As a user, you would expect roads be drawn on different scales according to their classification. SLD has elements to define a scale range where a rule must be applied; they are called `MinScaleDenominator` and `MaxScaleDenominator`. Let's use them!

1. Take the `RoadsThematic.xml` file, make a copy to `RoadsThematicScale.xml`, and then edit the new file in your text editor.

2. Go to line 9 and replace the text inside the `Name` element with the following code snippet:

    ```
    <Name>RoadsThematicScale</Name>
    ```

3. Go to line 11 and replace the text inside the `Title` element with the following code snippet:

    ```
    <Title>Geoserver Beginners Guide: Roads thematic map with
    scale ranges</Title>
    ```

4. We want Interstate roads to appear at any scale, so we leave the first `Rule` unchanged. Federal roads will appear only at 1:10,000,000 scale and closer. Go to line 50 and add following code just after the `Filter` section:

```
<MaxScaleDenominator>10000000</MaxScaleDenominator>
```

5. Go to line 74 and add a scale condition filter to make State roads only visible from a 1:1,500,000 scale:

```
<MaxScaleDenominator>1500000</MaxScaleDenominator>
```

6. Other and Under Construction roads would only be visible from a 1:500,000 scale. Go to lines 98 and 122 to add a scale condition filter as:

```
<MaxScaleDenominator>500000</MaxScaleDenominator>
```

7. Save your document and upload it to the Style Editor in GeoServer.

8. Click on **Validate** to check if you misspelled something. When it returns no errors, click on the **Submit** button.

9. Now go to the **Data | Layers** section and click on the **10m_roads_north_america** layer to open the layer properties form.

10. Go to the **Style** section and add **RoadsThematicScale** to the **Selected Styles** list. Click on the **Save** button.

11. Open the **Layer Preview** map and zoom to scale 1:12,000,000. Open the controls and select the **RoadsThematicScale** style from the drop-down list. As the map redraws, you can see that a lot of roads disappear.

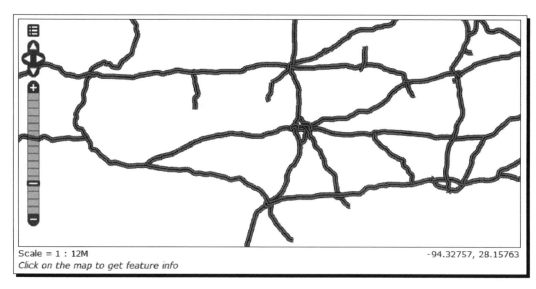

Scale = 1 : 12M   -94.32757, 28.15763
Click on the map to get feature info

12. Zoom in to get closer and you will see that other road classes appear. At 1:376,000 scale, all roads are drawn as in the previous example.

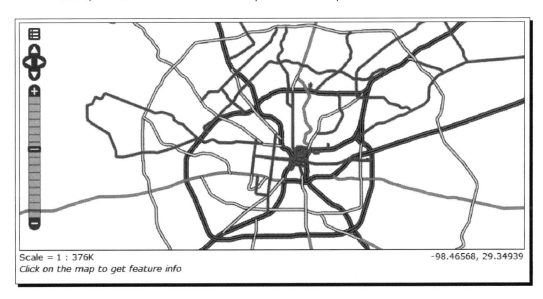

What just happened?

You made road maps much more readable by setting scale range for your feature classes. Setting scale range is a powerful tool and it is almost always required in maps, unless you are composing a map with a tiny number of features. Using scale range is quite easy; you just add it inside your rule.

Besides `MaxScaleDenominator`, there is another element to set scale range, `MinScaleDenominator`. Using them together you can define the upper and lower scale where a rule has to be applied. You may define two rules for the same layer with different scale ranges; this way, as the user zooms in or out, the symbols applied to features will change.

Putting it all together

A common map contains more than a layer, each one styled with one or more symbol according to its complexity and the map purpose. How can you create a multilayer document with SLD? Indeed you can't. As the acronym states, an SLD document can contain a rule relative to just one layer.

By publishing your layers with one or more styles associated on GeoServer, you can compose a map with an external client supporting a WMS protocol (for example, an OpenLayers JavaScript client or a desktop GIS such as QGIS).

Another possibility offered by GeoServer is the layer group. A layer group is a set of layers with a drawing order. Using layer groups, you can compose and publish a full map. Your client will have to do a single WMS request to get all the layers.

Time for action – grouping layers

To compose a full map, we will use a couple of styles created in this chapter and one bundled with GeoServer. We won't create new styles; it is just a matter of selecting layers and setting map properties:

1. On the GeoServer web interface, go to **Data | Layer Groups**.

2. Click on the **Add new layer group** link:

3. Insert the name you would like to give to the new layer group, for example, `myLayerGroup`.

4. Select the **Add layer...** link and choose the **states** layer from the list:

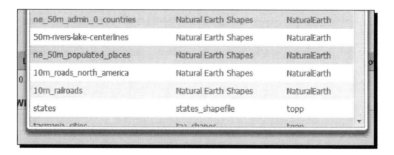

5. Repeat the previous step to add **10m_roads_north_america** and **50m_-rivers-lake-centerlines** layers.

6. In the **Coordinate Reference System** textbox, insert the **EPSG:4326** string. Then click on the **Generate Bounds** button.

You could also build a map with a different SRS than that of layers. In this case, data will be projected at runtime.

7. You composed the map, but as you selected the layers, they were added with their default style. Click on the style name for the roads layer and select the **RoadsThematicScale** style, then click on **Save**.

8. Go to the **Layer Preview** section and search for your new layer group. Note the different icon showing you that the item is composed of multiple layers:

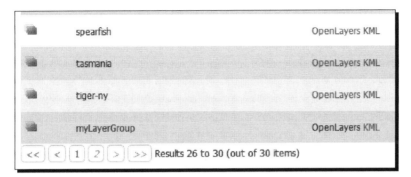

9. Explore your map, and zoom in closer to make all roads appear in the map.

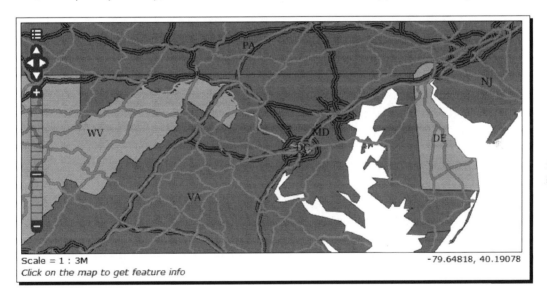

What just happened?

We composed a nice starting point for a map of the USA. It has thematic mapping, scale range, and different layers properly overlapped.

Have a go hero – composing a full map

You learned a lot about styling in this chapter, and you should now be ready to build your first real map. Take the layer group created in the last *Time for action* section and add populated places with points classified according to the SCALERANK field.

Summary

We had a complete introduction to styling in this chapter. Although there are some features we didn't explore, you learned techniques that will help you build 90 percent of your maps, and your comprehension of styling should make you comfortable with looking for more in rare cases where you need it.

Styles and layers are the building blocks of maps. You are now ready to jump to the client-side and create a code that can use what you are configuring on your GeoServer.

In the next chapter, we will use the maps you could compose on GeoServer. There are a few options to build a client application that will be able to deal with WMS protocol. We will explore client-side JavaScript with some specialized libraries. In detail, we will create examples using **Google Map API**, **OpenLayers**, and **LeafLet** library.

7
Creating Simple Maps

In the previous chapter you learned how to style your layers. You also composed maps by combining more layers. It is now time to learn how you can use maps on the client side.

In this chapter, we will explore how to build client applications with a few JavaScript frameworks. JavaScript is a powerful and widespread language and unsurprisingly it is one of the best choices when developing a web application. We will build some sample maps using Google Maps API (`https://developers.google.com/maps/`*), OpenLayers (*`http://openlayers.org/`*), and Leaflet (*`http://leafletjs.com/`*)—the new kid on the block. Throughout the chapter we will use a lot of simple yet useful code examples. We're going to use many of the layers you configured in the previous chapters.*

In this chapter, we will cover the following topics:

- Google map with GeoServer layer
- Google map with GeoServer as base layer
- Google map with GeoServer as base layer and Google as overlay
- OpenLayers map with GeoServer layer
- OpenLayers map with GeoRSS
- Leaflet map

Start up your favorite IDE or text editor. These sample maps will show you how to use GeoServer layers on your website.

Exploring Google Maps API

If you've been reading this book from the beginning, you probably remember that we have already encountered Google Maps previously, and as a map geek it is almost certain that you have already used Google Maps.

The web map application uses the Google Maps API, a JavaScript framework that you can incorporate in your application to build maps. Google Maps API lets you build maps with the data sets from Google, the same that you can see when using the Google application. In fact, it also supports the WMS standard, thereby enabling you to get data from any MapServer compliant with the standard. We'll go over several examples using version 3 of the Google Maps API, and how to incorporate GeoServer layers.

Let's start with a very simple map.

Time for action – adding a GeoServer layer as overlay

One of the most common things you can do with Google Maps API is use their data set as a basemap and add a GeoServer layer on top of the basemap.

You will use the sample code of this chapter, which you can download from the Packt Publishing website.

The Google Maps API doesn't have a method to calculate the BBOX parameters to query GeoServer's WMS server. So we'll need to calculate those on our own based on the x and y coordinates and the zoom level:

1. Once downloaded, the sample code has to be installed on your server. We can use Tomcat as a web server. Unpack the archive in the `/webapps/ROOT` folder inside the Tomcat installation folder.

2. Open your browser and point it to
   `http://localhost:8080/chapter7/index.html`.

3. The page shows a list of links to the sample maps that we will use in this chapter. We will start with a simple map showing the Google basemap with the USA counties layer on top of it. Click on the **GeoServer as overlay** link to open the map:

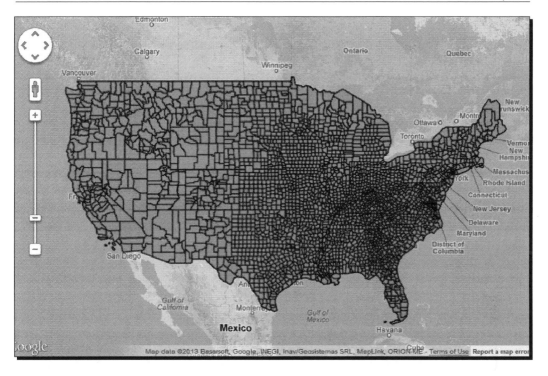

4. The map includes standard navigation tools. The map is redrawn each time it is mapped and/or zoomed, sending requests to the Google servers for the basemap and to your GeoServer for the USA counties layer.

5. Now we will explore the code. Open the `chapter7/google/geoserver_layer/index.html` file in your favorite text editor. The very simple HTML code loads the Google Maps API at line 10:

```
<script type="text/javascript" src="http://maps.google.
com/maps/api/js?sensor=false&language=en"></script>
```

6. Immediately after this, three other JavaScript files are loaded. `base.js` and `maps.js` are the common files for all Google samples. The `base.js` file contains values for the GeoServer location and the layers to load; you can edit them in case you are using a different configuration. The `wms.js` file contains some utility functions. The `map.js` file is the heart of our map and we will explore it in detail:

```
<script type="text/javascript" src="../base.js"></script>
<script type="text/javascript" src="../wms.js"></script>
<script type="text/javascript" src="map.js"></script>
```

7. The `body` tag just contains a placeholder for the map itself and a call to the `mapinitialize` function, a JavaScript function included in the `map.js` file:

```
</head>
<body onload="mapinitialize();">
    <div id="map"></div>
</body>
```

8. Now open the `map.js` file. It includes the code for the `mapinitialize` function. We will discuss the relevant section. At the beginning, you find a declaration for a set of parameters that will be used in the WMS request to GeoServer. The `transparent` parameter makes it possible to overlay the GeoServer layer on the basemap. Also note the `SRS` parameter that sets the projection to the Web Mercator value, which is the one used by Google Maps' data sets:

```
var wmsparams = [
  "REQUEST=GetMap",
  "SERVICE=WMS",
  "VERSION=1.1.1",
  "BGCOLOR=0xFFFFFF",
  "TRANSPARENT=TRUE",
  "SRS=EPSG:3857",
  "WIDTH=255",
  "HEIGHT=255",
  "format=image/png"
  ];
```

9. Just after setting WMS, we set a few parameters for Google Map. Note that we set the type to `roadmap`:

```
var mapOptions = {
    zoom: 4,
    center: new google.maps.LatL
ng(37.609066626725,-97.423977848479),
    mapTypeControl:false,
    draggableCursor: 'crosshair',
    mapTypeId:'roadmap',
    backgroundColor: "#badbff"
}
```

10. Now we create the `map` object:

```
map = new google.maps.Map(document.getElementById("map"),mapOption
s);
```

11. And then we define the parameters for the overlay layer. Note the GEOSERVERBASE and CountyLayer variables that you set previously:

```
var overlayMaps =[
{
    getTileUrl: function(coord, zoom)
    {
        var lULP = new google.maps.Point(coord.x*256,(coord.
y+1)*256);
        var lLRP = new google.maps.Point((coord.
x+1)*256,coord.y*256);

        var projectionMap = new MercatorProjection();

        var lULg = projectionMap.fromDivPixelToSphericalMercator(l
ULP, zoom);
        var lLRg = projectionMap.fromDivPixelToSphericalMercator(
lLRP, zoom);

        var lUL_Latitude = lULg.y;
        var lUL_Longitude = lULg.x;
        var lLR_Latitude = lLRg.y;
        var lLR_Longitude = lLRg.x;

        if (lLR_Longitude < lUL_Longitude){
        lLR_Longitude = Math.abs(lLR_Longitude);
    }
    return GEOSERVERBASE + "/geoserver/wms?" + wmsparams.join("&")
+ "&layers=" + CountyLayer + "&bbox=" + lUL_Longitude + "," + lUL_
Latitude + "," + lLR_Longitude + "," + lLR_Latitude;

},
tileSize: new google.maps.Size(256, 256),
isPng: true,
maxZoom: 15,
minZoom: 4,
alt: 'Counties'
}
];
```

12. Finally we add all the overlay layers (only one in this case) to the map:

```
for (i=0; i<overlayMaps.length; i++){
    var overlayMap = new google.maps.
ImageMapType(overlayMaps[i]);
        map.overlayMapTypes.push(overlayMap);
        map.overlayMapTypes.setAt(overlayMaps[i],overlayMap);
}
```

13. We used the default style for the counties layer; although we set it as `transparent`, it hides the basemap. Let's use a different style. Return to the sample maps home page and click on **GeoServer as transparent overlay** link. Once the map opens, zoom in to the **San Francisco** bay area:

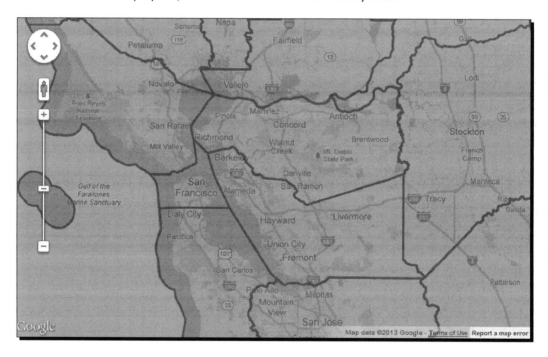

14. How does it work? Open the `map.js` file inside the `geoserver_transparent_layer` folder. Go to line 52. Adding a new parameter, `sld`, does the trick. With it we can reference an external sld to overwrite the default style:

```
return GEOSERVERBASE + "/geoserver/wms?" + wmsparams.join("&")
+ "&layers=" + CountyLayer + "&bbox=" + lUL_Longitude + "," +
lUL_Latitude + "," + lLR_Longitude + "," + lLR_Latitude + "&sld="
+ GEOSERVERBASE + "/chapter7/google/geoserver_transparent_layer/
counties.xml";
```

What just happened?

We built a basic Google Map and calculated the bbox parameters to query GeoServer's WMS server. Just like the other examples in this chapter, you'll see the WMS parameters that we pass to GeoServer. Another way to do this would be to use the GeoServer reflector, which can take the x, y, and zoom parameters instead of bbox.

Time for action – adding a GeoServer layer as a base layer

One lesser-known method allows you to use a GeoServer layer as a base layer with Google Maps, even without a Google Map layer. This example shows you how to use a GeoServer layer as a base layer:

1. Open your browser and point it to
   http://localhost:8080/chapter7/index.html.

2. Then open GeoServer as the base layer link:

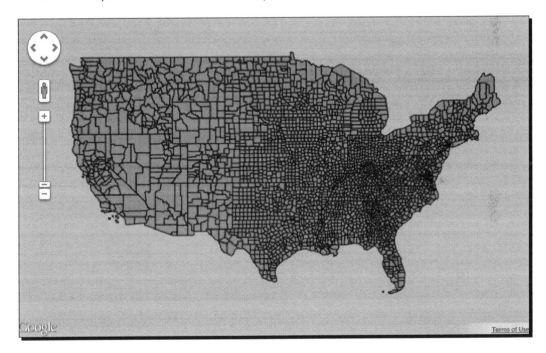

3. Now look at the `map.js` file. It is very similar to that of the previous sample, but in this case we are creating `custommap` and we are passing the GeoServer's layer when creating the `map` object and an overlay:

```
//custom base layer options
var maptypeOptions = {
    getTileUrl: function(coord, zoom)
    {
        var lULP = new google.maps.Point(coord.x*256,(coord.
y+1)*256);
        var lLRP = new google.maps.Point((coord.
x+1)*256,coord.y*256);

        var projectionMap = new MercatorProjection();

        var lULg = projectionMap.fromDivPixelToSphericalMercat
or(lULP, zoom);
        var lLRg  = projectionMap.fromDivPixelToSphericalMerca
tor(lLRP, zoom);

        var lUL_Latitude = lULg.y;
        var lUL_Longitude = lULg.x;
        var lLR_Latitude = lLRg.y;
        var lLR_Longitude = lLRg.x;

        if (lLR_Longitude < lUL_Longitude){
          lLR_Longitude = Math.abs(lLR_Longitude);
        }
        return GEOSERVERBASE + "/geoserver/wms?" + wmsparams.
join("&") + "&layers=" + CountyLayer + "&bbox=" + lUL_Longitude +
"," + lUL_Latitude + "," + lLR_Longitude + "," + lLR_Latitude;

    },
    tileSize: new google.maps.Size(256, 256),
    isPng: true,
    maxZoom: 15,
    minZoom: 4,
    alt: ''
};
//Create a custom map with base layer options
var custommap = new google.maps.ImageMapType(maptypeOptions);

var mapOptions = {
    zoom: 4,
```

```
        center: new google.maps.LatL
ng(37.609066626725,-97.423977848479),
        mapTypeControl:false,
        draggableCursor: 'crosshair',
        mapTypeId:'mapid',
        backgroundColor: "#badbff"
    }

    //Create a google map using custom base layer
    map = new google.maps.Map(document.getElementById("map"),mapOp
tions);
    map.mapTypes.set('mapid', custommap);
} //end init
```

What just happened?

You saw an example of how you can use a GeoServer layer as a base layer using the Google Maps API. Normally you would have specified ImageMapType of ROADMAP, SATELLITE, HYBRID, or TERRAIN. In our example, we created our own ImageMapType called custommap.

Using pre-calculated maps

We have already mentioned GeoWebCache. It is a caching software integrated in GeoServer. We will cover it in detail in *Chapter 8, Performance and Caching*. Now we will have a look at how you can use a cached layer with Google Maps.

Time for action – adding a GeoServer cached layer as overlay

Adding a GeoServer cached layer as an overlay is very similar to the other examples, but in this case we will use the GeoWebCache address as a base tile. We will also use the gmap service:

1. Open chapter7/index.html in your favorite browser.
2. Click on the GeoServer using GWC and the gmap service example.
3. Open /chapter7/google/geoserver_gwcgmap/index.html and /chapter7/google/geoserver_gwcgmap/map.js.
4. Review the map.js file:

```
var map;

function mapinitialize() {

    //custom base layer options
```

```
var maptypeOptions = {
    getTileUrl: function(coord, zoom) {
        return GEOSERVERBASE + "/geoserver/gwc/service/gmaps" +
        "?layers=" + CountyLayer + "&zoom=" + zoom + "&x=" +
coord.x + "&y=" + coord.y + "&format=image/png";
    },
    tileSize: new google.maps.Size(256, 256),
    isPng: true,
    maxZoom: 15,
    minZoom: 4,
    alt: ''
};

//Create a custom map with base layer options
var custommap = new google.maps.ImageMapType(maptypeOptions);

var mapOptions = {
    zoom: 4,
    center: new google.maps.LatL
ng(37.609066626725,-97.423977848479),
    mapTypeControl:false,
    draggableCursor: 'crosshair',
    mapTypeId:'mapid',
    backgroundColor: "#badbff"
}

//Create a google map using custom base layer
map = new google.maps.Map(document.getElementById("map"),mapOp
tions);
map.mapTypes.set('mapid', custommap);
}
```

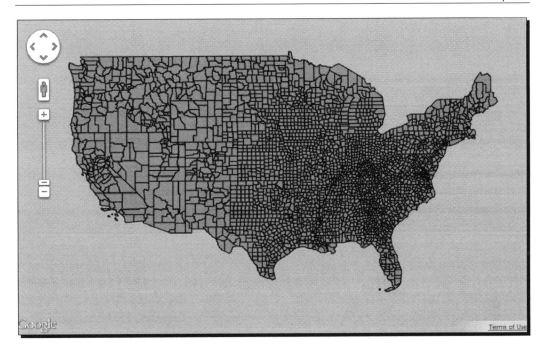

What just happened?

As we have seen in the previous *Time for action* sections, we used the GeoWebCache URI to cover yet another method to access your layers. This is the method you would likely want to use on high-traffic web applications. The good thing is that you can easily change the URL to point to the GeoWebCache as you go to production.

> We'll go over the GeoWebCache in future chapters. Remember that you can pass through WMS using this address too, so use it for WMS queries as well.

Time for action – customizing Google basemap

Google Maps have a lot of detail, so you might want to come up with a custom Google map style to overlay over the GeoServer base layer:

1. Open `chapter7/index.html` in your favorite browser.

2. Click on the GeoServer base layer with the Google layer example.

3. Open `/chapter7/source/google/geoserver_baselayergooglelayer/index.html` and `/chapter7/source/google/geoserver_baselayergooglelayer/map.js`.

4. Review the map.js file:

```
var map;

function mapinitialize() {

    var wmsparams = [
     "REQUEST=GetMap",
     "SERVICE=WMS",
     "VERSION=1.1.1",
     "BGCOLOR=0xFFFFFF",
     "TRANSPARENT=TRUE",
     "SRS=EPSG:3857",
     "WIDTH=255",
     "HEIGHT=255",
     "format=image/png"
     ];

    //custom base layer options
    var maptypeOptions = {
        getTileUrl: function(coord, zoom)
        {
            var lULP = new google.maps.Point(coord.x*256,(coord.
y+1)*256);
            var lLRP = new google.maps.Point((coord.
x+1)*256,coord.y*256);

            var projectionMap = new MercatorProjection();

            var lULg = projectionMap.fromDivPixelToSphericalMercat
or(lULP, zoom);
            var lLRg  = projectionMap.fromDivPixelToSphericalMerca
tor(lLRP, zoom);

            var lUL_Latitude = lULg.y;
            var lUL_Longitude = lULg.x;
            var lLR_Latitude = lLRg.y;
            var lLR_Longitude = lLRg.x;

  if (lLR_Longitude < lUL_Longitude){
            lLR_Longitude = Math.abs(lLR_Longitude);
        }
            return GEOSERVERBASE + "/geoserver/wms?" + wmsparams.
join("&") + "&layers=" + CountyLayer + "&bbox=" + lUL_Longitude +
"," + lUL_Latitude + "," + lLR_Longitude + "," + lLR_Latitude;
```

```
        },
        tileSize: new google.maps.Size(256, 256),
        isPng: true,
        maxZoom: 15,
        minZoom: 4,
        alt: ''
    };

    //Create a custom map with base layer options
    var custommap = new google.maps.ImageMapType(maptypeOptions);

    var mapOptions = {
        zoom: 4,
        center: new google.maps.LatL
ng(37.609066626725,-97.423977848479),
        mapTypeControl:false,
        draggableCursor: 'crosshair',
        mapTypeId:'mapid',
        backgroundColor: "#badbff"
    }

    //Create a google map using custom base layer
    map = new google.maps.Map(document.getElementById("map"),mapOp
tions);
    map.mapTypes.set('mapid', custommap);

    //add all the custom overlays we want.
    var overlayMaps =[
    {
        // Google Roads layer
        getTileUrl: function(coord, z) {
            var x = coord.x % (1 << z);
            var y = coord.y;

            return "http://mt0.google.com/vt/v=apt.116&hl=en-
US&x="
            + x + "&y=" + y + "&z=" + z + "&src=apiv3&s=G&lyrs=
r&apistyle=s.t:33|p.v:off&apistyle=s.t:49|s.e:l|p.v:on|p.l:50|
p.s:24,s.t:5|p.v:off,s.t:6|p.v:off,s.t:1|p.v:off,s.t:5|p.v:off-
,s.t:2|p.v:off"
        },
        tileSize: new google.maps.Size(256, 256),
        isPng: false,
        maxZoom: 18,
        name: "Roads",
```

```
              alt: "Custom Roads"
        }
        ];

        //add all overlays to the map
        for (i=0; i<overlayMaps.length; i++){
            var overlayMap = new google.maps.
ImageMapType(overlayMaps[i]);
            map.overlayMapTypes.push(overlayMap);
            map.overlayMapTypes.setAt(overlayMaps[i],overlayMap);
        }
    } //end init
```

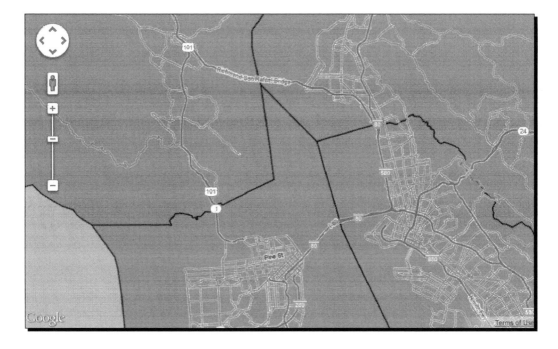

What just happened?

We created a custom Google Maps overlay using a Google map style to the base GeoServer map. The Google layer is displayed as you zoom into the map.

 This add-on Drupal module uses OpenLayers to do the same thing. Check out the **GitHub** project README.md for details on how to use it at https://github.com/brianyoungblood/google-map-styled.

Have a go hero – creating a custom Google map layer

Create your own custom Google map layer using the Google Maps API-styled wizard. Use Firebug to get the needed URL parameters (`http://gmaps-samples-v3.googlecode. com/svn/trunk/styledmaps/wizard/index.html`).

Interacting with the user

Publishing a beautiful map is a good starting point for your site, but you probably want to have some interaction with your users. JavaScript, and many frameworks built on it, gives you a lot of ways to customize your interface and how to react to a user action. We will see a short example in the next section.

Time for action – intercepting the Click event

If you want to query your GeoServer's WMS, you need to get the latitude and longitude. You can use this example map:

1. Open `chapter7/index.html` in your favorite browser.

2. Click on the **Google lat/lng on click event** example.

3. Open `/chapter7/source/google/geoserver_latlonclickevent/index. html` and `/chapter7/source/google/geoserver_latlonclickevent/map. js`.

4. Review the `map.js` file:

   ```
   var map;
   var geocoder;
   var overlay;

   function mapinitialize() {

       //add all the overlays we want
       var overlayMaps =[
       {
           // Google Roads layer
           getTileUrl: function(coord, z) {
               var x = coord.x % (1 << z);
               var y = coord.y;
               return "http://mt0.google.com/vt/v=apt.116&hl=en-
   US&x="
               + x + "&y=" + y + "&z=" + z + "&src=apiv3&s=G&lyrs=
   r&apistyle=s.t:33|p.v:off&apistyle=s.t:49|s.e:1|p.v:on|p.l:50|
   p.s:24,s.t:5|p.v:off,s.t:6|p.v:off,s.t:1|p.v:off,s.t:5|p.v:off-
   ,s.t:2|p.v:off"
   ```

```
        },
        tileSize: new google.maps.Size(256, 256),
        isPng: false,
        maxZoom: 18,
        name: "Roads",
        alt: "Custom Roads"
    }
    ];

    //custom base layer options
    var maptypeOptions = {
        getTileUrl: function(coord, zoom) {
            return GEOSERVERBASE + "/geoserver/gwc/service/gmaps"
+
            "?layers=" + CountyLayer +"&zoom=" + zoom + "&x=" +
coord.x + "&y=" + coord.y + "&format=image/png";
        },
        tileSize: new google.maps.Size(256, 256),
        isPng: true,
        maxZoom: 15,
        minZoom: 4,
        alt: ''
    };

    //Create a custom map with base layer options
    var commap = new google.maps.ImageMapType(maptypeOptions);

    var mapOptions = {
        zoom: 4,
        center: new google.maps.LatL
ng(37.609066626725,-97.423977848479),
        mapTypeControl:false,
        draggableCursor: 'crosshair',
        mapTypeId:'mapid',
        backgroundColor: "#badbff"
    }

    //Create a google map using custom base layer
    map = new google.maps.Map(document.getElementById("map"),mapOp
tions);
    map.mapTypes.set('mapid', commap);

    //need a overlay object to get the object being clicked on
using the click listener. this is a google api v3 requirement
    overlay = new google.maps.OverlayView();
```

```
    overlay.draw = function() {};
    overlay.setMap(map);
    //end overlay object

    //add all overlays to the map
    for (i=0; i<overlayMaps.length; i++){
        var overlayMap = new google.maps.
ImageMapType(overlayMaps[i]);
        map.overlayMapTypes.push(overlayMap);
        map.overlayMapTypes.setAt(overlayMaps[i],overlayMap);
    }

    //click listener
    google.maps.event.addListener(map, 'click',
        function(event) {
            var point = overlay.getProjection().fromLatLngToContai
nerPixel(event.latLng);
            alert("latlng: " + event.latLng + "\npoint: " +
point);
        }
        );
}
```

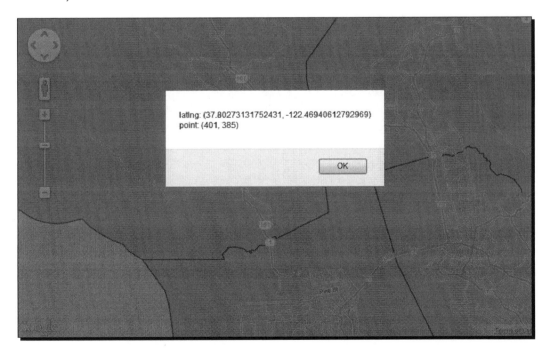

What just happened?

The key here is to create an `overlay` object and call the `getProjection()` method. This is something new for version 3 of the Google Maps API. This is useful for sending the latitude and longitude to GeoServer to query for the features.

Using OpenLayers

Google Maps API is not the only option for developing a JavaScript mapping application. OpenLayers is one of the oldest and frequently used frameworks. It is an open source project constantly maintained and developed by a growing crowd of enthusiast developers. As you've noticed, it is used with the GeoServer previews.

Copying the OpenLayers previews don't do much good, so let's go over some basics with OpenLayers.

Time for action – integrating GeoServer and OpenLayers

Once again, let's dive into the source code and see how OpenLayers works with GeoServer:

1. Open `chapter7/index.html` in your favorite browser.

2. Click on the **OpenLayers Basic Map** example:

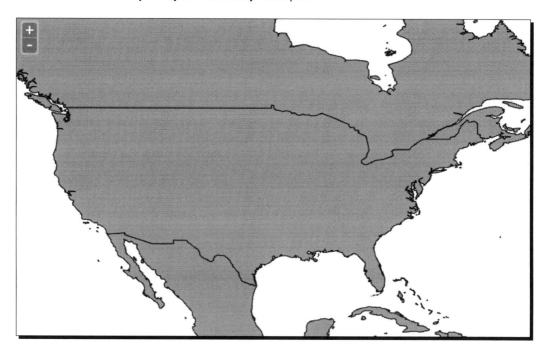

3. Open `chapter7/openlayers/geoserverbase/index.html` and `/chapter7/ openlayers/geoserverbase/map.js`. The `index.html` file is very similar to the previous one. The difference is the loading of the OpenLayers API code:

```
<script type="text/javascript" src="http://openlayers.org/
api/2.12/OpenLayers.js"></script>
```

4. The `map.js` file is quite different. First we define the map options, that is, bounds and `projection`:

```
var map;

function mapinitialize() {
    var bounds = new OpenLayers.Bounds(
        -180.0, -90.0, 180.0, 90.0
        );

    var options = {
        maxExtent: bounds,
        projection: 'EPSG:4326',
        units: 'degrees'
    };
```

5. Then we create a new `map` object:

```
    map = new OpenLayers.Map('map', options);
```

6. Create a new layer object and define its parameters:

```
    var countries = new OpenLayers.Layer.WMS(
        CountriesLayer, GEOSERVERBASE + '/geoserver/NaturalEarth/
wms',
        {
            layers: CountriesLayer,
            format: 'image/png'
        }
        );
```

7. Eventually we add it to the map and center it on the USA:

```
    map.addLayer(countries);
    map.zoomTo(4);
    map.panTo(new OpenLayers.LonLat(-95.0,40.0));
}
```

8. Of course a map with a single layer is almost useless. Let's add the layers of rivers and lakes from Natural Earth. Add the following code lines after the `countries` layer definition:

```
var rivers = new OpenLayers.Layer.WMS(
    RiversLayer, GEOSERVERBASE + '/geoserver/NaturalEarth/
wms',
    {
        layers: RiversLayer,
        transparent: 'true'
    },
    {
        isBaseLayer: false,
    }
);

map.addLayer(countries);
map.addLayer(rivers);
```

9. Now open the map sample:

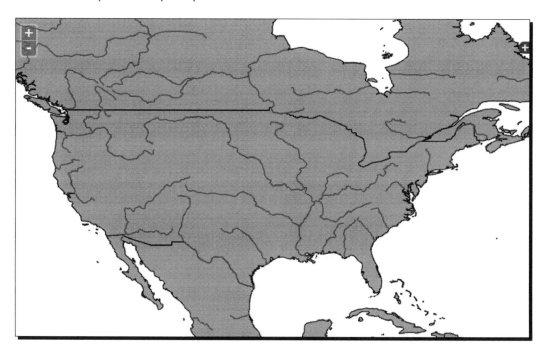

What just happened?

We created a basic OpenLayers map using GeoServer to serve as tiles. This is a good place to start when we want to use OpenLayers with GeoServer, as the GeoServer previews don't work if you copy and paste them into your own applications.

Time for action – using GeoRSS with OpenLayers

We're going to show a number of features represented as points:

1. Open `chapter7/index.html` in your favorite browser.

2. Click on the **OpenLayers GeoRSS** example.

3. Open `/chapter7/openlayers/georss/index.html` and `/chapter7/openlayers/georss/map.js`.

4. Review the `map.js` file:

```
var map, rss;

function mapinitialize() {

    map = new OpenLayers.Map('map', {
        maxResolution:'auto',
        projection: 'EPSG:4326'
    });
    layer = new OpenLayers.Layer.WMS(
        CountyLayer, GEOSERVERBASE + "/geoserver/tiger/wms",
        {
            LAYERS: CountyLayer,
            format: 'image/png'
        }
        );
    map.addLayer(layer);
    map.zoomTo(9);
    map.panTo(new OpenLayers.LonLat(-73.99, 40.75));
    addGeoRSS();
}

function addGeoRSS() {
```

```
        var value = GEOSERVERBASE + '/geoserver/tiger/wms?service
=WMS&version=1.1.0&request=GetMap&layers=tiger:poi&styles=&bb
ox=-74.0118315772888,40.70754683896324,-74.00153046439813,
40.719885123828675&width=427&height=512&srs=EPSG:4326&format=
application%2Frss%2Bxml';
        var georss = new OpenLayers.Layer.GeoRSS('Tiger POI', value);
        map.addLayer(georss);
}
```

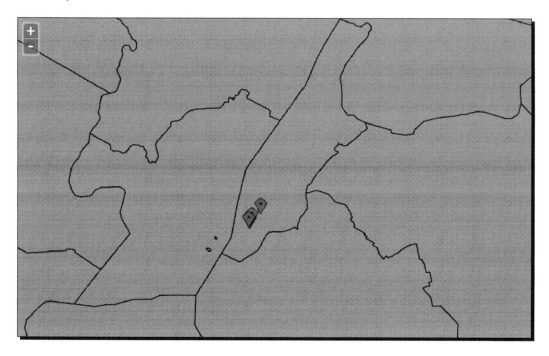

What just happened?

We're still viewing the counties data for the basemap, but we've overlayed the Tiger POI
layer using the GeoRSS output format. Remember to use `ProxyPass` to avoid any XSS
errors when serving example files from a different URL than your GeoServer.

Check out the examples for GeoRSS for more information, at
http://openlayers.org/dev/examples/georss.html.

Exploring Leaflet

The Leaflet project came out of the depths of OpenLayers. It's still young and being developed, but many desktop and mobile developers are moving towards a more compacted library that's easy to implement and understand. Mobile devices are given equal attention with bug fixes and features. These examples will work well on iOS, Android, and other HTML5 mobile browsers.

Time for action – using Leaflet with GeoServer layers

Check out the sample code folder for a quick example of Leaflet:

1. Open `chapter7/index.html` in your favorite browser.

2. Click on the **Leaflet basic map** example.

3. Open `/chapter7/leaflet/index.html` and `/chapter7/leaflet/map.js`.

4. Review the `map.js` file:

```
var map;

function mapinitialize() {

    counties = new L.TileLayer.WMS(GEOSERVERBASE + "/geoserver/
tiger/wms",
        {
            layers: "tiger:tl_2011_us_county",
            format: 'image/png',
            transparent: true,
            attribution: ""
        });

    rivers = new L.TileLayer.WMS(GEOSERVERBASE + "/geoserver/
NaturalEarth/wms",
        {
            layers: "NaturalEarth:50m-rivers-lake-centerlines",
            format: 'image/png',
            transparent: true,
            attribution: ""
        });

    populatedplaces = new L.TileLayer.WMS(GEOSERVERBASE + "/
geoserver/NaturalEarth/wms",
        {
```

```
        layers: "NaturalEarth:ne_50m_populated_places",
        format: 'image/png',
        transparent: true,
        attribution: ""
    });

map = new L.Map('map',
    {
        center: new L.LatLng(30.609, -87.424),
        zoom: 6,
        layers: [counties,rivers,populatedplaces],
        zoomControl: true
    });
}
```

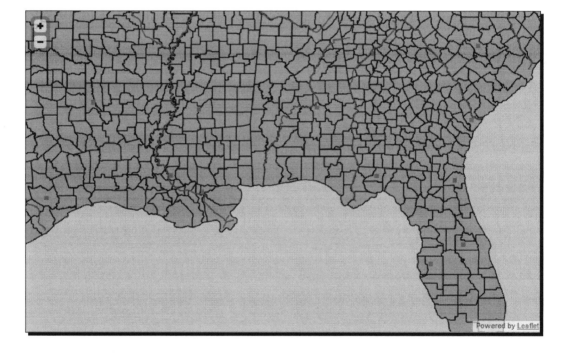

What just happened?

The shortest of the examples is the Leaflet map. We use the `gmap` service, which is something not often found in the other examples online. This allows you to use the XYZ format without translating a bounding box, as shown in the other examples. You can also use this GeoServer service with the Google Maps API.

For more information take a look at the Leaflet project on **GitHub**: `https://github.com/CloudMade/Leaflet`.

Pop quiz – creating mapping apps

Q1. Can you use any programming language for building a map client?

1. No, you may only use JavaScript/HTML.

2. Yes, you can use any language/framework supporting HTTP requests.

3. Yes, but you should build a web application.

Q2. When building a JavaScript application, can you mix more than one mapping framework (for example, OpenLayers and Leaflet)?

1. No, you have to select one and stick to it.

2. Yes, for example, if you want to integrate Google Maps data in an OpenLayers-based app.

3. It is technically possible but it is a bad idea and you won't gain any advantages from using more than one framework.

Summary

By now, you should be able to select among several choices to build your web-based GeoServer maps.

Specifically, in this chapter, we covered how to use Google Maps API to show a GeoServer layer as a base layer and an overlay. We also covered OpenLayers and Leaflet, two open source projects that offer you a ready-to-use framework. OpenLayers, at the moment, is considered more powerful but a little bit harder to learn. Leaflet is really straightforward to use and its capabilities are growing more and more.

In the next chapter, we will cover the cached layers in detail. We will describe why caching is important and how can you configure it in GeoServer. We will also explore the integrated GeoWebCache that ships with GeoServer in greater detail.

8
Performance and Caching

In previous chapters, you learned how to style layers for composing maps. Then you built a JavaScript code snippet, exploring several possibilities for including maps in your web application.

Whatever technology you prefer, or are constrained to use, you will have to submit a GetMap request to GeoServer. For each request GeoServer has to perform a complex set of operations: loading data, applying styles, rendering the result to a bitmap, and pushing it back to the client who performed the request. As your web application gains popularity, more and more concurrent requests will be added and you may run out of resources to satisfy them all.

Having to build the map from scratch every time does not make sense, especially if your web application does not offer the user the possibility to modify styles for layers. In many cases, the styles are defined just once, or very rarely, updated. So your GeoServer instance will render lots of identical maps.

This is, of course, a great place to do something to boost performance. As with other web document sharing the keyword here is caching.

Indeed when you are requesting a map to GeoServer, chances are that the same map was already produced before. We need a procedure to store and retrieve maps when needed and to match them for equality. This is a more general problem, not specifically linked to GeoServer. Several systems to implement map caching exist. Earlier GeoServer releases didn't include any caching mechanism and you had to set software in front of GeoServer, intercepting map requests and forwarding only those that can't get a hit from the cache to GeoServer.

In his chapter, we will cover the following topics in detail:

- What GeoWebCache is and how you can use it
- Setting general parameters for integrating GWC
- Configuring new gridsets
- Configuring tile layers

Exploring GeoWebCache

A prominent member of the tile map caching software family is GeoWebCache (http://geowebcache.org/), a Java open source project. Just as any caching system, it acts as a proxy between the clients and the map server. If you use the standalone version, your map server can be any that is in compliance with WMS standard. Indeed, GeoWebCache uses the WMS syntax to retrieve tiles from the map server. It exposes the tiles in several ways; with the GeoServer integrated version you can use the following:

- **WMS (Web Mapping Service)**
- **WMS-C (WMS Tiling Client Recommendation)**
- **WMTS (Web Map Tiling Service)**
- **TMS (Tile Map Service)**

You can use an external instance of GeoWebCache, disabling the one that is included, but there are many advantages in using the internal one. You can use a single interface to administer both GeoServer and GeoWebCache and you don't have to use a custom URL or a special endpoint; all the layers you publish on GeoServer are automatically configured as cached. You just have to set the caching properties on layers and layer groups.

Time for action – configuring GeoWebCache storage

Running the GeoWebCache shipped with GeoServer is very simple. All the layers are already configured for caching; we just need to modify some details of the configuration.

1. Caching will produce a lot of files, and storage requires quite a lot of space on your disk. By default, all the files are stored on the same filesystem where you installed GeoServer. A common issue is that you can run out of free space or available inodes on Linux filesystems. The result is the same: you won't be able to store anything more on the filesystem and you may also crash your system. We are going to use a custom location for cache files.

2. Locate your `webapps` folder inside the Apache Tomcat installation folder:

```
~$ cd /opt/apache-tomcat-7.0.27/webapps/
```

3. Go to the `geoserver/WEB-INF` folder:

```
/opt/apache-tomcat-7.0.27/webapps$ cd geoserver/WEB-INF/
```

4. Open the `web.xml` file and locate the line containing the following code:

```
<display-name>GeoServer</display-name>
```

5. After this, there are several parameters defined. We will insert a new parameter to set the `GeoWebCache` folder location. You can enter the following code just after the previous line. The `param-value` syntax is valorized with a folder location that is valid on the Linux filesystem. On a Windows filesystem, use proper syntax.

```
<!-- Setting GeoWebCache folder  -->
  <context-param>
    <param-name>GEOWEBCACHE_CACHE_DIR</param-name>
    <param-value>/opt/gwc</param-value>
  </context-param>
```

6. Save the file and close it.

7. Now go to the Tomcat Manager Application to reload GeoServer. The parameters that you change from the web administration interface don't need a reload to be effective. GeoServer reads the `web.xml` file on startup, so any changes to the file are effective only after an application reload.

8. Open your browser and enter the URL, `http://localhost:8080/manager/html/list`.

9. Locate **GeoServer** in the application list and click on the **Reload** button:

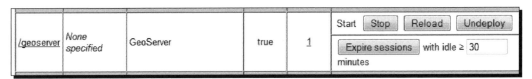

10. After a while, depending on the complexity of your configuration, a success message will appear:

11. Now, go to the **Tile Layers** section on the web administration interface of GeoServer and browse through the list to find the **NaturalEarth:ne_50_m_populated_places** layer:

12. From the drop-down list, select a combination of SRS and image format (for example, **EPSG:4326/jpeg**); a new map preview will show up in the browser window.

 This preview is not the same as the one you can access from the **Layer Preview** page. While both use JavaScript code with the OpenLayers library, the latter is optimized to use the integrated GeoWebCache.

13. Navigate the map by panning and zooming it. Each operation will request tiles from GeoWebCache. For the first time you use it, they have to be requested to GeoServer and stored for future reuse.

14. Now close the map and click again on the **Tile Layers** link in the administration interface. Going to the row that shows information for your layer, you can see that there is now a number showing the disk storage used by tiles:

15. Open a system console and go to the folder you configured for GeoWebCache in step 5. You should see that it contains a folder for the tiles of the layer:

```
/opt/gwc$ ls -al
total 32
drwxr-xr-x 5 root root 4096 Sep 30 18:12 ./
drwxr-xr-x 4 root root 4096 Sep 25 21:37 ../
drwxr-xr-x 2 root root 4096 Sep 30 17:48 diskquota_page_store/
-rw-r--r-- 1 root root  406 Sep 27 00:33 geowebcache-diskquota.xml
-rw-r--r-- 1 root root 4879 Sep 25 21:55 geowebcache.xml
drwxr-xr-x 2 root root 4096 Sep 30 17:48 meta_jdbc_h2/
drwxr-xr-x 8 root root 4096 Sep 30 18:18 NaturalEarth_ne_50m_
populated_places/
```

16. Open the folder and check whether the folder content actually uses the size that GeoServer showed you:

```
/opt/gwc/NaturalEarth_ne_50m_populated_places$ du -sh
1.4M    .
```

What just happened?

You configured the storage location for your tiles. By default, GeoWebCache stores them in the `temp` folder located inside Tomcat installation location. For production site, it is a good idea to use a folder on a different device. Also, try to avoid storing tiles on the same disk where the data is stored.

Time for action – configuring Disk Quota

Whether you prefer seeding your layers or you just set the cache on and wait for your clients' requests to populate it, the tiles can grow to a huge number of files and sizes. The folder configured for containing them may fill and you may run the filesystem on a shortage of resources. By default, the integrated GeoWebCache comes with unlimited disk usage for cached tiles. It is a good practice to configure it to a known value and to set a policy for tiles recycling.

1. From the GeoServer administration interface go to **Disk Quota** under the **Tile caching** section:

2. As you can see, there is an upper limit for cache size, that is, **500.0 MB**, but the **Enable disk quota** flag is unchecked; you might wonder what happens when your cache size hits the limit. Set the limit at 5 megabytes and click on the **Submit** button.

3. Now go to the **Tile layers** form and open the cache preview for **myLayerGroup**, which you created in *Chapter 6, Styling Your Layers*. Browse the map, panning and zooming a little, until you see that the layer's cache size exceeds 5 megabytes (you have to manually refresh the interface for the new size value to show up).

4. What will be shown now is the **Disk Quota** form. Go back to it and you will see that all your tiles are there, the total size is over the upper bound and the maximum size value acts just as a warning.

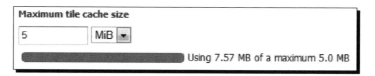

5. Now check the **Enable disk quota** flag and click on the **Submit** button. Go back to the **Disk Quota** form; all your tiles are now gone. This is because 5 megabytes is a very low limit and tiles are marked for removal in groups.

6. Now you will set the parameters to more realistic values. The first parameter is the block size used by the filesystem where you are storing tiles. The provided default is quite common, but if you are unsure you can check it. For example, on Linux you may use the `dumpe2fs` utility:

```
/opt/gwc$ sudo dumpe2fs -h /dev/mapper/ubuntu1204x64vm-root | grep
'Block size'
dumpe2fs 1.42 (29-Nov-2011)
Block size:               4096
```

7. Then you may want to set the time interval for GeoWebCache performing checks on the cache size. Although 10 seconds is a good trade–off, you might want to insert a higher value as a very low value will degrade performance.

8. Now you have to set the upper limit for your cache size. This depends on how many layers you have to cache and, of course, on how much space is available. If you are using a non-dedicated filesystem for your tiles, consider that there may be other processes creating temporary objects on the filesystem and select a conservative value that leaves at least 20 percent of the filesystem always free. On the other hand, if you have a dedicated filesystem for your cache you may insert a value near to 99 percent of the total size. Avoid setting it to a value equal to the size of the filesystem, as filling it completely may produce weird errors and corruption. We assume here that you are fine with a 5 gigabyte cache size.

9. Lastly, you have to choose the criteria for tile removal when the upper limit is hit. The default option selects **Least frequently used**, which is usually a good choice as long as your site contains a static set of layers. If you frequently add new layers, there is a chance that older layers are used less, so select the **Least recently used** option.

10. Now that all the parameters are valorized, you can click the **Submit** button:

What just happened?

You completed the storage configuration for GeoWebCache. Now you are ready to review general settings and layer parameters.

Setting caching defaults

As mentioned previously, the included GeoWebCache comes with a default configuration. From the web interface you can manage almost all parameters; this is a brand new feature of the GeoServer 2.2 release. In earlier releases, you had to go to the GeoWebCache web interface or open the configuration files.

The **Caching Defaults** form includes general parameters. The first section is about services used to expose tiles.

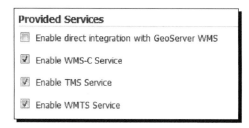

Direct integration

By default, the first option is disabled. Direct integration is about the endpoint used in WMS GetMap requests. If you go with the default option, you will have to use a custom endpoint to tell GeoServer that you want to retrieve a map from the cache, if there are tiles available to fulfill your request.

```
http://localhost:8080/geoserver/gwc/service/wms?
```

Enabling direct integration lets you use the same syntax you would use against a non-cached layer:

```
http://localhost:8080/geoserver/<workspace>/wms?tiled=true
```

Apart from the endpoint, there are a set of conditions that a request has to meet in order to use tiles from the cache. We will explore both methods in a later section querying layers with an OpenLayers-based application.

WMS-C

The second option listed is for the WMS-C service. **WMS-C** is the acronym for **Web Mapping Services Cached**. It is the default way to query for tiles and is available at the endpoint.

```
http://localhost:8080/geoserver/gwc/service/wms
```

If you disable the option when performing a request to the endpoint, you will receive a **Service is disabled** message and a **400 (Bad request) HTTP response** code from GeoServer.

TMS and WMTS

These two options enable endpoints specific to the **TMS (Tiled Map Services)** and **WMTS (Web Map Tiled Services)**. Both are OGC standards for retrieving tiled maps; the main difference is the incorporation of a query by location request (`GetFeatureInfo`) in WMTS. The endpoints are as follows:

```
http://localhost:8080/geoserver/gwc/service/tms/1.0.0
http://localhost:8080/geoserver/gwc/service/wmts?
```

Default layers options

The next section is about parameters for layers.

By default, each time you add a layer on GeoServer it is configured for caching. Configuring a layer for caching doesn't use space on your cache storage, until someone starts requesting maps of it. You may consider removing this option if, on your site, you are going to add a large number of frequently updated layers. Note that disabling this flag you should manually enable caching for the layers.

As you did in *Chapter 6, Styling Your Layers*, you can configure more than one style for your layers; by default all the styles are enabled to be cached. If you add a lot of styles but only one is important, you may want to avoid wasting space in your cache storage and store only tiles rendered with the default style.

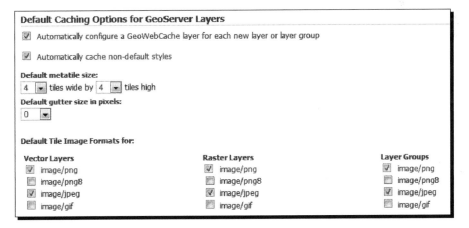

The default metatile size sets dimensions of the map produced by GeoServer when it gets a request for a tile not already stored in cache. By default, the map produced is composed of 16 tiles. When a request hits a tile not stored, a GeoWebCache sends a `GetMap` request for a map with dimension equal to 4x the tile's height size and 4x the tile's width size. Once produced, the map is sliced and each tile is stored in the GeoWebCache repository. Using a metatile is useful to reduce a layer's seeding time and for label placement. When you ask GeoWebCache to seed a layer (we will discuss this in detail later), all the tiles are produced, so a lot of `GetMap` requests are sent to GeoServer. It is much more efficient to produce larger maps and then slice them, than producing a lot of tiny maps.

With regards to label placement, you have to consider that GeoServer's labeling engine places the label according to the map's dimension. So with bigger maps you have a small chance of label duplication and overlapping.

So you may wonder why the default metatile size is not bigger than a mere 4 x 4. The problem is that when producing a map's memory, the consumption grows proportionally to the map's dimensions; having a big metatile size may produce errors in caching. According to the memory resource on your installation, you may increase the size but be careful with a metatile size higher than 8 x 8.

The gutter size defines an extra edge on the map used for label and feature placements. The edges won't be rendered in the map but setting it larger than zero may help reducing the label's conflicts.

In the **Default Tile Image Formats for** section, you can set those formats you want to enable. It is a good idea to go with the default here as **png8** (an 8-bit color depth version of PNG) and **gif** are not much used in web mapping.

Default Cached Gridsets

This section shows the gridsets that will be automatically configured for cached layers. A gridset is a schema for tiles; it contains CRS, tile dimensions, and zoom levels.

We will see how to create custom gridset in the very next paragraph.

By default there are two gridsets configured for all layers. They are the ones most commonly used in web mapping:

- **EPSG:4326** (geographic) with **22** maximum **Zoom levels** and **256 x 256** pixel tiles
- **EPSG:900913** (spherical Mercator) with **31** maximum **Zoom levels** and **256 x 256** pixel tiles

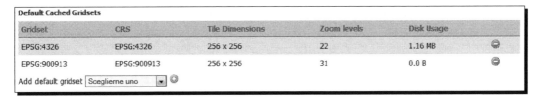

Configuring gridsets

Gridsets are caching schemas. When you decide to store tiles for a layer, you have to define the common properties for the tiles set. The logical entities where you store those properties are the gridsets.

The properties you can configure in a gridset are the CRS, the tile sizes in pixels, the number and scale of zoom levels, and the bounds of the gridset. Once you define a gridset and bind it to a layer, your client requests must conform to the caching schema, that is, the gridset or GeoWebCache will be unable to fulfill your request.

For your convenience, GeoServer comes with a common gridset already configured.

Time for action – creating a custom gridset

In *Chapter 5*, *Adding Your Data*, we add the tiger county shapefiles. The CRS for this is **EPSG:4269**. If we want to create a cache for it without projection, we need to create a specific gridset.

1. In the GeoServer web interface, select the gridset URL on the left panel.

2. GeoServer will show you a list of existing gridsets. Click on the **Create a new gridset** link:

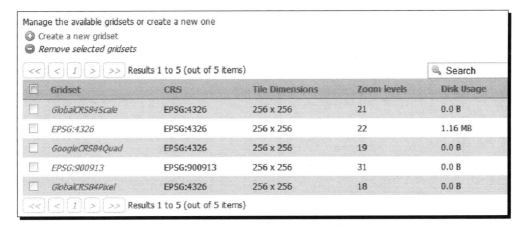

3. In the creation form, you have to insert the values for creating parameters. Choose a name for the new gridset; using the CRS is a good idea so insert `EPSG:4269`.

4. In the **Coordinate Reference System** section, enter `EPSG:4269`. The **Units** and **Meters per unit** parameters are updated from GeoServer as it retrieves the projection parameters. Please note that we inserted the same string in the title and CRS textbox but they have completely different meanings; the title is just a label that you can set to a string convenient for you, while the CRS has to be a value recognized from GeoServer projection engine:

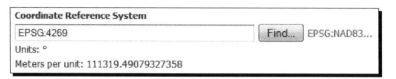

5. Click on the **Compute from maximum extent of CRS** link; the gridset bounds will be automatically calculated by GeoServer. If you want your gridset limited to a smaller extent, you may manually insert values in the textboxes. As we are going to use this gridset for the USA inland counties, we will enter custom bounds values as shown in the following screenshot:

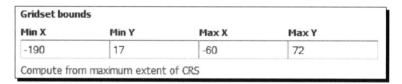

6. Each gridset must have a fixed tile size. GeoServer will prompt you to have the default values of 256 x 256 pixels; this is usually a good choice so we will leave it unchanged. Note that you may want to set a smaller or greater size and you can also have rectangular tiles, but you might run into trouble with clients requesting your tiles.

7. You now have to set the zoom levels for your gridsets. Keep in mind that when using cached maps, you are constrained to pre-calculated zoom levels. Here you have the opportunity to set what and how many they are. Creating levels is quite simple; first you need to decide how many levels you need. Click on the **Add zoom level** link. A new line is added showing you the level's parameters. The first column shows you the level's index (the list is zero based) and then you find **Pixel Size**. GeoServer calculates first level for having a single row of tiles covering all of your layer extent. Optionally, you may set a name for the level. In the **Tiles** column, you can see how many tiles would compose the levels; the syntax is *column x rows*. The red symbol at the end of the row lets you remove a level.

Tile Matrix Set				
Define grids based on: ● Resolutions ○ Scale denominators				
Level	Pixel Size	Scale	Name	Tiles
0	0.25390625	1: 100,945,408.78296293	EPSG:4269:0	2 x 1

8. Keep adding levels until you add level 10. As you can see each level is calculated doubling the columns and the rows, hence it contains 4x the tiles of the previous level. The total number of tiles grows fast; at level 10 you already have almost 2 million tiles, plus those of the other levels:

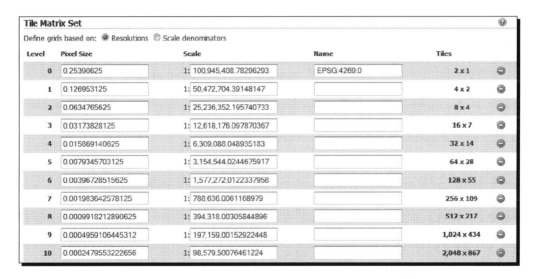

Tile Matrix Set				
Define grids based on: ● Resolutions ○ Scale denominators				
Level	Pixel Size	Scale	Name	Tiles
0	0.25390625	1: 100,945,408.78296293	EPSG:4269:0	2 x 1
1	0.126953125	1: 50,472,704.39148147		4 x 2
2	0.0634765625	1: 25,236,352.195740733		8 x 4
3	0.03173828125	1: 12,618,176.097870367		16 x 7
4	0.015869140625	1: 6,309,088.048935183		32 x 14
5	0.0079345703125	1: 3,154,544.0244675917		64 x 28
6	0.00396728515625	1: 1,577,272.0122337958		128 x 55
7	0.001983642578125	1: 788,636.0061168979		256 x 109
8	0.0009918212890625	1: 394,318.00305844896		512 x 217
9	0.0004959106445312	1: 197,159.00152922448		1,024 x 434
10	0.0002479553222656	1: 98,579.50076461224		2,048 x 867

9. Now click on the **Save** button. The gridset is added to the list. You may also want to add a custom gridset to the default gridset list, but this is not the case with the **EPSG:4269** that we created for the county layer.

10. Now go to the layer panel and select the **tiger:tl_2011_us_county**. In the **Configuration** form, go to the **Tile Caching** tab. At the end of the page, there is the **Gridset** section; here you can configure the available gridsets for your layer. Please note that all the default settings we configured in the previous paragraph may be overridden in the layer configuration. From the drop-down list, select the **EPSG:4269** gridset you just created, then click on the plus symbol on the right:

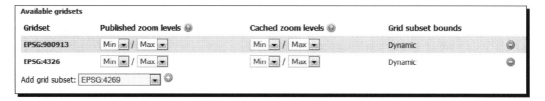

11. The new gridset is added to the list of those available for your layer. Note that you can optionally have only a subset of the levels published and/or cached.

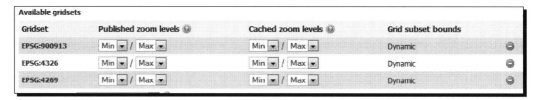

What just happened?

We created a new gridset with custom properties for caching a specific layer and a specific area of the world. You can have as many gridsets as you need for your layers. Please remember that clients requesting maps shall conform to the gridset's properties (for example, tile sizes), otherwise you will get an error from GeoWebCache.

Configuring tile layers

From the web interface, you can access the **Tile layers** section. All the layers published on GeoServer and configured for caching are listed in this section, and you can review the status and the main parameters for each layer.

The first two columns display the **Type** and **Layer Name**, and the third is for per layer **Disk Quota**. In GeoServer 2.2, the per layer disk quota is not checked and cannot be configured as in the GeoWebCache standalone version, so you can only see an **N/A** value here. The next column contains the size occupied on disk by the layer's tiles.

The next column shows you if the layer, configured for caching, is enabled to store tiles in the cache. Disabling caching on a layer without removing it from cached layers is useful when you want to temporarily disable layers from caching without losing the configuration.

If caching is enabled on a specific layer, you see a drop-down list with the gridsets associated to that layer, and by clicking on it you can open a new web page with a preview application. It is very similar to the page raised by the layer preview list, but it ensures that the request conforms to the caching schema, that is, the gridset and maps that are requested are retrieved from the cache.

Eventually you find the link to **Seed** or **Truncate** one or more levels of the cache.

The **Empty** link will erase all tiles for that specific layer, including all gridsets and styles.

Time for action – configuring layers and layer groups for caching

By default, each layer you publish on GeoServer is added to GeoWebCache's configuration. If your layer contains data that is updated very often, caching may be a bad idea. You would waste space to store tiles that will soon become outdated. Let's see how to configure caching on a specific layer.

1. From the web interface, open the **Tile layers** section.

2. Scroll the list to find the **NaturalEarth:10m_roads_north_america** layer and click on the layer name.

3. The layer configuration page opens with a focus on the **Tile Caching** tab.

4. The very first section contains flags for inserting layers among the cached layers and for enabling caching. If you uncheck the first radio button, all the other settings become unavailable, and the caching configuration is lost. By default, unless you modified the **Caching Defaults** section, all layers added to GeoServer configuration are also configured as cached layers.

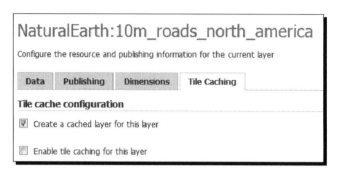

5. Metatiling factors, gutter size, and image formats let you override the values set for these parameters in the **Caching Defaults** section. For example, you may want to increase metatiling sizes and gutter sizes on layers where labeling is really critical. Acting on a per layer basis avoids stress on overall performance.

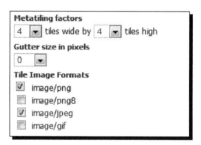

6. The next section lets you choose whether GeoWebCache will create a separate cache for each style associated to the layer. You can also set a separate cache for time and elevation. These options make sense only if you configured time and elevation support.

 Time and elevation configurations are out of the scope of this book. You can configure them in the **Dimension** tab of the layers web page. Note that your data, raster or vector, should have attributes holding meaningful time or elevation values.

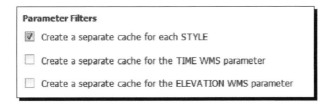

7. You can set which gridset will be used for caching your layer. By default, both the gridsets defined in the **Caching Defaults** section are enabled. You can add others or remove the defaults. You can also set zoom levels for each gridset that you want to be published and/or cached:

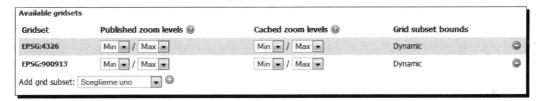

What just happened?

You reviewed all the options available for fine tuning on cache configuration. While caching defaults are fine for having a working set of properties, each time you add a new layer, you should configure it to maximize performance and optimize disk space.

Time for action – using tiles with OpenLayers

Now that you know how to manage caching configuration, we will explore how to use it. In this section, you will use an OpenLayers client to consume cached layers. You had a look at OpenLayers library in the previous chapter, but if you are not yet an expert, don't worry, we will guide you to fully understand the basic code of the following example:

1. We will create a new HTML file. It should be published with Apache Tomcat, so you can create it in the `webapps/ROOT` folder inside your Tomcat installation.

2. Insert the following code. As we are creating an HTML file, the code contains some mandatory elements. We also want to include a title for our page:

```
<html>
  <head>
    <title>Creating a simple map</title>
    <meta http-equiv="Content-Type" content="text/html;
charset=UTF-8">
```

3. Now add the following CSS code to add a style to the `html` element that will host the map canvas:

```
<style type="text/css">
  #myMap {
    clear: both;
    position: relative;
    width: 750px;
    height: 450px;
    border: 1px solid black;
  }
</style>
```

4. Now we have to include a reference to the OpenLayers library. We use a reference to the online release. Note that this only works if you are connected to the Internet in your development environment; otherwise you may want to download the library and deploy it on Tomcat:

```
<script type="text/javascript" src="http://openlayers.org/
api/2.12/OpenLayers.js"></script>
```

5. Now add the code to create a `map` object. We first create a `mapOptions` collection to set some map properties, that is, the projection, the extent, and the units. Take note of the first parameter passed to `Map` constructors in the last line; it is a reference to a `dom` element where the map will be placed:

```
<script type="text/javascript">
  function init() {
    var mapOptions = {
      projection: "EPSG:4326",
      maxExtent: new OpenLayers.Boun
ds(-180.0,-90.0,180.0,90.0),
      units: "degrees"
    };
    map = new OpenLayers.Map('myMap', mapOptions );
```

6. Now you have to add a layer object. We create it by pointing to `ne_50m_populated_places`. We pass some properties to the constructor, for example, for using a different style from default:

```
demolayer = new OpenLayers.Layer.WMS(
    'NaturalEarth:ne_50m_populated_places', '../geoserver/
NaturalEarth/wms',
    {layers: 'NaturalEarth:ne_50m_populated_places',
     styles: 'PopulatedPlacesStroke',
     format: 'image/png' },
    {singleTile: 'True'}
);
```

7. Then, we add the layer to the map and add code to set a zoom level and center the map on a specific point:

```
map.addLayer(demolayer);
map.zoomTo(4);
map.panTo(new OpenLayers.LonLat(12.0,42.0));
}
</script>
</head>
```

8. The JavaScript code for the page is complete. Now add a call to the `init` function when the browser loads the page and a `div` element for the map:

```
<body onload="init()">
  <div id="myMap"></div>
</body>
</html>
```

9. Save the file as `wmsPlain.html`. Now open your browser and enter `http://localhost:8080/wmsPlain.html` as the URL.

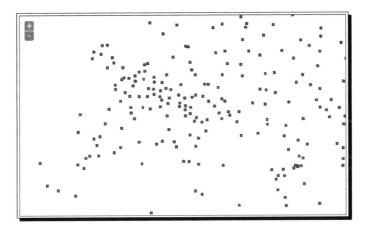

10. Now zoom and pan a little with the map, then go to the **Tile layers** web page and look if the map produced by your requests was stored as a map:

	Type	Layer Name	Disk Quota	Disk Used	Enabled	Preview	Actions
☐	●	NaturalEarth:ne_50m_populated_places	N/A	0.0 B	✓	Select One ▾	Seed/Truncate | Empty

11. It seems like your requests are not stored in the cache. Can you identify what went wrong? Think about it before going ahead with the exploration.

12. Go back to the folder where you saved the `wmsPlain.html` file, make a copy of it, and rename the copy to `wmsExplicitCached.html`.

13. Open the new file with your editor, go to line 3, and replace it with the following:

```
<title>Creating a simple map for cached layers</title>
```

14. For a `GetMap` request to hit the cache, you have to constrain it to the gridset properties. We are using the **EPSG:4326** projection, so we need to use the same zoom levels of the **EPSG:4326** gridset. Go to line 18 and just after it add a new item to `mapOptions`. It contains all resolutions for the gridset:

```
resolutions: [
    0.703125, 0.3515625, 0.17578125,
    0.087890625, 0.0439453125, 0.02197265625,
    0.010986328125, 0.0054931640625, 0.00274658203125,
    0.001373291015625, 0.0006866455078125, 0.0003433227539062,
    0.0001716613769531, 0.0000858306884766, 0.0000429153442383,
    0.0000214576721191, 0.0000107288360596, 0.0000053644180298,
    0.0000026822090149, 0.0000013411045074, 0.0000006705522537,
    0.0000003352761269
],
```

 You don't really need to add all the zoom levels to your maps; you can select a subset of them. This way you can constrain your user to explore data only at a specific zoom range.

15. Our request needs to be directed to the GeoWebCache endpoint. Go to line 33 and modify the layer creator as in the following code fragment:

```
demolayer = new OpenLayers.Layer.WMS(
    'NaturalEarth:ne_50m_populated_places',
    '../geoserver/gwc/service/wms',
```

16. We also need to match the tile sizes. On line 30 replace the `singleTile: 'True'` line of code with the following:

```
{tileSize: new OpenLayers.Size(256,256)}
```

17. Save the file. Now open your browser and enter `http://localhost:8080/wmsExplicitCached.html` as the URL. As before, navigate your maps by panning and zooming around the world, then go back to the **Tile layers** web page and see if your tiles are stored in the cache.

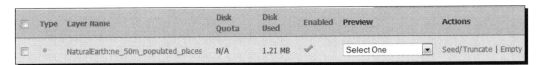

Type	Layer Name	Disk Quota	Disk Used	Enabled	Preview	Actions
○	NaturalEarth:ne_50m_populated_places	N/A	1.21 MB	✓	Select One ▾	Seed/Truncate | Empty

As you can see from the **Disk Used** value, this time your requests matched the gridset properties and the tiles produced were stored properly. Are you wondering how to check exactly what your requests are requests and what responses you are getting from GeoWebCache?

There are several tools/techniques that you can use to do this; a widely used and popular one is **Firebug**. Firebug is Firefox's extension that offers you a powerful set of tools for developing and debugging web apps. In our case, you can use the web console to see complete details about requests and responses for your application.

More info is available at `https://www.getfirebug.com`.

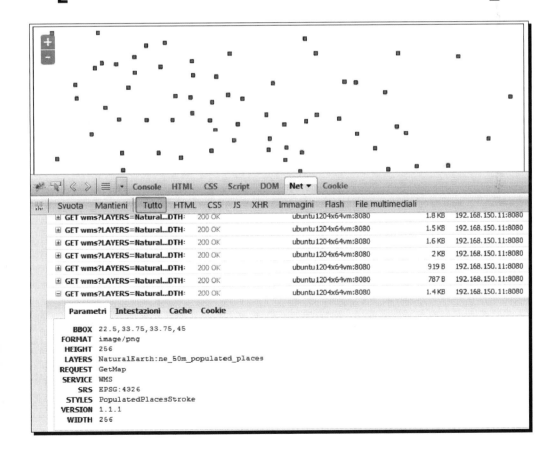

18. We need to go a step further. Do you remember we talked about direct integration? Go back to the **Caching defaults** section and check the flag. Then click on the **Save** button.

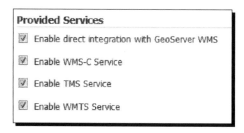

19. Go back to the folder where you saved the wmsExplicitCached.html file, make a copy of it, and rename the copy to wmsDirectIntegrationCached.html.

20. Open the new file with your editor, go to line 3, and replace it with the following:

```
<title>Creating a simple map for cached layers with direct
integration</title>
```

21. Our request needs to be directed to the GeoServer WMS endpoint. Go to line 33 and modify the layer creator as in the following code fragment:

```
demolayer = new OpenLayers.Layer.WMS(
    'NaturalEarth:ne_50m_populated_places',
    '../geoserver/NaturalEarth/wms',
```

22. On line 37, just after the style setting, add a code to specify the map request that has to be tiled:

```
styles: 'PopulatedPlacesStroke',
tiled: 'true',
```

23. Save the file and close it.

24. Go to the **Tile layers** page and click on the **Empty** link for the **NaturalEarth:ne_50m_populated_places** layer. When prompted about deleting all tiles click on the **OK** button.

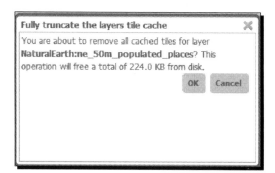

25. Save the file. Now open your browser and point it to `http://localhost:8080/wmsDirectIntegrationCached.html`. As before, navigate your map's panning and zoom around the world, then go back to the **Tile Layers** web page and see if your tiles are stored in the cache again.

	Type	Layer Name	Disk Quota	Disk Used	Enabled	Preview	Actions
☐	◦	NaturalEarth:ne_50m_populated_places	N/A	1.02 MB	✔	Select One ▾	Seed/Truncate | Empty

What just happened?

You built a very simple web mapping application and integrated it with GeoWebCache. Apart from the trivial interface, you explored how to properly build map requests that can access a cache. You can use this knowledge to apply caching in real application.

Have a go hero – building a client for tiger county layer

In the previous *Time for action – creating a custom gridset* section, you built a custom gridset. You named it **EPSG:4269** and added to the `tl_2011_us_county` layer's configuration. It is now time to use it. Based on the JavaScript code of the previous *Time for action – using tiles with OpenLayers* section, build a simple application using the cache for the layer. Just in case you need some hints, you can have a look at `wmsExplicitCached4269.html` file in the chapter's resource.

Time for action – seeding a layer

As of now we have used the GeoWebCache for storing tiles produced by user request. Of course following requests with equal parameters will hit the cache and GeoServer won't render a new map for them.

But you can also pre-calculate the tiles for a layer to avoid some users experiencing a delay when requesting zoom levels and areas not yet cached.

The process of pre-calculating tiles is called **seeding**. This section will guide you to understand how it works.

1. Go to the **Tile layers** page and look for the **tl_2011_us_county** layer. Click on the **Seed/Truncate** link for it:

☐	▨	tiger:tl_2011_us_county	N/A	0.0 B	✔	Select One ▾	Seed/Truncate | Empty

2. A new page will open. The GeoWebCache seeding is not integrated in the GeoServer web interface. What you see is the GeoWebCache interface:

3. Scroll to the **Create a new task** section. You have to set the parameters for the seeding. The first one is the number of parallel processes, that is, threads that will request maps to GeoServer. As we have a single GeoServer instance, there is no gain in running too many processes. Select **04** from the drop-down list:

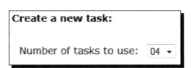

4. Then select the operation type. You can select **Seed**, which will generate only the missing tiles, or **Reseed** to regenerate all tiles. This is the case if you changed the style for the layer and don't want your user to see a mixed map. Note that the **Truncate** operation is a little different from the **Empty** operation integrated in the GeoServer interface. Here you will have the option to select a set of zoom levels for truncating, while the **Empty** operation will always remove all tiles. Select **Seed – generate missing tiles**:

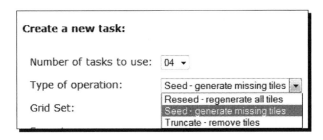

5. You have to select a gridset and an image format for the seeding. If you want to pre-calculate cache for more than one gridset and/or image format, you can start another operation just after starting this. Select **Grid Set** as **EPSG:4269** and **Format** as **image/png**:

6. You can start a seeding operation only on a subset of the specified gridset. You can select a levels range and an area. If you don't want to restrict seeding to a specific area, leave the **Bounding box** textboxes empty, and the operation will use the gridset bounds. Select **00** as **Zoom start:** and **10** as **Zoom stop:**. Now start the seeding operation by clicking on the **Submit** button:

7. Once the tasks start, the web interface shows you the list of currently running tasks. If you are seeding more layers concurrently, you can filter the tasks per layer and also kill one or all the tasks that are running. Clicking on the **Refresh list** link will update the list with the number of **Tiles completed**, **Time elapsed**, and **Time remaining** columns. The number of tiles grows quickly at more detailed zoom levels. Seeding not only requires a lot of disk space, it also requires a lot of time, depending on your system's capacity.

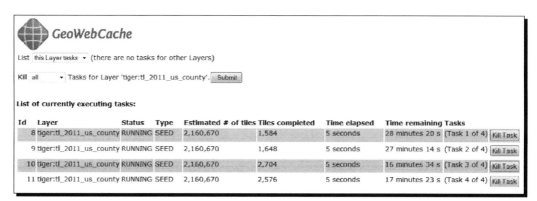

8. When your tasks end, you should see an empty list. Go back to the **Tile layers** page and now there will be a lot of disk space allocated for your layer's tiles:

What just happened?

Seeding your layers can have a huge impact on performances. Every map request from your clients, in the levels range you pre-calculated, will hit the cache now. You can expect performances to increase from 10 to 90 times.

Pop quiz – configuring integrated GeoWebCache

Q1. Can you have more than one gridset for a layer?

1. No, you have to select one caching schema for each layer.

2. Yes, you can add any gridsets you need and use them concurrently.

3. Yes, but you can store tiles in the cache for just one gridset.

Q2. Can you cache a layer with more than one style?

1.   Yes, you can store tiles rendered with several different styles.

2.   No, you have to configure the same data as a new layer to use a different style.

3.   Yes, but you can't use the same layer with different styles concurrently in the same map request.

Q3. Can your client use both cached and plain layers?

1.   No, you have to set the caching properties in the map and all layers are constrained to those settings.

2.   Yes, but for each layer you have to decide if you want it cached or not.

3.   Yes, and you can also add the same layer on your client's map in a plain and cached way.

Using an external GeoWebCache

The integrated GeoWebCache is a convenient way to use a powerful caching tool while avoiding the complexity of an external installation and configuration. So what's the point of using an external instance of GeoWebCache?

In a production environment, you will often have to deal with multiple GeoServer instances, running in parallel like a cluster. Indeed we will see how to configure such a scenario in *Chapter 11, Tuning GeoServer in a Production Environment*. When more than one GeoServer publishes the same data, you can't efficiently use the integrated GeoWebCache. There is no way to connect all the GeoServers to a single GeoWebCache. Anyway it would make no sense as you will introduce a single point of failure in your architecture.

So you have two ways to go: using the integrated GeoWebCache on each GeoServer node, duplicating the tiles and wasting a lot of space, or installing an external GeoWebCache and linking it to each GeoServer node.

Installing and configuring an external GeoWebCache is out of the scope of this book. You have to turn off the integrated GeoWebCache. You can do this from the **Caching Defaults** page, disabling all services and turning off the automatic creation of a cache configuration for each new layer.

Caching Defaults

Configure the global settings for the embedded GeoWebCache
Go to the embedded GeoWebCache home page

Provided Services

☐ Enable direct integration with GeoServer WMS

☐ Enable WMS-C Service

☐ Enable TMS Service

☐ Enable WMTS Service

Default Caching Options for GeoServer Layers

☐ Automatically configure a GeoWebCache layer for each new layer or layer group

If you used the integrated GeoWebCache before, you may also want to disable each layer and remove tiles.

The standalone GeoWebCache is a Java web application that you can deploy on a Tomcat instance, the same as we did for GeoServer in *Chapter 2, Installing Geoserver*. Once installed, you have to manually configure each layer by editing the `geowebcache.xml` file.

Refer to the project online documentation for detailed instructions and reference (`http://geowebcache.org/docs/current/index.html`).

Summary

We explored the integrated GeoWebCache and how it may impact on GeoServer performances. Deploying a properly configured production site requires caching, unless your planned users are very few.

Configuring a map cache requires you to act not only on the server side but also on the client side. Clients should know how you cached the data and compile proper map requests for the benefit of pre-calculated tiles. We used JavaScript and OpenLayers to have a look at the client side.

GeoServer integrates a pretty interface for configuring cache, but as your site grows and you find yourself increasingly adding and removing layers, you may wonder if a way of automating the configuration exists.

In the next chapter, we will explore the GeoServer REST interface. REST exposes most of the GeoServer interface through HTTP calls. Using a scripting language, you can build simple procedures that help you in performing repetitive tasks.

We will see how to use the REST interface to add data stores and workspaces, publish layers, and apply changes to your configuration.

9
Automating Tasks: GeoServer REST Interface

In the previous chapters you learned how to connect GeoServer to your data.

Creating data stores or feature types, configuring layers, and uploading styles can be tedious and overwhelming tasks as soon as your site grows from the data we used in the examples.

If your site intends to deliver a professional map service, it will probably be replicated on more instances. We will see in detail how this can be done, but for now you will probably have guessed that it means more effort to configure and synchronize all nodes.

When you are dealing with a repetitive task, you usually look at how you can automate it.

GeoServer's developers didn't leave you alone in the dark. GeoServer includes a REST interface that lets you perform most administrative tasks. In this chapter we will see how you can add, update, and delete your data configuration.

In this chapter we will cover the following topics in detail:

- ◆ Defining REST
- ◆ Using REST with cURL and Python
- ◆ Configuring Workspaces, Data Stores, and Feature Types
- ◆ Configuring Styles and Layers

Introducing REST

So, what is REST? The acronym stands for **REpresentational State Transfer**, and defines client-server interaction in terms of state transitions. Each request from the client is a transition to a new state. The response sent by the server represents the application state after the transition.

Does it sound too complicated? From a theory point of view you may find it unconventional, especially if you are used to a client/server with a stateful interaction. REST is stateless, and once you get the general idea you will discover that it is very simple.

Although REST is commonly thought of as a web interface, actually it is much more. The term REST was defined by Roy T. Fielding—one of the most important people behind HTTP protocol design—in his PhD thesis. REST describes the interaction between clients and servers, and does it by abstracting from any protocol. It describes a set of operations that a server has to implement and that a client can use. Of course in implementations, a protocol, for example, HTTP, has to be selected. You could also develop a REST interface without HTTP.

Refer to the following links to find out more on REST:

- ◆ http://www.ics.uci.edu/~fielding/pubs/ dissertation/top.htm
- ◆ http://en.wikipedia.org/wiki/Representational_ State_Transfer

GeoServer's REST interface uses HTTP and defines a set of operations and resources. Operations are derived from HTTP so you can perform GET, POST, PUT, and DELETE operations. Resources are the building blocks of GeoServer's configuration, which includes workspaces, data stores, layers, and so on.

Using REST

REST defines a set of operations defined from the HTTP protocol; so how can you interact with it? Using a browser can be a common way to send HTTP requests to a server; you do it almost every day when you browse the Internet and you do it with the GeoServer web interface! But using a browser is not a simple way to automate tasks; it requires human interaction. We need something that enables us to build small programs.

A lot of different tools exist that enable you to interact with REST. You can use programming languages such as Java or PHP, or script languages such as PowerShell in Windows or any Linux shell. In this chapter we will see examples in the programming language, Python, and with cURL. Python is a programming language that leverages on simplicity and code readability, and hence it is very easy to create small programs with it. cURL is a library and a command-line tool that can be easily incorporated in simple shell scripts. Both of these tools allow users to create REST requests in a very simple manner, that is, by writing a few lines of code. This avoids you getting distracted by a complex syntax.

In this chapter, it is assumed that you have a working installation of Python and cURL. If you are using a Linux box, it is quite likely that you already have both installed and configured, or you can rely on your distribution package system to install a recent release.

For Windows, you can get Python from the project site at `http://python.org/`.

cURL is available as a source, for the brave, or as a binary package from `http://curl.haxx.se/download.html`.

Time for action – installing the Requests library

We stated before that Python mainly aims at simplicity and code readability, but unfortunately this is not always the case. Interacting with REST using the standard Python libraries can be painfully laborious. Luckily, there is an open source project that can solve this. The project produced a library called **Requests**, and I have to say it really is an appropriate name. So let's install it!

1. As the first step, you need to download the ZIP or TAR archive containing the library code:

    ```
    ~$ wget https://github.com/kennethreitz/requests/tarball/master -O
    master.tar.gz

    ~$ ls -al
    drwxrwxr-x 2 stefano stefano    4096 Oct 15 08:01 ./
    drwxr-xr-x 9 stefano stefano    4096 Oct 15 07:41 ../
    -rw-rw-r-- 1 stefano stefano 720204 Oct 15 08:02 master.tar.gz
    ```

2. Now extract the archive content:

    ```
    ~$ tar xvfz master.tar.gz
    ...
    ```

3. Enter the new folder and install it into your site package:

```
~$ cd kennethreitz-requests-c03e893
~$ sudo python setup.py install
```

4. Installation is now complete. Check it by opening Python and importing the new library in the following manner:

```
~$ python
Python 2.7.3 (default, Aug  1 2012, 05:14:39)
[GCC 4.6.3] on linux2
Type "help", "copyright", "credits" or "license" for more
information.
>>> import requests
>>>
```

What just happened?

You installed the Requests library as a site package inside your Python installation. You can now use it inside any Python program, leveraging on its powerful objects for the purpose of interacting with the HTTP protocol.

Requests is an open source project started by Kenneth Reitz. You can download and use it in a very liberal way. It is released under the ISC license. You can also fork it on GitHub and add features. The following link will lead you to the Requests download page:

http://docs.python-requests.org/en/latest/

Managing data

The core of each map service is data. We need to create workspaces for grouping together data sets, connecting databases and folders containing data, adding feature types, and configuring their options. GeoServer's REST interface exposes resources for each one of them.

Working with workspaces and namespaces

A **workspace** is a logical entity you can use to group data. A workspace is always linked to a **namespace URI** that defines a web reference for it. The REST interface defines two resources that you can use to access these elements. They are as follows:

+ /workspaces
+ /namespaces

GET, POST, PUT, and DELETE operations are defined for both of these resources, which allows you to view, create, update, and delete workspaces and namespaces.

Time for action – managing workspaces

We are going to use REST operations with workspaces. In this section, as in the others contained in this chapter, we will use both cURL and Python to perform the same operation. The examples are shown in a Linux shell, but cURL and Python syntaxes are identical in a Windows shell.

1. The first step looks at which workspaces are defined in your GeoServer instance. This requires a GET operation. The following code shows you the syntax. cURL has a lot of options, you can have a look at all of them running it with the `curl --help` command from Linux and Windows. On Linux you can also have a look at the manual with the command `man curl`. The first option we use is `-u`. It stands for user authentication and you have to insert the user ID and password you set in *Chapter 2, Getting Started with GeoServer*, when we modified the default password.

   The `-v` option tells cURL to run verbosely, so it will output detailed information on the request processing. The `-X` option defines which HTTP operation you want to use to send your requests. If you don't insert it, cURL assumes GET as its default. You can avoid writing the option, although inserting it may make the code clearer. The `-H` option lets you add headers to your requests. You may repeat this option as many times as you need, to specify multiple headers. In this case we are using it to make the server know that we would accept an XML format as a response. After that, we have the URL we want requested. The URL is composed of a base part that will be the same for all the operations, that is, `http://yourhostname:yourport/geoserver/rest`, and an operation part that specifies the operation. Finally, we add the `-o` option to write the response to a file:

   ```
   curl -u admin:password -v -XGET -H 'Accept: text/xml' http://
   localhost:8080/geoserver/rest/workspaces -o workspaces.xml
   ```

2. A lot of information is displayed. This may be very useful when in trouble, and you need to debug what is wrong. A line starting with > means "header data sent by cURL", while < means "header data received by cURL". In this case, we just look at the status code received from GeoServer; it reports 200, that is, the HTTP code for OK:

   ```
   * About to connect() to localhost port 8080 (#0)
   *   Trying 127.0.0.1...   % Total    % Received % Xferd  Average
   Speed   Time    Time     Time  Current
                                   Dload  Upload   Total   Spent
   Left  Speed
     0     0    0     0     0     0      0      0 --:--:-- --:--:--
   --:--:--    0connected
   * Server auth using Basic with user 'admin'
   ```

```
> GET /geoserver/rest/workspaces HTTP/1.1
> Authorization: Basic YWRtaW46Y29yZS4yMDEy
> User-Agent: curl/7.22.0 (x86_64-pc-linux-gnu) libcurl/7.22.0
OpenSSL/1.0.1 zlib/1.2.3.4 libidn/1.23 librtmp/2.3
> Host: localhost:8080
> Accept: text/xml
>
< HTTP/1.1 200 OK
< Date: Tue, 16 Oct 2012 19:59:27 GMT
< Server: Noelios-Restlet-Engine/1.0..8
< Content-Type: application/xml
< Transfer-Encoding: chunked
<
{ [data not shown]
100  1100    0  1100    0    0  18648      0 --:--:-- --:--:--
--:--:-- 19642
* Connection #0 to host localhost left intact
* Closing connection #0
```

3. You may want to check if the `workspaces.xml` file was created. In order to do that, run the following command:

```
~/REST$ ls -al
total 12
drwxrwxr-x 2 stefano stefano    4096 Oct 16 21:59 ./
drwxr-xr-x 9 stefano stefano    4096 Oct 16 21:11 ../
-rw-rw-r-- 1 stefano stefano    1100 Oct 16 21:59 workspaces.xml
```

4. Before analysing the response file content, let's do the same request using Python. From your console, launch it and import the `requests` module as shown:

```
~/REST$ python
Python 2.7.3 (default, Aug  1 2012, 05:14:39)
[GCC 4.6.3] on linux2
Type "help", "copyright", "credits" or "license" for more
information.
>>> import requests
```

5. Now define a new string variable for the URL:

```
>>> myUrl = 'http://localhost:8080/geoserver/rest/workspaces'
```

6. Also, a Python dictionary for the headers:

```
>>> headers = {'Accept': 'text/xml'}
```

7. We are ready to send the request; the `requests` object has a method for each HTTP operation, and in a really "Pythonic" way, the name is the operation. You have to call the method by passing the parameters for the URL, headers, and authentication:

```
>>> resp = requests.get(myUrl,auth=('admin','password'),headers=he
aders)
```

8. So the response was saved in the new variable called `resp`. The Python interpreter didn't throw any exception, so things should be ok; but how can we check what GeoServer replied? The `resp` variable is indeed a response object defined in the requests library, and it has methods to extract information about the response. Start by looking at the status code of the response.

```
>>> resp.status_code
200
```

9. Nice! It succeeded. But what if you would like to extract the response body to list it or to save it to a file? The `response.text` method is what you are looking for, so let's save the result in a file:

```
file = open('workspaces_py.xml','w')
file.write(resp.text)
file.close()
```

10. Now you should have two XML files looking absolutely identical. Open one of them and look at its content. It lists the workspaces defined on your GeoServer, and it also gives you a URL to reference each one of them. This is shown as follows:

```
<workspaces>
  <workspace>
    <name>NaturalEarth</name>
    <atom:link xmlns:atom="http://www.w3.org/2005/Atom"
rel="alternate" href="http://localhost:8080/geoserver/rest/
workspaces/NaturalEarth.xml" type="application/xml"/>
  </workspace>
  <workspace>
    <name>tiger</name>
    <atom:link xmlns:atom="http://www.w3.org/2005/Atom"
rel="alternate" href="http://localhost:8080/geoserver/rest/
workspaces/tiger.xml" type="application/xml"/>
  </workspace>
  ...
</workspaces>
```

11. Now use the information from the XML file to retrieve information about the first workspace. In cURL, type the following command:

```
curl -u admin:password -XGET -H 'Accept: text/xml' http://
localhost:8080/geoserver/rest/workspaces/NaturalEarth -o
NaturalEarth.xml
```

12. Do the same in Python:

```
>>> myUrl = 'http://localhost:8080/geoserver/rest/workspaces/
NaturalEarth'
>>> headers = {'Accept': 'text/xml'}
>>> resp = requests.get(myUrl,auth=('admin','password'),headers=he
aders)
```

13. The information retrieved contains the URL to explore data stores linked to the workspace:

```
<workspace>
  <name>NaturalEarth</name>
  <dataStores>
    <atom:link xmlns:atom="http://www.w3.org/2005/Atom"
rel="alternate" href="http://localhost:8080/geoserver/rest/
workspaces/NaturalEarth/datastores.xml" type="application/xml"/>
  </dataStores>
  <coverageStores>
    <atom:link xmlns:atom="http://www.w3.org/2005/Atom"
rel="alternate" href="http://localhost:8080/geoserver/rest/
workspaces/NaturalEarth/coveragestores.xml" type="application/
xml"/>
  </coverageStores>
  <wmsStores>
    <atom:link xmlns:atom="http://www.w3.org/2005/Atom"
rel="alternate" href="http://localhost:8080/geoserver/rest/
workspaces/NaturalEarth/wmsstores.xml" type="application/xml"/>
  </wmsStores>
</workspace>
```

14. Now retrieve information about namespaces in cURL:

```
curl -u admin:password -XGET -H 'Accept: text/xml' http://
localhost:8080/geoserver/rest/namespaces -o namespaces.xml
```

15. Retrieve the same in Python:

```
>>> myUrl = 'http://localhost:8080/geoserver/rest/namespaces'
>>> headers = {'Accept': 'text/xml'}
>>> resp = requests.get(myUrl,auth=('admin','password'),headers=he
aders)
```

16. In the response, you can see the namespace list, which is pretty similar to the workspace list. As we wrote before, they are bounded together:

```
<namespaces>
  <namespace>
    <name>NaturalEarth</name>
    <atom:link xmlns:atom="http://www.w3.org/2005/Atom"
rel="alternate" href="http://localhost:8080/geoserver/rest/
namespaces/NaturalEarth.xml" type="application/xml"/>
  </namespace>
  <namespace>
    <name>tiger</name>
    <atom:link xmlns:atom="http://www.w3.org/2005/Atom"
rel="alternate" href="http://localhost:8080/geoserver/rest/
namespaces/tiger.xml" type="application/xml"/>
  </namespace>
  ...
</namespaces>
```

17. Now have a look at information about a single namespace. First in cURL:

```
curl -u admin:password -XGET -H 'Accept: text/xml' http://
localhost:8080/geoserver/rest/namespaces/tiger -o tigerNamespace.
xml
```

18. Then in Python:

```
>>> myUrl = 'http://localhost:8080/geoserver/rest/namespaces/
tiger'
>>> headers = {'Accept': 'text/xml'}
>>> resp = requests.get(myUrl,auth=('admin','password'),headers=he
aders)
```

19. The response contains the prefix name for the namespace, that is, the linked workspace, the namespace URI, and a URL to retrieve feature types linked to the namespace:

```
<namespace>
  <prefix>tiger</prefix>
  <uri>http://www.census.gov</uri>
  <featureTypes>
    <atom:link xmlns:atom="http://www.w3.org/2005/Atom"
rel="alternate" href="http://localhost:8080/geoserver/rest/
workspaces/tiger/featuretypes.xml" type="application/xml"/>
  </featureTypes>
</namespace>
```

20. Until now, you have retrieved the information; now try to create a new namespace. In cURL, we need to specify a different operation with the `-X` option and send some data to GeoServer, that is, XML code containing the information about the namespace to be created. We use the `-d` option for this:

```
curl -u admin:password -XPOST -H 'Content-type: text/xml' -d '<na
mespace><prefix>newWorkspace</prefix><uri>http://geoserver.org</
uri></namespace>' http://localhost:8080/geoserver/rest/namespaces
```

21. To do the same in Python, you can save the XML code beforehand in a file:

```
>>> myUrl =  'http://localhost:8080/geoserver/rest/namespaces'
>>> file = open('requestBody.xml','r')
>>> payload = file.read()
>>> headers = {'Content-type': 'text/xml'}
>>> resp = requests.post(myUrl, auth=('admin','password'),
data=payload, headers=headers)
>>> resp.status_code
500
```

22. Huh! We got an error. 500 is the HTTP code for an internal server error. Indeed, you can't create a duplicated namespace. On looking at the GeoServer log, you should see something like the following:

```
org.geoserver.rest.RestletException: java.lang.
IllegalArgumentException: Namespace with prefix 'newWorkspace'
already exists.
   at org.geoserver.rest.ReflectiveResource.handleException(Reflect
iveResource.java:325)
   at org.geoserver.rest.ReflectiveResource.
handlePost(ReflectiveResource.java:123)
   …
```

23. Open the GeoServer web interface and look at the workspace list; you can now see the one you created, and if you click on it you will see the namespace URI you defined:

Edit Workspace

Edit existing workspace

Name

newWorkspace

Namespace URI

http://geoserver.org

The namespace uri associated with this workspace

Default Workspace

24. Now we want to set a more appropriate URI for the new workspace. To do so, we will use the PUT operation. In cURL, it is as follows:

```
curl -u admin:password -XPUT -H 'Content-type: text/xml' -H
'Accept: text/xml' -d '<namespace><prefix>newWorkspace</
prefix><uri>http://localhost:8080/geoserver</uri></namespace>'
http://localhost:8080/geoserver/rest/namespaces/newWorkspace
```

25. In Python, it is as follows:

```
>>> myUrl =  'http://localhost:8080/geoserver/rest/namespaces/
newWorkspace'
>>> file = open('requestBody.xml','r')
>>> payload = file.read()
>>> headers = {'Content-type': 'text/xml'}
>>> resp = requests.put(myUrl, auth=('admin','password'),
data=payload, headers=headers)
```

26. This time we didn't get an error. You can update the same namespace as many times as you need.

27. The last operation is DELETE. To remove the new workspace from the GeoServer configuration in cURL, run the following command:

```
curl -u admin:password -XDELETE -H 'Accept: text/xml' http://
localhost:8080/geoserver/rest/workspaces/newWorkspace
```

28. In Python, run the following code:

```
>>> myUrl =  'http://localhost:8080/geoserver/rest/workspaces/
newWorkspace'
>>> headers = {'Accept': 'text/xml'}
>>> resp = requests.delete(myUrl, auth=('admin','password'),
headers=headers)
>>> resp.status_code
404
```

29. And, of course, you can't remove the same workspace twice; that is why you got an error. 404 is the HTTP code for a nonexistent document.

What just happened?

You learned how to interact with the REST interface. You did it for namespaces and workspaces, but the basic concepts you learned apply to all REST operations. It is important that you understand that REST is stateless. Each request you sent in the examples were absolutely unaware of what you did previously. You can link REST operations in a chain, but is up to you to extract information from the responses and build requests accordingly.

If you were a little confused by the Python code, there are a lot of free resources to explore this language. You will learn it very fast and add a powerful tool to your GIS skill. The following links will help you learn Python:

- http://www.greenteapress.com/thinkpython
- http://docs.python.org/tutorial

Using data stores

Data stores connect GeoServer to your data. You can't use data that is not supported by GeoServer with a built-in connector or plugin. Of course, the REST interface supports all operations on data stores. The resource exposed is in the form shown as follows:

/workspaces/<ws>/datastores

Here, ws stands for the workspace to which the data store is linked.

Time for action – managing data stores

Did you enjoy using cURL and Python? Where we are again with cURL and Python, since you are now so skilled! So let's get information about data stores:

1. The GET operation lets you know which data stores are available in the configuration. Retrieve the information in Python using the following code:

```
>>> myUrl = 'http://localhost:8080/geoserver/rest/workspaces/
NaturalEarth/datastores'
>>> headers = {'Accept': 'text/xml'}
>>> resp = requests.get(myUrl,auth=('admin','password'),headers=he
aders)
```

2. In cURL, use the following command:

```
curl -u admin:password -XGET -H 'Accept: text/xml' http://
localhost:8080/geoserver/rest/workspaces/NaturalEarth/datastores
-o naturalEarthDataStores.xml
```

3. The response contains all the data stores linked to the workspace. The only attribute is the name and the link to retrieve the detailed information about each one:

```
<dataStores>
  <dataStore>
    <name>Natural Earth Shapes</name>
    <atom:link xmlns:atom="http://www.w3.org/2005/Atom"
rel="alternate" href="http://localhost:8080/geoserver/rest/
workspaces/NaturalEarth/datastores/Natural+Earth+Shapes.xml"
```

```
type="application/xml"/>
  </dataStore>
</dataStores>
```

 If you are wondering what the request is to get a list of all data stores configured on GeoServer, I am sorry to tell you it does not exist. You have to query each workspace. You may request the workspace list and iterate on items to retrieve all data stores.

4. You created the Natural Earth data store in *Chapter 6*, *Styling Your Layers*. In case you don't remember what it is about, let's request the information in Python:

```
>>> myUrl = 'http://localhost:8080/geoserver/rest/workspaces/
NaturalEarth/datastores/Natural+Earth+Shapes'
>>> headers = {'Accept': 'text/xml'}
>>> resp = requests.get(myUrl,auth=('admin','password'),headers=he
aders)
```

5. And in cURL:

```
curl -u admin:password -XGET -H 'Accept: text/xml' http://
localhost:8080/geoserver/rest/workspaces/NaturalEarth/datastores/
Natural+Earth+Shapes -o naturalEarthShapes.xml
```

6. Open the XML file. It contains much more information than the previous responses. Data stores are more complicated objects than workspaces. Keep in mind that data stores are heterogeneous; the connection parameter tag may contain very different elements depending on the data store type, for example, a PostGIS data store will have user ID, password, and a TCP port:

```
<dataStore>
  <name>Natural Earth Shapes</name>
  <type>Directory of spatial files (shapefiles)</type>
  <enabled>true</enabled>
  <workspace>
    <name>NaturalEarth</name>
    <atom:link xmlns:atom="http://www.w3.org/2005/Atom"
rel="alternate" href="http://localhost:8080/geoserver/rest/
workspaces/NaturalEarth.xml" type="application/xml"/>
  </workspace>
  <connectionParameters>
    <entry key="memory mapped buffer">false</entry>
    <entry key="timezone">Europe/Rome</entry>
    <entry key="create spatial index">true</entry>
    <entry key="charset">ISO-8859-1</entry>
    <entry key="filetype">shapefile</entry>
```

```
      <entry key="cache and reuse memory maps">true</entry>
      <entry key="url">file:///home/stefano/naturalEarth</entry>
      <entry key="namespace">http://www.naturalearthdata.com/</
entry>
    </connectionParameters>
    <__default>false</__default>
    <featureTypes>
      <atom:link xmlns:atom="http://www.w3.org/2005/Atom"
rel="alternate" href="http://localhost:8080/geoserver/rest/
workspaces/NaturalEarth/datastores/Natural+Earth+Shapes/
featuretypes.xml" type="application/xml"/>
    </featureTypes>
  </dataStore>
```

7. It is now time to create a new data store. We will start with a single shapefile by duplicating `tiger counties`. You have to provide a lot of information, hence create a new XML file, insert the following code, and save it as `tigerCounties. xml`. You should recognize many parameters; you valorised them in *Chapter 5, Adding Your Data*, when adding the data store from the WEB interface. The key part is the `type` element, where you specify which kind of data you are adding. The connection parameters collection is also important, where you insert information on how GeoServer could retrieve the data from the filesystem or a DB:

```
<dataStore>
  <name>tiger_counties_REST</name>
  <description>tiger counties created from REST</description>
  <type>Shapefile</type>
  <enabled>true</enabled>
  <connectionParameters>
    <entry key="memory mapped buffer">false</entry>
    <entry key="create spatial index">true</entry>
    <entry key="charset">ISO-8859-1</entry>
    <entry key="filetype">shapefile</entry>
    <entry key="cache and reuse memory maps">true</entry>
    <entry key="url">file:///home/stefano/shapes2/tl_2011_us_
county.shp</entry>
    <entry key="namespace">http://www.census.gov</entry>
  </connectionParameters>
  <__default>false</__default>
</dataStore>
```

8. Now call the REST interface in cURL and add the data store:

```
curl -u admin:password -XPOST -T tigerCounties.xml -H 'Content-
type: text/xml' -H 'Accept: text/xml' http://localhost:8080/
geoserver/rest/workspaces/tiger/datastores
```

9. Open the web interface and list the configured data store. Was your add request successful?

10. Do the same in Python. Note that in a Python dictionary, for example, the headers variable, you can add more than a key-value pair. In this case, you specify two header values:

```
>>> myUrl = 'http://localhost:8080/geoserver/rest/workspaces/
tiger/datastores'
>>> file = open('tigerCounties.xml','r')
>>> payload = file.read()
>>> headers = {'Content-type': 'text/xml','Accept': 'text/xml'}
>>> resp = requests.post(myUrl, auth=('admin','password'),
data=payload, headers=headers)
>>> resp.status_code
>>> 500
```

11. And, of course, you can't add two identical data stores; that is why you got an internal server error code. In the GeoServer log, you will find the following:

```
2012-10-20 17:52:56,682 ERROR [geoserver.rest] -
org.geoserver.rest.RestletException: java.lang.
IllegalArgumentException: Store 'tiger_counties_REST' already
exists in workspace 'tiger'
        at org.geoserver.rest.ReflectiveResource.handleException(R
eflectiveResource.java:325)
        at org.geoserver.rest.ReflectiveResource.
handlePost(ReflectiveResource.java:123)
    ...
```

12. Adding a shapefile data store was quite easy. Let's try to add a new PostGIS source to our configuration. Again, it is better to create an XML file holding all the parameters, name it `postgis.xml`, and insert the code. The mandatory connection parameters are `host`, `port`, `database`, `schema`, `user`, and `password`. In this case, we inserted all the default values you would find by adding the data store from the web interface:

```
<dataStore>
  <name>myPostGIS</name>
  <description>PostGIS local instance</description>
  <type>PostGIS</type>
  <enabled>true</enabled>
  <connectionParameters>
    <entry key="host">localhost</entry>
```

```
        <entry key="port">5432</entry>
        <entry key="database">postgis20</entry>
        <entry key="schema">public</entry>
        <entry key="user">postgres</entry>
        <entry key="passwd">postgres</entry>
        <entry key="dbtype">postgis</entry>
        <entry key="validate connections">true</entry>
        <entry key="Connection timeout">20</entry>
        <entry key="min connections">1</entry>
        <entry key="max connections">10</entry>
        <entry key="Loose bbox">true</entry>
        <entry key="fetch size">1000</entry>
        <entry key="Max open prepared statements">50</entry>
        <entry key="Estimated extends">true</entry>
    </connectionParameters>
    <__default>false</__default>
</dataStore>
```

13. Now use a cURL call to create your new PostGIS source:

```
curl -u admin:password -XPOST -T postgis.xml -H 'Content-type:
text/xml' -H 'Accept: text/xml' http://localhost:8080/geoserver/
rest/workspaces/tiger/datastores
```

14. You can use the following Python syntax to send the same requests. As usual, if you already created it with cURL, you will get an HTTP 500 error code:

```
>>> myUrl = 'http://localhost:8080/geoserver/rest/workspaces/
tiger/datastores'
>>> file = open('postgis.xml','r')
>>> payload = file.read()
>>> headers = {'Content-type': 'text/xml','Accept': 'text/xml'}
>>> resp = requests.post(myUrl, auth=('admin','password'),
data=payload, headers=headers)
>>> resp.status_code
>>> 500
```

15. You can update a data store configuration. If your PostGIS password was changed from the DBA, you can send a request to update it on GeoServer. Create an XML file with the modified value:

```
<dataStore>
  <name>myPostGIS</name>
  <description>PostGIS local instance</description>
  <type>PostGIS</type>
  <enabled>true</enabled>
  <connectionParameters>
    <entry key="host">localhost</entry>
```

```
        <entry key="port">5432</entry>
        <entry key="database">postgis20</entry>
        <entry key="schema">public</entry>
        <entry key="user">postgres</entry>
        <entry key="passwd">new_pwd</entry>
        <entry key="dbtype">postgis</entry>
        <entry key="validate connections">true</entry>
        <entry key="Connection timeout">20</entry>
        <entry key="min connections">1</entry>
        <entry key="max connections">10</entry>
        <entry key="Loose bbox">true</entry>
        <entry key="fetch size">1000</entry>
        <entry key="Max open prepared statements">50</entry>
        <entry key="Estimated extends">true</entry>
    </connectionParameters>
    <__default>false</__default>
</dataStore>
```

16. Then send it in a PUT request. In cURL, it is as follows:

```
curl -u admin:password -XPUT -T updPostGIS.xml -H 'Content-type:
text/xml' -H 'Accept: text/xml' http://localhost:8080/geoserver/
rest/workspaces/tiger/datastores/myPostGIS
```

17. And in Python, the syntax is as follows:

```
>>> myUrl = 'http://localhost:8080/geoserver/rest/workspaces/
tiger/datastores/myPostGIS'
>>> file = open('updPostGIS.xml','r')
>>> payload = file.read()
>>> headers = {'Content-type': 'text/xml','Accept': 'text/xml'}
>>> resp = requests.put(myUrl, auth=('admin','password'),
data=payload, headers=headers)
```

18. The last supported operation is DELETE, for dropping a data store. Clean your configuration by removing the duplicated data store for the tiger counties we created:

```
curl -u admin:password -XDELETE -H 'Accept: text/xml' http://
localhost:8080/geoserver/rest/workspaces/tiger/datastores/tiger_
counties_REST
```

19. And the same operation in Python:

```
>>> myUrl = 'http://localhost:8080/geoserver/rest/workspaces/
tiger/datastores/tiger_counties_REST'
>>> headers = {'Accept': 'text/xml'}
>>> resp = requests.delete(myUrl, auth=('admin','password'),
headers=headers)
```

What just happened?

You learned how to play with data stores, but there is another way of creating it. In some cases you may create it implicitly while creating a feature type. We will look at it in the very next paragraph.

Using feature types

Feature types are strictly related to data stores; the latter are the data containers and the former are geometrical homogenous data sets. In some cases there is a one-to-one relation among feature types and data stores, as in the data store for the single shapefile of tiger counties we created. More often, a data store is connected to many feature types. As with other resources, you can use REST operations to list information, add and delete items, and modify the configuration.

The resources are exposed as follows:

```
/workspaces/<ws>/datastores/featuretypes/<ft>
```

Here, `ws` means a workspace existing in your system and `ft` is the feature type on which you want to perform the operation.

Retrieving information about feature types uses the GET operation as used by the previous resources. The output is quite long, depending on how many attributes it holds. It looks as follows:

```
<featureType>
  <name>ne_110m_admin_0_countries</name>
  <nativeName>ne_110m_admin_0_countries</nativeName>
  <namespace>
    <name>NaturalEarth</name>
    <atom:link xmlns:atom="http://www.w3.org/2005/Atom"
rel="alternate" href="http://localhost:8080/geoserver/rest/namespaces/
NaturalEarth.xml" type="application/xml"/>
  </namespace>
  <title>ne_110m_admin_0_countries</title>
  <description>Contents of file</description>
  <keywords>
    <string>features</string>
    <string>ne_110m_admin_0_countries</string>
  </keywords>
  <nativeCRS>GEOGCS[&quot;GCS_WGS_1984&quot;,
  DATUM[&quot;D_WGS_1984&quot;,
    SPHEROID[&quot;WGS_1984&quot;, 6378137.0, 298.257223563]],
  PRIMEM[&quot;Greenwich&quot;, 0.0],
  UNIT[&quot;degree&quot;, 0.017453292519943295],
```

```
  AXIS[&quot;Longitude&quot;, EAST],
  AXIS[&quot;Latitude&quot;, NORTH]]</nativeCRS>
  <srs>EPSG:4326</srs>
  <nativeBoundingBox>
    <minx>-179.99999999999997</minx>
    <maxx>180.00000000000014</maxx>
    <miny>-90.00000000000003</miny>
    <maxy>83.64513000000001</maxy>
    <crs>GEOGCS[&quot;GCS_WGS_1984&quot;,
  DATUM[&quot;D_WGS_1984&quot;,
    SPHEROID[&quot;WGS_1984&quot;, 6378137.0, 298.257223563]],
  PRIMEM[&quot;Greenwich&quot;, 0.0],
  UNIT[&quot;degree&quot;, 0.017453292519943295],
  AXIS[&quot;Longitude&quot;, EAST],
  AXIS[&quot;Latitude&quot;, NORTH]]</crs>
  </nativeBoundingBox>
  <latLonBoundingBox>
    <minx>-179.99999999999997</minx>
    <maxx>180.00000000000014</maxx>
    <miny>-90.00000000000003</miny>
    <maxy>83.64513000000001</maxy>
    <crs>GEOGCS[&quot;WGS84(DD)&quot;,
  DATUM[&quot;WGS84&quot;,
    SPHEROID[&quot;WGS84&quot;, 6378137.0, 298.257223563]],
  PRIMEM[&quot;Greenwich&quot;, 0.0],
  UNIT[&quot;degree&quot;, 0.017453292519943295],
  AXIS[&quot;Geodetic longitude&quot;, EAST],
  AXIS[&quot;Geodetic latitude&quot;, NORTH]]</crs>
  </latLonBoundingBox>
  <projectionPolicy>NONE</projectionPolicy>
  <enabled>true</enabled>
  <store class="dataStore">
    <name>Natural Earth Countries</name>
    <atom:link xmlns:atom="http://www.w3.org/2005/Atom"
rel="alternate" href="http://localhost:8080/geoserver/rest/
workspaces/NaturalEarth/datastores/Natural+Earth+Countries.xml"
type="application/xml"/>
  </store>
  <maxFeatures>0</maxFeatures>
  <numDecimals>0</numDecimals>
  <attributes>
    <attribute>
      <name>the_geom</name>
      <minOccurs>0</minOccurs>
```

```
        <maxOccurs>1</maxOccurs>
        <nillable>true</nillable>
        <binding>com.vividsolutions.jts.geom.MultiPolygon</binding>
    </attribute>
...
    </attributes>
</featureType>
```

Time for action – adding a new shapefile

We already added a single shapefile data store, now we want to upload a new shapefile and configure it on GeoServer. And, of course, we are going to use only HTTP operations to accomplish the task.

1. We will use a new layer from the Natural Earth repository. We will use a small shapefile, that is, the small-scale world admin boundaries:

```
~$ wget http://www.naturalearthdata.com/http//www.
naturalearthdata.com/download/110m/cultural/110m-admin-0-
countries.zip
```

2. Don't uncompress the archive; we will forward it to GeoServer in the ZIP format, and we will use a PUT operation. Note that to the header specifying the content type, we are transferring a zip file to GeoServer; this way we can publish a data set on a remote node without accessing the remote filesystem. We are also creating a new data store, `Natural+Earth+Countries`; the URL points to this nonexistent data store:

```
curl -u admin:password -XPUT -H 'Content-type: application/
zip' -T /home/stefano/110m-admin-0-countries.zip http://
localhost:8080/geoserver/rest/workspaces/NaturalEarth/datastores/
Natural+Earth+Countries/file.shp
```

3. Of course you can do the same with Python. Note that reading the ZIP file is pretty much the same as reading an XML file. The `rb` parameter specifies that we are going to read a binary file:

```
>>> myUrl = 'http://localhost:8080/geoserver/rest/workspaces/
NaturalEarth/datastores/Natural+Earth+Countries/file.shp'
>>> file = open('110m-admin-0-countries.zip','rb')
>>> payload = file.read()
>>> headers = {'Content-type': 'application/zip'}
>>> resp = requests.put(myUrl, auth=('admin','password'),
data=payload, headers=headers)
```

4. Now look at the web interface and list the data stores; there is a new one:

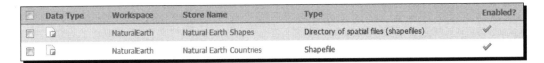

	Data Type	Workspace	Store Name	Type	Enabled?
		NaturalEarth	Natural Earth Shapes	Directory of spatial files (shapefiles)	✓
		NaturalEarth	Natural Earth Countries	Shapefile	✓

5. If you look at the details, you can see that the shapefile is now stored in the GeoServer data folder:

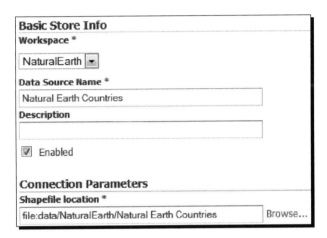

6. And, of course, GeoServer created a new layer for the feature type, populating all parameters and enabling them:

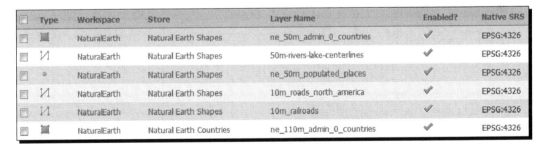

	Type	Workspace	Store	Layer Name	Enabled?	Native SRS
		NaturalEarth	Natural Earth Shapes	ne_50m_admin_0_countries	✓	EPSG:4326
		NaturalEarth	Natural Earth Shapes	50m-rivers-lake-centerlines	✓	EPSG:4326
		NaturalEarth	Natural Earth Shapes	ne_50m_populated_places	✓	EPSG:4326
		NaturalEarth	Natural Earth Shapes	10m_roads_north_america	✓	EPSG:4326
		NaturalEarth	Natural Earth Shapes	10m_railroads	✓	EPSG:4326
		NaturalEarth	Natural Earth Countries	ne_110m_admin_0_countries	✓	EPSG:4326

7. According to the geometry type, GeoServer assigns a default style so that you can also look at the data preview:

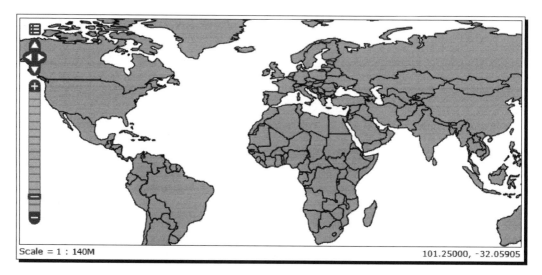

Scale = 1 : 140M   101.25000, -32.05905

What just happened?

You created the data store, the feature type, and the layer with just one operation. GeoServer can manage retrieving all the needed information from your data set and can manage using many default values. Of course, you may want to use different styles, but the REST interface truly makes remote administration very easy.

Time for action – adding a PostGIS table

PostGIS data store is one of those connected to many feature types. You will probably have new spatial data to add after creating the data store. Let's see how to do so:

1. In *Chapter 5*, *Adding Your Data*, you loaded the tiger counties in PostGIS. Now do the same with the admin boundaries shapefile from Natural Earth; call the table `ne_110m_admin`. Then use the PostGIS connection to add the table as a new feature type in the workspace **NaturalEarth**. Note that we are delivering very little information about the feature type to GeoServer; the table name is the only mandatory field:

```
curl -u admin:password -XPOST -H 'Content-type: text/xml' -d
'<featureType><name>ne_110m_admin</name></featureType>' http://
localhost:8080/geoserver/rest/workspaces/NaturalEarth/datastores/
myPostGIS/featuretypes
```

2. The Python syntax is as follows:

```
>>> myUrl =  'http://localhost:8080/geoserver/rest/workspaces/
NaturalEarth/datastores/myPostGIS/featuretypes'
>>> payload = '<featureType><name>ne_110m_admin</name></
featureType>'
>>> headers = {'Content-type': 'text/xml'}
>>> resp = requests.post(myUrl, auth=('admin','password'),
data=payload, headers=headers)
```

3. Looking at the layers list, we can see the newly added workspace:

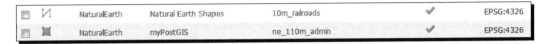

4. The new feature type works perfectly, and of course we can add more parameters to the XML code to have a better layer configuration. These examples add a more detailed description, some keywords, and a style other than the default one:

```
<featureType>
  <name>World boundaries</name>
  <nativeName>ne_110m_admin</nativeName>
  <title>World boundaries</title>
  <abstract>World administrative boundaries at small scale</
abstract>
  <keywords>
    <string>Political</string>
    <string>World</string>
  </keywords>
<featureType>
```

5. But there's more. Not only can you add an existing table, you can also create a new one. When creating a new table, you have to specify all the attributes required for the layer:

```
<featureType>
  <name>rivers</name>
  <nativeName>rivers</nativeName>
  <title>World River</title>
  <srs>EPSG:4326</srs>
  <attributes>
    <attribute>
      <name>geom</name>
      <binding>com.vividsolutions.jts.geom.Polyline</binding>
    </attribute>
    <attribute>
      <name>name</name>
```

```
        <binding>java.lang.String</binding>
        <length>30</length>
    </attribute>
    <attribute>
     <name>country_code</name>
     <binding>java.lang.String</binding>
        <length>8</length>
    </attribute>
   </attributes>
</featureType>
```

6. Now you have to send a POST request to create the feature. Of course, you have to send it to a PostGIS data store:

```
curl -u admin:password -XPOST -T rivers.xml -H 'Content-type:
text/xml' http://localhost:8080/geoserver/rest/workspaces/
NaturalEarth/datastores/myPostGIS/featuretypes
```

7. The same request in Python looks like the following code:

```
>>> myUrl =  'http://localhost:8080/geoserver/rest/workspace/
NaturalEarth/datastores/myPostGIS/featuretypes'
>>> file = open('rivers.xml','r')
>>> payload = file.read()
>>> headers = {'Content-type': 'text/xml'}
>>> resp = requests.post(myUrl, auth=('admin','password'),
data=payload, headers=headers)
```

8. Now look at the layers list; there is a new item:

9. If you go to the layer's detail page, you can see that the SRS was correctly set to 4326. But as an empty feature type, the bounding boxes are inconsistent. The attributes mentioned in the following screenshot are the ones you specified:

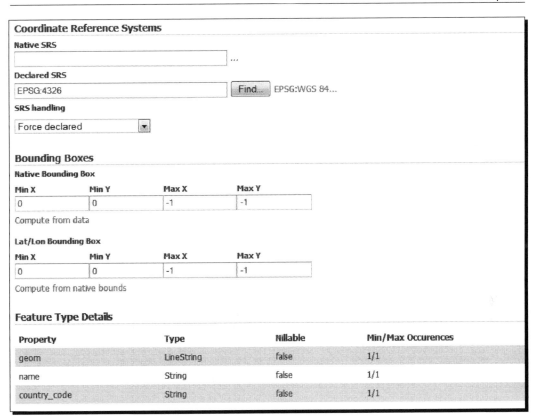

What just happened?

You learned how to manage feature types—the link to your data. A feature type is strictly connected to a layer, the map representation. You already implicitly created a layer when you added or created a new feature type. To modify the way your data is published, you have to manage the publishing elements.

Have a go hero – create a new shapefile

It was really simple to create a new table in PostGIS. Now it is time to explore other data stores. Create the new shapefile's folder data store and create a new shapefile inside it. Use a polygon geometry and three attributes, a date type for the object creation date, a Boolean for the validation field, and a string field for the object code.

Publishing data

Once you have configured your data on GeoServer, it is time to publish it. The REST interface gives you resources for managing layers, styles, and layer groups.

Working with styles

You learned a lot about styles and SLD in *Chapter 6, Styling Your Layers*. Configuring proper visualization requires you to create and publish proper styles.

REST offers you two resources for managing styles. They are as follows:

♦ `/styles`

♦ `/workspaces/<ws>/styles`

The former points to styles that are not associated to a workspace, while the latter contains the workspaces with associated styles.

Time for action – adding a new style

Adding a new style is a routine task if you are going to publish data with REST. We will retrieve an existing style from GeoServer, update it, and then upload to GeoServer as a new one.

1. We will use `PopulatedPlacesLabeled` as a template for our new style. Send a request to GeoServer to retrieve it and save to the `PopulatedPlacesBlueLabeled.xml` file. Please note that we are sending a header to tell GeoServer that we want the SLD format. If you specify `text/xml`, you will get only a description of what the SLD is:

```
curl -u admin:password -XGET -H 'Accept: application/vnd.
ogc.sld+xml' http://localhost:8080/geoserver/rest/styles/
PopulatedPlacesLabeled -o PopulatedPlacesBlueLabeled.xml
```

2. In Python, the code is as follows:

```
>>> myUrl = 'http://localhost:8080/geoserver/rest/styles/
PopulatedPlacesLabeled'
>>> headers = {'Accept: application/vnd.ogc.sld+xml'}
>>> resp = requests.get(myUrl, auth=('admin','password'),
headers=headers)
```

3. Now, open the `PopulatedPlacesBlueLabeled.xml` file, go to line 46, and replace the RGB code for black with that for blue:

```
<sld:CssParameter name="fill">#0000FF</sld:CssParameter>
```

4. Go to line 9 and replace the old name with the new name as shown in the following line of code:

```
<sld:Name>PopulatedPlacesBlueLabeled</sld:Name>
```

5. Save the file and close it. Now we will create a new style with this file. Send a POST request to create a `PopulatedPlacesBlueLabeled` style.

```
curl -u admin:password -XPOST -H 'Content-type: application/
vnd.ogc.sld+xml' -T PopulatedPlacesBlueLabeled.xml http://
localhost:8080/geoserver/rest/styles
```

6. Or in Python:

```
>>> myUrl = 'http://localhost:8080/geoserver/rest/styles'
>>> file = open(PopulatedPlacesBlueLabeled.xml','r')
>>> payload = file.read()
>>> headers = {'Content-type': 'application/vnd.ogc.sld+xml'}
>>> resp = requests.post(myUrl, auth=('admin','password'),
data=payload, headers=headers)
```

7. Go to the WEB interface and list the styles; you should see the new one:

	PopulatedPlaces
	PopulatedPlacesBlueLabeled
	PopulatedPlacesComplex
	PopulatedPlacesGraphics
	PopulatedPlacesLabeled
	PopulatedPlacesStroke

What just happened?

We review just the GET and POST operations for styles, but you can also use DELETE when you want to remove a style from your configuration, or PUT when you want to change an existing style. You can mimic the syntax learned in the previous sections.

Working with layers

Once you are done with configuring styles, you probably want to apply them to layers. Creating or modifying styles is the last step for data publication. Unsurprisingly, it is possible to perform layer operations with the REST interface.

Time for action – managing layers

In the previous section, you created a new style; but it's useless if you can't add a layer to it. We will now update the populatedplace layer by adding the new style.

1. Retrieve information on the layer ne_50m_populated_places.

```
curl -u admin:password -XGET -H 'Accept: text/xml' http://
localhost:8080/geoserver/rest/layers/ne_50m_populated_places -o
ne_50m_populated_places.xml
```

2. In Python, it is written as follows:

```
>>> myUrl =  'http://localhost:8080/geoserver/rest/layers/ne_50m_
populated_places'
>>> headers = {'Accept: text/xml'}
>>> resp = requests.get(myUrl, auth=('admin','password'),
headers=headers)
```

3. Open the ne_50m_populated_places.xml file; it starts with a styles collection. You need to insert the code for the new style you created. We don't need all the elements returned from GeoServer. Modify the file as in the following code. (Please note that we inserted the enabled element; the default value being false for it. If you make a PUT and don't explicitly set it to true, your layer will be modified and disabled):

```
<layer>
  <styles>
    <style>
      <name>PopulatedPlacesComplex</name>
    </style>
    <style>
      <name>PopulatedPlacesGraphics</name>
    </style>
    <style>
      <name>PopulatedPlacesStroke</name>
    </style>
    <style>
      <name>PopulatedPlacesLabeled</name>
    </style>
    <style>
      <name>PopulatedRotateTransparent</name>
    </style>
    <style>
      <name>PopulatedPlacesBlueLabeled</name>
    </style>
  </styles>
  <enabled>true</enabled>
</layer>
```

4. Now save the file as `addStyle.xml` and send the PUT request to GeoServer, to modify the layer's configuration:

```
curl -u admin:password -XPUT -H 'Content-type: text/xml' -T
addStyle.xml http://localhost:8080/geoserver/rest/layers/ne_50m_
populated_places
```

5. In Python, the code is as follows:

```
>>> myUrl =  'http://localhost:8080/geoserver/rest/layers/ne_50m_
populated_places'
>>> file = open(addStyle.xml','r')
>>> payload = file.read()
>>> headers = {'Content-type: text/xml'}
>>> resp = requests.put(myUrl, auth=('admin','password'),
data=payload, headers=headers)
```

6. Now go to the **Layer Preview** interface and open the **OpenLayers** preview for the `ne_50m_populated_places` layer; then open the tools and look at the drop-down list for styles. Is the new one there? Select it and your map should look like the following screenshot:

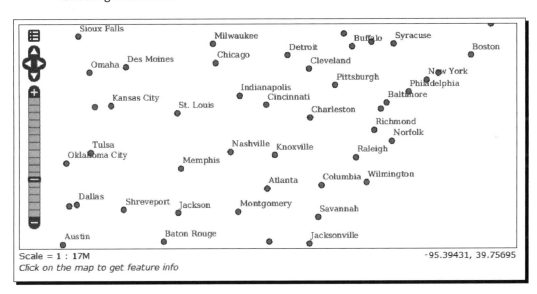

```
Scale = 1 : 17M                                              -95.39431, 39.75695
Click on the map to get feature info
```

What just happened?

You added a new style to an existent layer. You can also change the default style just by adding the XML code for it in the code sent with the PUT request.

We covered the essential operation you should know to use GeoServer's REST interface. The online documentation covers all of the allowed operations on each resource. A good approach, when you are not sure what your XML code should look like to perform a request, is to check the syntax with a GET request on the same object. When creating your application, you may want to have a look at the following reference page:

```
http://docs.geoserver.org/stable/en/user/restconfig/
rest-config-api.html#
```

Pop quiz – reviewing REST operations

Q1. Can you use REST for stopping publication of data?

1. No, you have to remove a layer for it to no longer be visible.

2. Yes, you can update a layer to "not enabled" with a POST operation.

3. Yes, you may disable a layer with a PUT operation.

Q2. which operations are available on the `geoserver/rest/workspaces/<ws>/styles` resource?

1. You can perform GET, POST, DELETE, and PUT.

2. You can perform GET and POST.

3. You can perform GET and DELETE.

Q3. Which protocol can you use with GeoServer's REST interface?

1. Any of the following protocols: HTTP, HTTPS, FTP. REST is an architectural model implemented on several protocols.

2. HTTP for GET and HTTPS for POST, PUT, and DELETE.

3. The HTTP protocol.

Summary

In this chapter we learned how to automate configuration tasks. Using the REST interface, you can publish data from a remote procedure that check for updates, extract, transform, and load the data on a filesystem or a spatial database, and then send a request to GeoServer for configuring and publishing the data.

In the next chapter, we will explore security—a real issue if you are going to deploy your GeoServer to the Internet.

We will explore how to create a set of users and link them to security policies. Each user can be profiled to access only a set of data. The most important keywords are users, groups, and roles. Understanding these topics will enable you to fine-tune the GeoServer's security system.

10
Securing GeoServer Before Production

In the previous chapters you've always needed a user ID and password to manage the GeoServer configuration. However, you could acquire the layers and maps with anonymous access. For GeoServer security, you used the default settings that are configured to provide free access to your data for everyone.

While this is quite understandable when you are developing your application, it is not often a good idea for a real site.

There could be many different reasons for you wanting to hide your services or at least a part of them. Your maps could be integrated into a site with a security system requiring your user to log on.

Why should maps be freely available? Users may be linked to different roles, with some confidential data only visible from a few of them. GeoServer security can help you secure your data, both in simple and complex cases. If you just want to publish your maps or if you are going to work with the data of a large corporation, you should read this chapter carefully.

In this chapter we will cover in detail how to do the following:

- Add strong cryptography support
- Add users and set their properties
- Define groups of users
- Define roles and link them to groups
- Filter data access with specific roles

Basic security settings

In *Chapter 2*, *Getting Started with GeoServer*, we changed the administrator password from the default of "geoserver" while installing GeoServer. Basic security settings will move you a little further down the path to building a secure site.

On the panel you will find a drop-down list showing you the active role service. This time you have just one choice; we will create more role services when we deal with users and roles. Note that you may have just one active role service.

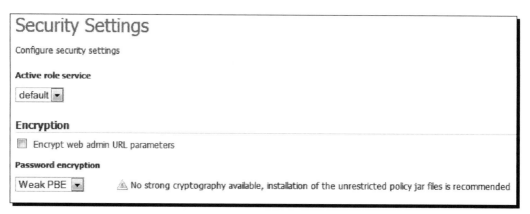

Next there is a section about encryption. Encrypting parameters in a URL is a good idea. If you click on the web interface on the styles list and select one, your browser's address bar should contain this URL:

```
http://localhost:8080/geoserver/web/?wicket:bookmarkablePage=:org.
geoserver.wms.web.data.StyleEditPage&name=PopulatedPlacesBlueLabe
led
```

The parameters' names and values are plain text. If you check the flag for encryption and browse to the same page, you should see something similar to the following URL:

```
http://localhost:8080/geoserver/web/?x=WK8KbnWoyAA*Q3OCKWLyddwndQL
Z9Nt6J7Y-1UM6swM3VW8ph6pSjk3d0fACbvjC1y5OORzTKp*78*UMVpUW5ZIGJEnVU
Qe54I2bnpTWj6tEe8bLoclmUg
```

If there is someone sniffing packets, it is a little bit harder to understand the parameters.

Time for action – enabling strong encryption

GeoServer can store passwords in an encrypted format. You can select the encryption type from the basic security settings page. We will enable strong encryption by adding a couple of files to our installation.

1. The first step is getting the files you need. Open your browser and point to
    `http://www.oracle.com/technetwork/java/javase/downloads/jce-6-download-429243.html`.

> We are assuming that you are using Oracle Java™ 6; we installed it in *Chapter 2, Getting Started with GeoServer*. If you are using Oracle Java™ 7, download the files at `http://www.oracle.com/technetwork/java/javase/downloads/jce-7-download-432124.html`. You should not use Java™ 5 or the previous versions with GeoServer.

2. Accept the license agreement and then the download link will be available. Save the archive to a convenient folder and explore it:

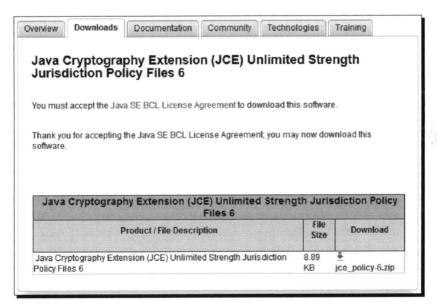

3. There are three files inside the archive. You need to copy the two JAR files to your `<java-home>/lib/security` folder:

```
~/JCE6$ ls -l *jar
-rw-rw-r-- 1 stefano stefano 2500 May 31  2011 local_policy.jar
-rw-rw-r-- 1 stefano stefano 2487 May 31  2011 US_export_policy.jar
~/JCE6$ sudo mv *jar /usr/lib/jvm/jre1.6.0_37/lib/security/.
```

4. Now restart Tomcat using the following command:

```
~/JCE6$ sudo service tomcat restart
```

5. Open the **Security Setting** page in the GeoServer web interface. Now you shouldn't see any warning about strong PBE not being available:

6. Select **Strong PBE** from the drop-down list and click on the **Save** button.

What just happened?

Passwords are saved on a filesystem or inside a database and should always be encrypted to avoid usage by unauthorized users. A stronger encryption makes GeoServer safer, but it is not enough for a production site. Go to the next section for another hint.

Time for action – changing the master password

You used the admin account on GeoServer to administer it. Silently acting behind the scenes is another account in GeoServer, called the **root account**. It is the real super user account and it is present for your safety. If you disable the admin account, you may find yourself locked out of GeoServer. In this case you can use the root account to log in and restore the admin user.

By default the root password is equal to that of admin, but you can change it with the following steps:

1. Log in as admin or root.

2. Open the **Passwords** page.

3. On the top of the page, click on the link to change the master password:

4. Insert the current master password, which is the same as the admin password, and then a new one. Click on **Change Password**:

What just happened?

We changed the master password. If you are in charge of several GeoServer instances and are not the only one performing administrative tasks on them, the master password may help you when in need of a disaster recovery.

Defining users, groups, and roles

To ensure data security, you need to recognize who is accessing your layers and your services. Anonymous access can't be used on secured data.

Security in GeoServer is based on a role system where each role defines a specific function. You can assign roles to users and groups, that is, assigning functions to real people using your system.

To organize your real users, GeoServer provides you with the user, group, and role concept. With the first two, you can insert real people into the GeoServer security subsystem and with roles you can grant rights to real users.

User definition

In GeoServer, a user is someone who can use the system, a real person, or another system. GeoServer stores a username, uniquely identifying the user, a password, and a set of key/value pairs to store general information about it. A user can be disabled.

Group definition

A group is a set of users. GeoServer stores a list of usernames belonging to the group and a group name, uniquely identifying the group. A group can be disabled, but please note that this only removes the roles deriving from the disabled group and does not disable the users belonging to the group.

User/group services

Users and groups are stored in a user/group service. This defines the storage medium, XML files by default or a JDBC Database, the encryption type for passwords, and the password policy. Although you may have more than one user/group service, you will usually be fine with the default one.

Roles definition

GeoServer roles are associated with performing certain tasks or accessing particular resources. Roles are assigned to users and groups, authorizing them to perform the actions associated with the role.

Time for action – creating users and groups

In order to fully understand how security works in GeoServer, we will use a typical scenario. Consider an organization working with data in the `NaturalEarth` workspace. We want to restrict access to this data only to the organization's members. Inside the organization, there are a few people editing data to create new data sets or to update existing ones, and many more members who need to read data to compose maps. There is also a need for an administrator to keep it all working. Lastly, we need to consider that our GeoServer site also contains data that is freely available. We are now going to create the security organization from an unsecured GeoServer.

1. We will start creating groups. In the security section of the left pane, select the **Users, Groups, and Roles** link. The following screenshot shows you the **User Group Services** configured. You will find the **default** service shipped with GeoServer. We already changed it to use strong PBE encryption and that's fine. Click on the name to edit it:

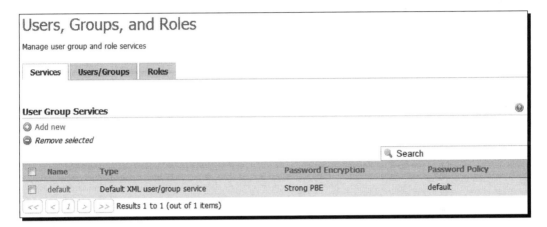

2. Select the **Groups** tab. The list is empty. Click on **Add a new group**.

3. Enter NE_Publishers as a group name and leave the group enabled. Don't assign any role to the new group as we will create specific roles later. Click on the **Save** button:

4. Repeat the previous step to create **NE_Editors** and **NE_Admins** groups. Your list now shows the three groups as follows:

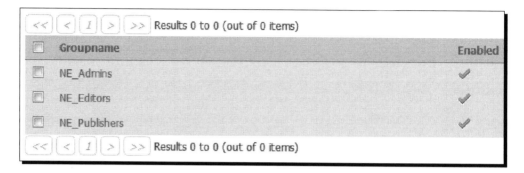

5. Now switch to the **Users** tab. Obviously it lists the only existing user, that is, **admin**, as shown in the following screenshot:

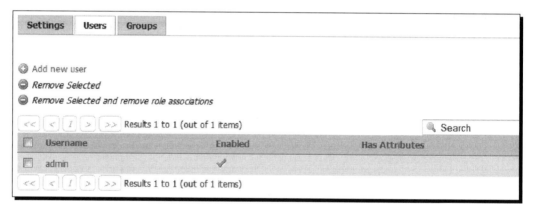

6. I am pleased to introduce you to **Steven Plant**, the Natural Earth Data Administrator. Click on the **Add new user** link, and add him with a password of your choice:

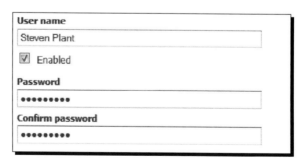

7. Add Steven to the **NE_Admins** group, then click on the **Save** button:

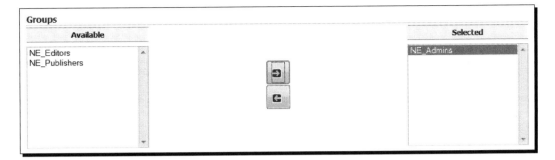

8. Repeat the previous step to create a user **Michael Ford**, a member of **NE_Editors** group, and **John Smith**, a **NE_Publishers** group member. Your list now shows the three users:

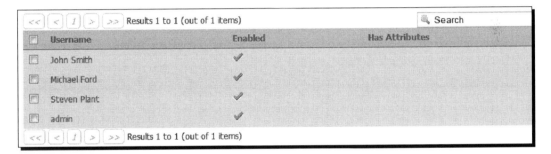

What just happened?

We just created three users for the three groups and this may seem overkill to you. Consider them as templates of the real users. While in the real word, we don't want to have too many administrators, we will probably need several Michaels and Johns processing the data. Now we need to define what they can do on GeoServer.

Time for action – defining roles

A user or a group without any role assigned is useless. It is now time to create roles and assign them to our users.

1. From the **Users, Groups, and Roles** section, select the **Roles** tab. You will find that two roles already exist. They are the administrative roles assigned to the admin, and they grant access to all GeoServer configuration. Click on the **Edit** link as shown in the following screenshot:

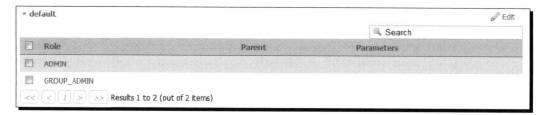

2. You entered the Role service definition. Leave the settings untouched and switch to the **Roles** tab. Click on **Add new role**.

3. Enter NE_VIEWER as a new role name. We don't need a parent role. A child role inherits all the grants from the parent role, making it useful when you want to extend a basic role with more grants. Indeed we are going to do this in the next step:

4. Click on the **Save** button and then repeat the previous step to create the **NE_EDITOR** role. This time select **NE_VIEWER** as the parent role as shown in the following screenshot:

5. Click on the **Save** button and then repeat the previous step to create the **NE_ADMIN** role. This time select **NE_EDITOR** as the parent role. Once saved, your role's list should look like the following screenshot:

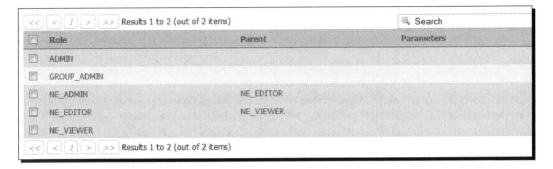

6. The final step is to associate a role to users or groups. Select the **User, Groups and Roles** page from the left pane, then select the groups list and click on the **NE_Publishers** group to edit it. Add the **NE_VIEWER** role to the group and save it:

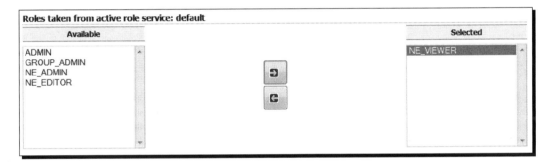

7. Now click on the **NE_Editors** group and associate it to the **NE_EDITOR** role.

8. Finally, associate the **NE_Admins** group to the **NE_ADMIN** role.

What just happened?

By defining roles and associating them to the users, we completed the definition of our organization. Now we need to explore how data are bound to roles and users.

Accessing data and services

GeoServer supports access and control, both at the service level, allowing for the lockdown of service operations to only authenticated users who have been granted a particular role, and on a per-layer basis.

The two approaches can't be mixed. If you lock down a service to a role, you can't grant the access on a specific layer to the same role.

When working with layers, you can define rules that specify what a role can do on any specific layer. The operations controlled are the view, write, and admin access. When granting read access on a layer, you enable a user to add it on a map; while granting write access you enable the user to update, create, and delete features contained in the layer. The admin access level enables the user to update the layer's configuration.

Have a go hero – creating a new shapefile

For the next *Time for action* section, we need a layer to perform editing. We already have a bunch of layers loaded from the Natural Earth data sets, but we will need a simpler layer. You will create a new shapefile inside the Natural Earth Shapes data store, called `myLocations`. Use point geometry and EPSG:4326 as the SRS. Add a string attribute and call it `NAME`.

Time for action – securing layers

We want to protect the Natural Earth data set from unauthorized access, while leaving the remaining layers freely available to all users. In this section we are going to associate layers and roles. We will also use the new layer you created for editing.

1. Select **Data**, under the **Security** section from the left pane. The rules list shows the two shipped with the default GeoServer's configuration. Click on the **Add a new rule** link.

2. In the rule editing page, select **NaturalEarth** as the workspace. Leave * as a layer. Since we want to protect all layers in this workspace, the access mode should be **Read**. Select the **NE_READER** role and move it to the right list by clicking on the arrow. Click on the **Save** button to create the reading rule:

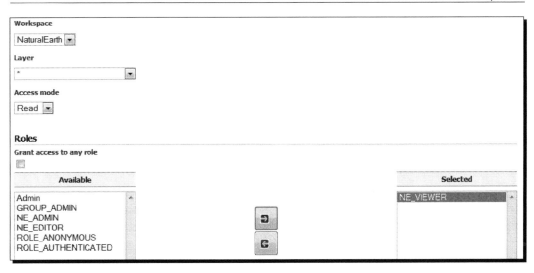

3. Repeat the previous step to create a writing rule. Select **Write** as the access mode and **NE_EDITOR** as the role.

4. Then create the administration rule. Select **Admin** as the access mode and **NE_ADMIN** as the role. After saving, you will see a rule list like the one displayed in the following screenshot:

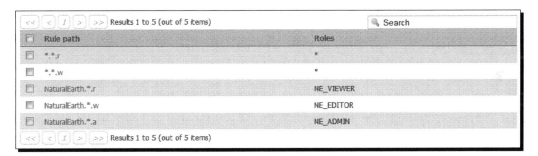

5. Now we will log off from the GeoServer web interface. If you try to access the layer preview anonymously, you won't see any layer from the Natural Earth workspace while all the others are still listed.

6. Now log on as John Smith, with the password you assigned to him. Going back to the layer preview, you should see the Natural Earth layers listed. Try the **Open Layers** preview page for the **10m_railroads** layer. It works and you can use the data to compose maps such as the following:

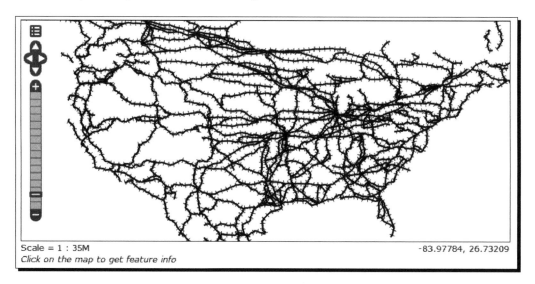

Scale = 1 : 35M   -83.97784, 26.73209
Click on the map to get feature info

7. But John Smith can't edit the styles associated to the layer or any other property. He would need admin rights granted for it; can you guess who the proper user will be?

8. Log on to GeoServer as Steve Plant. Now the left pane is richer than it was when you were John, but with fewer features than those visible to the admin. Click on the **Layer** link; you will see only the layers belonging to the Natural Earth workspace. You can split the admin responsibilities with GeoServer Security:

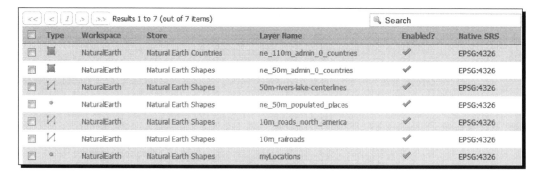

Results 1 to 7 (out of 7 items)   Search

Type	Workspace	Store	Layer Name	Enabled?	Native SRS
	NaturalEarth	Natural Earth Countries	ne_110m_admin_0_countries	✓	EPSG:4326
	NaturalEarth	Natural Earth Shapes	ne_50m_admin_0_countries	✓	EPSG:4326
	NaturalEarth	Natural Earth Shapes	50m-rivers-lake-centerlines	✓	EPSG:4326
	NaturalEarth	Natural Earth Shapes	ne_50m_populated_places	✓	EPSG:4326
	NaturalEarth	Natural Earth Shapes	10m_roads_north_america	✓	EPSG:4326
	NaturalEarth	Natural Earth Shapes	10m_railroads	✓	EPSG:4326
	NaturalEarth	Natural Earth Shapes	myLocations	✓	EPSG:4326

9. If you go on layer preview and select the **10m_railroads** layer again, can you see the map? You can, because of roles inheritance, which you set when creating the NE roles. So **NE_ADMIN** inherits all the grants from **NE_EDITOR**, and hence from **NE_VIEWER**.

10. We now want to check if Michael Ford can really edit the data. Log out from GeoServer.

11. From the left pane, select the **Demos** link. It gets you to a page containing links to demos applications. We will use the demo requests page to test the security.

GeoServer Demos

Collection of GeoServer demo applications

- Demo requests Example requests for GeoServer (using the TestServlet).
- SRS List List of all SRS known to GeoServer
- Reprojection console Simple coordinate reprojection tool
- WCS request builder Step by step WCS GetCoverage request builder

> **WFS** is an OGC standard for services delivering you features instead of their representations, which are maps. WFS-T is an extension to add features from the client to the server. This way you can perform editing, that is, creating, deleting, or updating features. We will cover WFS in *Chapter 12, Going Further: Getting Help and Troubleshooting*.

12. In the demo requests page, select the request for a WFS insert:

13. Remove the code in the body—it's an XML example for a layer shipped with the GeoServer default configuration—and replace it with the following code. You don't need to fully understand the code; it basically contains a GML fragment defining the feature we want to create:

```
<wfs:Transaction service="WFS" version="1.0.0"
    xmlns:wfs="http://www.opengis.net/wfs"
  xmlns="http://www.opengis.net/ogc" xmlns:NaturalEarth="http://
www.naturalearthdata.com/"
  xmlns:gml="http://www.opengis.net/gml" xmlns:xsi="http://www.
w3.org/2001/XMLSchema-instance"
  xsi:schemaLocation="http://www.opengis.net/wfs http://schemas.
opengis.net/wfs/1.0.0/WFS-transaction.xsd
    http://www.naturalearthdata.com/ http://localhost:8080/
geoserver/wfs?request=DescribeFeatureType&amp;service=wfs&amp;vers
ion=1.0.0&amp;typeName=NaturalEarth:myLocations">
  <wfs:Insert>
    <NaturalEarth:myLocations>
```

```
    <NaturalEarth:the_geom>
      <gml:Point srsName="EPSG:4326">
        <gml:coordinates decimal="." cs="," ts=" ">115.86,-
31.908</gml:coordinates>
      </gml:Point>
    </NaturalEarth:the_geom>
    <NaturalEarth:NAME>Perth</NaturalEarth:NAME>
  </NaturalEarth:myLocations>
 </wfs:Insert>
</wfs:Transaction>
```

Geography Markup Language (GML) is an OGC standard defining an XML grammar to describe geographical features. It is often used as an interchange format for spatial transactions.

For more information visit the following link:
http://www.opengeospatial.org/standards/gml.

14. Click on the **Submit** button. A form showing you the result will appear, shown as follows:

<servlet-exception> HTTP response: 401 Unauthorized </servlet-exception>

15. The message is not unexpected. We are trying to insert a point in a feature type with anonymous access, while we previously defined a rule granting write access only to the **NE_Editors** group's members. In the demo request page, enter the proper credentials and try editing again:

16. This time the response shows us that GeoServer has accepted our insert request:

```
-<wfs:WFS_TransactionResponse version="1.0.0" xsi:schemaLocation="http://www.opengis.net/wfs
  http://ubuntu1204x64vm:8080/geoserver/schemas/wfs/1.0.0/WFS-transaction.xsd">
  -<wfs:InsertResult>
      <ogc:FeatureId fid="new0"/>
   </wfs:InsertResult>
  -<wfs:TransactionResult>
    -<wfs:Status>
        <wfs:SUCCESS/>
      </wfs:Status>
   </wfs:TransactionResult>
 </wfs:WFS_TransactionResponse>
```

17. Repeat the previous step to insert other locations with the following values:

Brisbane	153.030 -27.450
Sydney	151.210 -33.868
Melbourne	144.974 -37.812
Darwin	130.839 -12.455

18. Now open the **myLocations** layer's configuration, update its Bounding Boxes, and set the style to **PopulatedPlacesLabeled**. Then open the layer preview for it; in the map you should see the five locations you created:

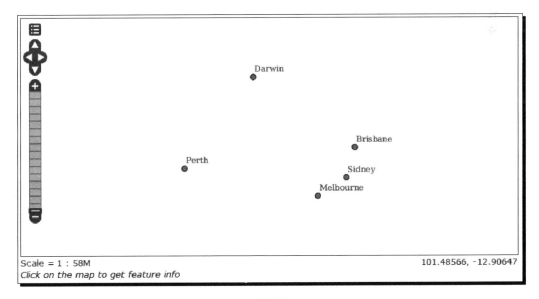

What just happened?

We completed the security scenario. By defining rules for data access, we restricted what a user can perform on the data and we also tried impersonating the users we created. Unless you know the admin password, there is no way to bypass the security system and access restricted data.

Pop quiz – reviewing security

Q1. Can you set grants on data directly to a user?

1. Yes, you can create a rule and link it to a single user.

2. No, you can only link a rule to a role.

3. Yes, but you have to define a group with a single user and then link the proper rule to that group.

Q2. How many groups can you define in GeoServer?

1. Three groups: one for data reading, one for data creation, and one for data administration.

2. Many groups for data reading but only one for data creation and administration.

3. You can have an unlimited set of groups in GeoServer.

Summary

We took a brief journey through GeoServer security. From the plain installation, which ships with a very low security level, we learned how to create users and give them grants to access data and perform tasks on GeoServer.

We have just covered a small subset of the wide range of topics that GeoServer has to offer.

GeoServer can integrate with Enterprise security. You can have users and roles defined in an external LDAP repository.

In the next chapter we will focus on performance, which is a big challenge when you eventually deploy your site in production. Users might wait in anticipation for your maps, but if it takes too long to download them, they will soon abandon your site.

11
Tuning GeoServer in a Production Environment

Everyone hates slow websites; web maps are no exception. Your users will look for a nice user experience with the map promptly reacting to their input.

Speed is not the only factor you need to take into account. As a user you will be expect that the site is usually available; frequent downtime will make your users go away to some other website.

In this chapter we will cover the configuration of GeoServer to optimize its speed and availability. We have already learned how to cache layers for optimizing the map speed using GWC. It is a great tool and proper configuration can boost your map's performances. However, caching is not always feasible, such as in cases of frequently changing data, hence GeoServer offers you other tools to increase performance.

In this chapter, we will cover the following topics in detail:

- Optimizing runtime parameters for JVM
- Improving image manipulation performance using JAI
- Using a proxy
- Creating a GeoServer cluster

Tuning Java

When we installed Tomcat, we didn't play with the JVM settings. Tomcat's startup script is configured for booting quickly, but of course it can't match all the requirements of the application. Tuning your Java runtime parameters can greatly increase performance. There are many runtime parameters you can set at JVM startup. In the following section you will set the parameters that are most effective on GeoServer performances. Note that the values may vary according to the hardware configuration on your site.

Unfortunately, there is no way to cut corners on the path of tuning parameters for a Java application. While the options presented in this chapter have been widely tested on GeoServer and are recommended by core developers, you should note that the best options may vary depending on your scenario. A valuable resource to understand how each parameter works is at `http://www.oracle.com/technetwork/java/javase/tech/vmoptions-jsp-140102.html`.

Time for action – configuring Java runtime parameters

In *Chapter 2, Getting Started with GeoServer*, we created a startup script for automated startup of GeoServer on Linux. Now you will edit the script and add proper values for the Java runtime parameters. Each parameter will be briefly described in the following steps:

1. Open the startup file for editing:

   ```
   ~$ sudo vi /etc/init.d/tomcat
   ```

   vi is one the most famous editors on Linux. System Administrators and developers often love it for its flexibility and power. On the other hand it has provides a steep learning curve, where newcomers may find its command mode/insert mode, dual nature uncomfortable. On Debian distribution you may find nano, which is a more user-friendly console editor. And it goes without saying that you can use a powerful IDE such as Gedit or Jedit if you can access a desktop environment.

2. Locate the following line; if you didn't modify the script created in *Chapter 2, Getting Started with GeoServer*, it should be on line 16:

   ```
   export JAVA_OPTS="-Djava.awt.headless=true"
   ```

3. Insert a new line just before it. The first parameter that you are going to tune is the HEAP size. It really depends on the available memory on your system. 2 GB, as indicated, is a good figure. You may want to decrease it if you are hosting it on a tiny cloud machine where the total memory size is limited. Type the following values on the new line:

```
HEAP="-Xms2048m -Xmx2048m"
```

4. Now add a second line and insert the following code. You are reserving space for the new objects created by GeoServer. These values shouldn't be more than a quarter of the heap size, so reduce them proportionally if you need to reduce your heap:

```
NEW="-XX:NewSize=256m -XX:MaxNewSize=256m"
```

5. Add a line and insert a value to avoid the RMI-induced Full GCs from running too frequently; once every 10 minutes should be more than enough:

```
RMIGC="-Dsun.rmi.dgc.client.gcInterval=600000 -Dsun.rmi.dgc.
server.gcInterval=600000"
```

6. Add a line to use the Parallel Garbage Collector that enables multithreaded garbage collection and improves performance if more than two cores are present:

```
PGC="-XX:+UseParallelGC"
```

7. Now increase the maximum size of the permanent generation (or permgen) allocated to GeoServer. This is the heap portion where the bytecode class is stored. GeoServer uses lots of classes, and hence it may exhaust that space quickly, leading to out of memory errors:

```
PERM="-XX:PermSize=256m -XX:MaxPermSize=256m"
```

8. Finally, add some tracing to help us in case things go astray:

```
DEBUG="-verbose:gc -XX:+PrintTenuringDistribution"
```

9. Always dump on **Out Of Memory (OOM)**. It does not cost anything unless triggered:

```
DUMP="-XX:+HeapDumpOnOutOfMemoryError"
```

10. The last set is for forcing the server JVM. On most Linux systems, it is the default, but having it explicitly set doesn't cause any harm:

```
SERVER="-server"
```

11. Now go to the line XX and add all the values you set in the JAVA_OPTS variable. The JVM reads it at startup and will use your values:

```
export JAVA_OPTS="-Djava.awt.headless=true $HEAP $NEW $RMIGC $PGC
$PERM $DEBUG $DUMP $SERVER"
```

12. Save the file and restart your Tomcat.

What just happened?

You customized the Java runtime environment hosting GeoServer. If you are on a Windows machine, you can insert the values in the Tomcat Configuration Console. Go to the **Java** tab and insert each parameter on a new line in the **Java Options** textbox. You can insert the heap size in the textboxes called **Initial memory pool** and **Maximum memory pool**.

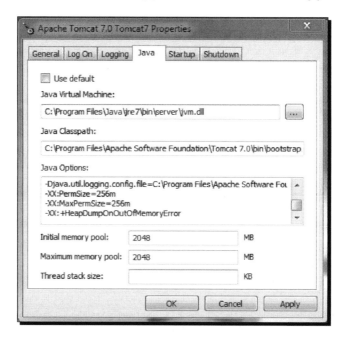

Time for action – installing native JAI

Java Advanced Imaging (JAI) is a library developed by Oracle for advanced image manipulation. GeoServer can run without it, as it is shipped with a pure Java version of JAI. Installing JAI greatly improves performance when working with images, that is, raster format data. If you are not going to use spatial raster data, GeoServer works with image formats when you ask for a map, for example, in a WMS GetMap request, so it is really worthwhile to have it on your production site:

1. Download the proper package for your system, Linux or Windows, from
   http://download.java.net/media/jai/builds/release/1_1_3/:

   ~$ wget http://download.java.net/media/jai/builds/release/1_1_3/
   jai-1_1_3-lib-linux-amd64-jre.bin

2. Copy the file into the folder where you installed the JRE and then run it:

```
~$ sudo cp jai-1_1_3-lib-linux-amd64-jre.bin /usr/lib/jvm/
jre1.7.0_04/.
~$ cd /usr/lib/jvm/jre1.7.0_04/
~$ sudo sh jai-1_1_3-lib-linux-amd64-jre.bin
```

3. The program prompts you for the license agreement; scroll down to read it and accept the agreement at the end:

```
UnZipSFX 5.50 of 17 February 2002, by Info-ZIP (Zip-Bugs@lists.
wku.edu).
   inflating: COPYRIGHT-jai.txt
   inflating: DISTRIBUTIONREADME-jai.txt
   inflating: LICENSE-jai.txt
   inflating: THIRDPARTYLICENSEREADME-jai.txt
   inflating: UNINSTALL-jai
   inflating: lib/amd64/libmlib_jai.so
   inflating: lib/ext/jai_core.jar
   inflating: lib/ext/jai_codec.jar
   inflating: lib/ext/mlibwrapper_jai.jar
Done.
```

4. Now copy the `JAI-IO` package from
`http://download.java.net/media/jai-imageio/builds/release/1.1/`:

```
~$ wget http://download.java.net/media/jai-imageio/builds/
release/1.1/jai_imageio-1_1-lib-linux-amd64-jre.bin
```

5. Again, copy the file into the folder where you installed the JRE and then run it. If you are running GeoServer on Ubuntu, you should add an environment variable as in the following lines. In this case too you are required to accept the license agreement:

```
~$ sudo cp jai_imageio-1_1-lib-linux-amd64-jre.bin /usr/lib/jvm/
jre1.7.0_04/.
~$ cd /usr/lib/jvm/jre1.7.0_04/
~$ sudo su
~$ export _POSIX2_VERSION=199209
~$ sh jai_imageio-1_1-lib-linux-amd64-jre.bin
UnZipSFX 5.50 of 17 February 2002, by Info-ZIP (Zip-Bugs@lists.
wku.edu).
   inflating: COPYRIGHT-jai_imageio.txt
   inflating: DISTRIBUTIONREADME-jai_imageio.txt
   inflating: ENTITLEMENT-jai_imageio.txt
```

```
inflating: LICENSE-jai_imageio.txt
inflating: THIRDPARTYLICENSEREADME-jai_imageio.txt
inflating: UNINSTALL-jai_imageio
inflating: lib/amd64/libclib_jiio.so
inflating: lib/ext/jai_imageio.jar
inflating: lib/ext/clibwrapper_jiio.jar
Done.
```

6. You can now remove the two archives you have downloaded:

```
~$ rm jai_imageio-1_1-lib-linux-amd64-jre.bin
~$ rm jai-1_1_3-lib-linux-amd64-jre.bin
```

7. Stop your Tomcat service:

```
~$ sudo service tomcat stop
```

8. Now remove the pure Java version of JAI:

```
~$ cd /opt/apache-tomcat-7.0.27/webapps/geoserver/WEB-INF/lib/
~$ sudo rm jai_codec-1.1.3.jar
~$ sudo rm jai_core-1.1.3.jar
~$ sudo rm jai_imageio-1.1.jar
```

9. Restart the Tomcat service:

```
~$ sudo service tomcat start
```

10. Open the GeoServer web interface and go to the **Server status** page. You can now see that it is using **Native JAI**:

Native JAI	true	
Native JAI ImageIO	true	
JAI Maximum Memory	181 MB	
JAI Memory Usage	0 KB	Free memory
JAI Memory Threshold	75.0	
Number of JAI Tile Threads	7	
JAI Tile Thread Priority	5	

What just happened?

You installed JAI libraries for advanced imaging manipulation. This will make your GeoServer faster at writing rasters, for example, when preparing a response to a `GetMap` request. Although tuning Java can greatly improve your server performances, there is another little step that is often forgotten: removing unneeded features.

Removing unused services

In this book we mainly used GeoServer as a map server. In fact, GeoServer ships with three OGC services enabled: **WMS**, **WFS**, and **WCS**. If you are only going to use GeoServer to produce maps, you should disable WCS and WFS, or at least set them to read-only mode. We use **WFS-T** for editing data in the chapter about security. If your data is static, the most secure way to avoid accidental updating or deleting is to disable WFS-T.

 Web Coverage Services is the analogue of WFS for raster. We will briefly introduce it in *Chapter 12, Going Further: Getting Help and Troubleshooting*, but chances are that you won't need it.

Time for action – disabling unused services

Now you should turn off WMS and WFS, or WFS-T, according to your needs:

1. Open the GeoServer web interface. On the left pane, you can see the **Services** category and under it **WCS**, **WFS**, and **WMS** are listed. Select **WCS**.

2. Remove the flag from the **Enable WCS** checkbox to disable the service and click on the **Submit** button:

3. Now select **WFS** in the **Services** category. If you don't want to deliver features to your users, disable the service as you did for WCS:

4. If you want to give your user an option to download geometry, leave the service enabled. Scroll down until you find the **Maximum number of features** textbox. This value limits the number of records returned on a single `GetFeature` request. Lower the default value to **10000**:

5. In the very next section, set the **Service Level** option. Select **Basic** and then click on the **Submit** button:

6. Now select **WMS** in the **Services** category. Of course you want to disable the WMS service, but you can set some values to optimize map rendering.

7. Scroll down to the **Resource consumption limits** section. The three values limit the amount of memory, time, and errors that GeoServer can use while rendering a map. Set the memory to **20480**, which is enough for a full screen map:

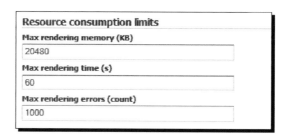

8. Click on the **Submit** button to save your settings.

What just happened?

Disabling unneeded services improves resource usage and helps you to avoid out of memory errors. The more features you discard from GeoServer, the fewer classes it will need to load in the memory.

Setting a proxy

Whether you are using GeoServer on Tomcat or you installed **Jetty,** it is not a good idea to expose it directly to your users, especially if they are on the Internet. A safer option is to use a more stable web server, such as **Apache httpd**—one of the most popular and widely used web servers across the Web. To expose GeoServer, or more generally, a Java application from the web server, you need to set a proxy on the web server. Users will point to an alias and their requests will be redirected to Tomcat, more safely deployed in a protected LAN.

Time for action – configuring a proxy

We will configure the Apache HTTP web server to act as a proxy for GeoServer. First of all we need to get it working; you will learn that just like many other open source projects, this is surprisingly simple!

1. To install Apache on Linux, you can use the distribution repository. At the time of writing, it installs release 2.2.22 for Ubuntu. You can also download and install a binary package from `http://httpd.apache.org/download.cgi`. The following line is the only way if you are on Windows:

    ```
    ~$ sudo apt-get install apache2
    ```

2. If your server is not registered on a DNS you should insert the full hostname inside the site's configuration file. Open the following file:

    ```
    ~$ sudo vi /etc/apache2/sites-available/default
    ```

3. Insert the following code as the first line of the file:

    ```
    ~$ ServerName ubuntu1204x64vm
    ```

    > Note that if you perform a manual installation of Apache or if you are on a Windows machine, the file and folder locations are different from those shown.

4. Point your browser to `http://localhost`. If the installation was successful, you should see the following **It works!** message:

    ## It works!

    This is the default web page for this server.

    The web server software is running but no content has been added, yet.

5. The proxy capabilities are contained in some optional modules. You can find which modules are available on your system:

    ```
    ~$ ls /etc/apache2/mods-available | grep proxy
    proxy_ajp.load
    proxy_balancer.conf
    proxy_balancer.load
    proxy.conf
    ```

```
proxy_connect.load
proxy_ftp.conf
proxy_ftp.load
proxy_http.load
proxy.load
proxy_scgi.load
```

6. For configuring a proxy, you need the `proxy` and `proxy_ajp` modules. Enable them using the command line tool `a2enmod`. After that you need to restart the Apache service:

```
~$ sudo a2enmod proxy proxy_ajp
~$ sudo service apache2 restart
```

7. Now you will configure a proxy; edit the `http.conf` file:

```
~$ sudo vi /etc/apache2/httpd.conf
```

8. You have to insert a `ProxyPass` directive in the Apache configuration file. With the following syntax, you are informing the web server that each incoming request for `/geoserver` will be forwarded to your host on port `8009` using the `ajp` protocol:

```
ProxyPass /geoserver ajp://localhost:8009/geoserver
<Location /geoserver>
    Order deny,allow
    Deny from all
    Allow from 127.0.0.1
</Location>
```

9. Now open your browser and point it to `http://localhost/geoserver/web/`:

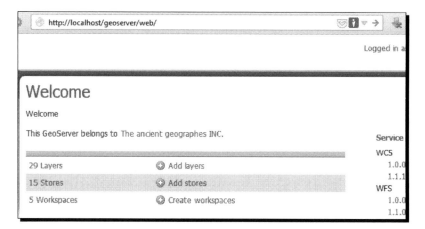

10. It works! You can now use GeoServer pointed to your web server and ignore where GeoServer is deployed.

What just happened?

You learned the basic method of configuring Apache to act as a proxy. Properly configuring a web server for security is far out of the scope of this book, but you should keep in mind that the HTTP protocol exposed by Tomcat and Jetty is not intended for real Internet use. You should always avoid deploying GeoServer in a DMZ (`http://en.wikipedia.org/wiki/ DMZ_(computing)`).

Avoiding service faults

GeoServer is a great software, and core developers hit bugs every day, enhance existing functions, and deliver new capabilities. Despite all of this, and the careful configuration of your site, it is just a matter of time before you will encounter a failure that prevents your GeoServer from delivering maps. In the simplest of cases, it will only affect some specific requests; more often it will halt it for a while, and sometimes you will need to restart it to get it working again.

It happens to almost all the software applications that you will have worked with, either proprietary or open source, free of charge or very expensive. Avoiding faults is out of your control, but you should learn how you can manage avoiding service interruption.

A high availability or fault tolerant configuration is what you need. Indeed, this a very common approach in software deployment and what you will learn here is best practice for any kind of software service, not only for the map services.

So how do you get a fault tolerant configuration? It's all about redundancy, if you can't avoid faults you can yet eliminate a single point of failure. In fault tolerant configurations, a single point of failure is a part of both hardware and software that doesn't have a spare companion to succeed in its job if it fails.

The basic idea is quite simple but very effective. If you have two GeoServers working in parallel, they probably won't break at the same time. So while you, or even better, an automated procedure, work to restore the broken instance, the other GeoServer will continue to process the users' requests. From the users' point of view, there is no fault; he can only experience a slowdown in the response time. Of course, this model can be implemented with far more than just two instances of GeoServer; you may have a lot of them. This model will not only make your system more reliable, but it will also greatly improve your site's performance.

Of course, having two GeoServers is not enough. First of all, their configuration needs to be synchronized; besides, you need a way to share requests among the instances. Indeed, you need a load balancer to distribute the request load across a pool of servers.

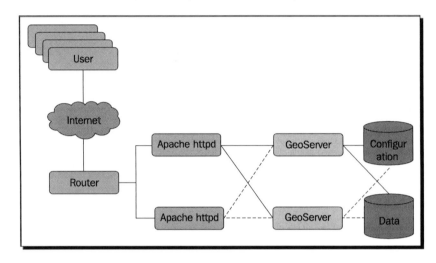

The previous diagram displays all the components of a fault tolerant configuration. Starting from the right, we find two repositories designed with the symbol usually used for databases: one holds the configuration files and the other stores the data. As you learned in the previous chapters, GeoServer's configuration is contained in a folder. This folder is contained inside `war`; so when you deploy it on Tomcat, it is contained in the `geoserver` folder. You can put it on an external filesystem to make it accessible by all instances.

Note that to avoid a single point of failure and corruption in access contention, you can't simply copy the configuration folder on a server and have all your GeoServers pointing to it. You need to copy it on a special filesystem thought to be simultaneously mounted on multiple servers; these filesystems are called **Cluster File System**. Of course, the same issue applies to data not in an **RDBMS**, for example, shapefiles. For more information, take a look at `http://en.wikipedia.org/wiki/Clustered_file_system`.

The data store may be an RDBMS, for example, a PostGIS server, or a folder containing shapefiles and georeferenced images.

Going leftwards, you will find two GeoServers. Note the lines connecting to both data and configuration. They are differently styled just to make the connected items clear, but their function is the same. Each GeoServer needs to access the same configuration store and data store to expose exactly the same layers.

On the left of the map servers there are a couple of web servers. You learned that they act as a proxy for GeoServer, here they also balance the load among them. We will see the configuration's details in the *Time for action – configuring a cluster* section; for now you should note that each web server is connected to each GeoServer. This way if one of them fails, the other will forward requests to the map servers.

In front of the web servers there is a component called **Router**. From a logical point of view, it is a balancer that associates all your web servers to a single IP address. It may be a hardware or a software component; see `http://en.wikipedia.org/wiki/Load_balancing(computing)` for a discussion and a list of implementations.

Eventually we find the users. They are unaware of the architectural complexity; they just have an entry point for the map service to forward the requests. The cluster configuration takes care of the requests, dispatching them to a GeoServer and returning the responses.

There is an important fact to keep in mind. WMS, WFS, and WCS are stateless. There is no session state to maintain across the client requests, so you don't need to synchronize session data among your servers. A user request may be filled by server1 and then dispatched to server2. The request's body contains all the information needed by server2 to process the request. This greatly reduces complexity and you can cluster your configuration just by implementing load balancing and redundancy.

Time for action – configuring a cluster

In the configuration schema, we didn't mention the hardware. Of course, having software redundancy while deploying all components on a single physical server is not a good idea. You can deploy each component on a separate server (and in modern server farm they will probably be virtual ones), but the basic idea is that you should never have all the instances of a component on a single machine.

For the sake of simplicity, and to save you having to buy a lot of hardware, we will use a single Linux machine in the following section:

1. As a first step, we will relocate the configuration folder out of the GeoServer web archive. Stop the Tomcat service:

   ```
   ~$ sudo service tomcat stop
   ```

2. Now move the folder to an external location:

   ```
   ~$ sudo mv /opt/apache-tomcat-7.0.27/webapps/geoserver/data /opt/geoserver_config
   ```

3. Now you have to edit the `web.xml` file to make GeoServer aware of the new configuration folder:

```
~$ sudo vi /opt/apache-tomcat-7.0.27/webapps/geoserver/WEB-INF/
web.xml
```

4. Locate the following commented code fragment:

```
<!--
  <context-param>
    <param-name>GEOSERVER_DATA_DIR</param-name>
    <param-value>C:\eclipse\workspace\geoserver_trunk\cite\
confCiteWFSPostGIS</param-value>
  </context-param>
-->
```

5. Remove the first and last line to uncomment it and insert the location of the new folder in the `param-value` element:

```
<context-param>
  <param-name>GEOSERVER_DATA_DIR</param-name>
  <param-value>/opt/geoserver_config</param-value>
</context-param>
```

6. Save the file and then restart the Tomcat service:

```
~$ sudo service tomcat start
```

7. Log in to GeoServer and check that the configuration was properly read. Now we need a second Tomcat instance. Again, stop the Tomcat service, and copy it to a new location:

```
~$ sudo cp -r /opt/apache-tomcat-7.0.27 /opt/new_apache-
tomcat-7.0.27
```

8. With two different servers you could leave the Tomcat configuration untouched and it would work perfectly. But when you have both on the same machine and you start them, they will try to bind to the same TCP port (for example, 8080 for HTTP protocol), and one of them will fail in doing so. Open the `server.xml` file of the new Tomcat with an editor:

```
~$ sudo vi /opt/new_apache-tomcat-7.0.27/conf/server.xml
```

9. Locate the following code—it is the first uncommented line—and modify `Server port` to 8105:

```
<Server port="8105" shutdown="SHUTDOWN">
```

10. Now look for the code section where the HTTP connector is configured. Change `connector port` to `8180`:

```
<Connector port="8180" protocol="HTTP/1.1"
           connectionTimeout="20000"
           redirectPort="8443" />
```

11. Scroll down until you find code for the `AJP` connector and modify the port number to `8109`:

```
<Connector port="8109" protocol="AJP/1.3" redirectPort="8443" />
```

12. Save the file and close it. Before starting the two Tomcat servers, we need to add a couple of parameters for JVM, otherwise integrated GWC will lock the `data` folder and only one GeoServer will be able to start:

```
~$ sudo vi /etc/init.d/tomcat
```

13. Just after the line setting the `-server` parameter, insert the following:

```
GWC="-DGWC_DISKQUOTA_DISABLED=true -DGWC_METASTORE_DISABLED=true"
```

14. Add the GWC variable in the line setting `JAVA_OPTS`:

```
export JAVA_OPTS="-Djava.awt.headless=true $HEAP $NEW $RMIGC $PGC
$PERM $DEBUG $DUMP $SERVER $GWC"
```

15. Save the file, then open the startup script for the new Tomcat server:

```
$ sudo vi /opt/new_apache-tomcat-7.0.27/bin/catalina.sh
```

16. Insert a new line, just after the initial comments, and set the same parameters:

```
JAVA_OPTS="-DGWC_DISKQUOTA_DISABLED=true -DGWC_METASTORE_
DISABLED=true"
```

17. Save the file.

18. Now we can start the two Tomcat servers. You can start the old one with the service command utility. To start the newly created one you will use the default startup script:

```
~$ sudo /opt/new_apache-tomcat-7.0.27/bin/startup.sh
```

19. Now open your browser and point to `http://localhost/geoserver`, and to `http://localhost:8180/geoserver`. Go to the **Layer Preview** page; now you see the same layers list as expected.

20. Now we need to set a proxy for both the Tomcat servers and add a balancer. This is delivered by `apache httpd mod_proxy_balancer`. Enable it using the following script:

```
~$ sudo a2enmod proxy_balancer
~$ sudo service apache 2 restart
```

21. In order to change the proxy configuration, you have to edit the `httpd.conf` file:

```
~$ sudo vi /etc/apache2/httpd.conf
```

22. We need to modify the `ProxyPass` directive. Comment the lines you inserted in the previous *Time for action – configuring a proxy* section, by inserting a # character at line start. Then insert the following code:

```
ProxyPass /geoserver balancer://geoserver
<Proxy balancer://geoserver>
    BalancerMember ajp://localhost:8009/geoserver
    BalancerMember ajp://localhost:8109/geoserver
    Order deny,allow
    Deny from all
    Allow from 127.0.0.1
</Proxy>
```

23. Save the file and restart the Apache service. Now open your browser and go to `http://localhost/geoserver`. Apache will forward your request to one of the two GeoServers.

24. You may wonder how the balancer works, how it balances requests, and what happens if a server fails. `Apache mod_proxy_balancer` comes with a practical interface to manage and monitor the balancer. You have to explicitly expose it in the `httpd.conf` file:

```
~$ sudo vi /etc/apache2/httpd.conf
```

25. Insert the following code:

```
<Location /balancer-manager>
    SetHandler balancer-manager
    Order Deny,Allow
    Deny from all
        Allow from 127.0.0.1
</Location>
```

26. From your browser, open `http://localhost/balancer-manager`:

Load Balancer Manager for localhost

Server Version: Apache/2.2.22 (Ubuntu)
Server Built: Nov 8 2012 21:37:37

LoadBalancer Status for balancer://geoserver

StickySession Timeout FailoverAttempts Method

-	0	1		byrequests

Worker URL	Route	RouteRedir	Factor	Set	Status	Elected	To	From
ajp://localhost:8009/geoserver	1	0	Ok	6		0	9.4K	
ajp://localhost:8109/geoserver	1	0	Ok	5		0	80K	

Apache/2.2.22 (Ubuntu) Server at ubuntu1204x64vm Port 80

27. From the web interface, you can monitor the main parameters for each node of the configuration. The status tells you if the node is working or if it is down. Right next to it you can find the number of requests that each node processed since the service started. The `method` field shows you how the requests are distributed. The default mode to perform weighted request counting is `byrequests`. You can also modify it to `bytraffic`, to perform weighted traffic byte count balancing. By default each node is assigned an equal load, but you can distribute traffic asymmetrically using the `loadfactor` parameter. Let's change our configuration to split 75 percent of the requests to one node and the remaining 25 percent to the other:

```
<Proxy balancer://geoserver>
    BalancerMember ajp://localhost:8009/geoserver loadfactor=1
    BalancerMember ajp://localhost:8109/geoserver loadfactor=3
    Order deny,allow
    Deny from all
    Allow from 127.0.0.1
</Proxy>
```

28. Restart the Apache service, then open the GeoServer web interface, and navigate it to send a few requests. If you now open the balancer-manager interface again, the page should look as follows:

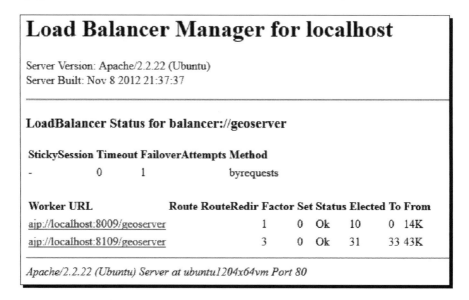

29. You can also set a node as a host stand-by. The balancer will fetch requests to it in case the node fails. To set a backup, you have to insert the `status=+H` parameter:

```
<Proxy balancer://geoserver>
    BalancerMember ajp://localhost:8009/geoserver status=+H
    BalancerMember ajp://localhost:8109/geoserver
    Order deny,allow
    Deny from all
    Allow from 127.0.0.1
</Proxy>
```

What just happened?

You learned how to configure a simple yet effective high availability configuration. In this section we didn't introduce any router; this task is usually performed by network engineers and you are safe knowing that it has to be done.

Pop quiz – production environment

Q1. How can you tune the environment for JVM?

1. You should use a 64-bit JVM version; it performs much better than the 32-bit one.

2. You have to launch a console window on your server and set the global environment variables.

3. You have to set custom values for JVM startup parameters in the script used to start GeoServer.

Q2. How can you reduce the downtime for your map service?

1. Using an improved hardware.

2. Optimizing your data.

3. Setting redundant items for each component of your configuration.

Summary

In this chapter we discussed basic considerations to safely deploy the GeoServer in production.

Deploying a successful configuration requires you to take care of several topics. JVM optimization may enhance performances, and a high availability configuration can rock your GeoServer. Although, as a beginner, some of the issues may seem out of your scope for now, it is important to know where to focus your attention when planning a new installation. Most of the times you will be working with system and network engineers knowing very little about map servers. You will be expected to guide them in identifying the critical details in the configuration.

In the next chapter, we will focus on the next steps to take once you are confident with GeoServer, how to get further help, and what else GeoServer can offer you that we didn't cover in this book.

12
Going Further: Getting Help and Troubleshooting

Our journey into GeoServer is coming to an end. What you have learned should enable you to create a map service and make your data accessible to everyone on the Internet.

GeoServer is far more complex than what we have covered so far. There are lots of advanced features for data sharing and performing spatial analysis.

In this chapter we will briefly cover some advanced features, for example, other standard protocols supported by GeoServer, and how to get help and also how to collaborate the project. We will cover the following topics in detail:

- ◆ Web Feature Service (WFS)
- ◆ Web Coverage Service (WCS)
- ◆ Online resources
- ◆ Future steps (maybe!)

Going beyond maps

We focused on the maps in the book and almost always used the WMS protocol in our examples. As you learned in *Chapter 1, GIS Fundamentals*, a map is a representation of data. A map can include vector or raster data, but it always represents them as a raster output, that is, an image. While maps are an easy and useful way to show your data, there are other scenarios where users need not use a representation, but the original data, for example, to process the data on a client-side task. Here, two other OGC protocols come into use: WFS and WCS.

Delivering vector data

If a user needs to get your vector data, for example, the USA railroads, he can use the **Web Feature Service** (**WFS**) protocol. It is a standard protocol defined by OGC that refers to the sending and receiving of geospatial data through HTTP.

When delivering data, the most important thing to define is the data format. Vector data is usually stored in a binary format—think of a shapefile or a PostGIS table—but for practical purposes we need a more standard approach. Indeed, WFS encodes and transfers information in **Geography Markup Language** (**GML**), based on XML.

There exist a few versions of WFS and GML. The current GeoServer release supports the 1.0.0, 1.1.0, and 2.0.0 WFS versions.

You can find the full reference for WFS and GML at the OGC repository at
`http://www.opengeospatial.org/standards/is`; look for:

♦ OpenGIS Geography Markup Language (GML) Encoding Standard
♦ OpenGIS Web Feature Service (WFS) Implementation Specification

WFS defines a set of operations that a user can perform on data. You used transactional operations in *Chapter 10, Securing Your GeoServer Before Production*, for data editing. We will now focus on retrieving data.

Time for action – retrieving vector data

We will use WFS to get vector data encoded in GML. In case you disabled it, as we did in *Chapter 11, Tuning GeoServer in a Production Environment*, you will need to enable the WFS in GeoServer. Open your command-line console; we are going to use `curl` for sending requests:

1. The first operation that we will use is `GetCapabilities`. It describes which feature types and operations are available on the server:

```
~$ curl -XGET "http://localhost/geoserver/wfs?service=wfs&version=
1.0.0&request=GetCapabilities" -o getCapabilities.xml
```

2. The XML returned is quite huge; the following lines show you the brief description for a `featuretype` element:

```
<FeatureType>
    <Name>NaturalEarth:10m_railroads</Name>
      <Title>10m_railroads</Title>
      <Abstract/>
      <Keywords>10m_railroads, features</Keywords>
```

```
      <SRS>EPSG:4326</SRS>
      <LatLongBoundingBox minx="-150.08159339101002"
miny="8.329046942181577" maxx="-59.94810950429127"
maxy="64.93097565311908"/>
</FeatureType>
```

3. If you need to use a `featuretype` element, for example, railroads, you probably need the full description. You can get it using the `DescribeFeatureType` operation, which returns an XML code containing a description for the `featuretype` element you requested. Note that you can omit the `TypeName` parameter; in this case you get the full list for the `featuretype` element, ordered by workspace:

```
~$ curl -XGET "http://localhost/geoserver/wfs?service=wfs&versi
on=1.0.0&request=DescribeFeatureType&TypeName=NaturalEarth:10m_
railroads" -o railroads.xml
```

4. The response contains that feature type's detailed description. You can find the `name` and `type` of each attribute:

```
<?xml version="1.0" encoding="UTF-8"?>
...
   <xsd:complexType name="10m_railroadsType">
     <xsd:complexContent>
       <xsd:extension base="gml:AbstractFeatureType">
         <xsd:sequence>
           <xsd:element maxOccurs="1" minOccurs="0" name="the_geom"
nillable="true" type="gml:MultiLineStringPropertyType"/>
           <xsd:element maxOccurs="1" minOccurs="0"
name="ScaleRank" nillable="true" type="xsd:int"/>
           <xsd:element maxOccurs="1" minOccurs="0"
name="FeatureCla" nillable="true" type="xsd:string"/>
           <xsd:element maxOccurs="1" minOccurs="0" name="SOV_A3"
nillable="true" type="xsd:string"/>
           <xsd:element maxOccurs="1" minOccurs="0" name="UIDENT"
nillable="true" type="xsd:int"/>
         </xsd:sequence>
       </xsd:extension>
     </xsd:complexContent>
   </xsd:complexType>
...
```

5. Now we will retrieve the features. The `GetFeature` operation retrieves them from the GeoServer. To avoid getting a huge number of features, you can limit the number of elements returned with the `maxFeatures` parameter:

```
~$ curl -XGET "http://localhost/geoserver/wfs?service=wfs&
version=1.1.0&request=GetFeature&TypeName=NaturalEarth:10m_
railroads&maxFeatures=1" -o getFeature.xml
```

6. The XML code returned contains GML for the single feature that we specified. In this case we have a single `lineString` element with a lot of vertices listed in the `gml:coordinates` element:

```
<gml:boundedBy>
    <gml:null>unknown</gml:null>
</gml:boundedBy>
<gml:featureMember>
    <NaturalEarth:10m_railroads fid="10m_railroads.1">
        <NaturalEarth:the_geom>
            <gml:MultiLineString srsName="http://www.opengis.net/
gml/srs/epsg.xml#4326">
                <gml:lineStringMember>
                    <gml:LineString>
                        <gml:coordinates xmlns:gml="http://
www.opengis.net/gml" decimal="." cs="," ts=" ">-
147.67979896,64.81824372 -147.69432532,64.83020661
-147.70750892,64.83808015
...

  -148.96648109,60.85010407 -148.9647721,60.83167145</
gml:coordinates>
                    </gml:LineString>
                </gml:lineStringMember>
            </gml:MultiLineString>
        </NaturalEarth:the_geom>
        <NaturalEarth:ScaleRank>8</NaturalEarth:ScaleRank>
        <NaturalEarth:FeatureCla>Railroad</
NaturalEarth:FeatureCla>
        <NaturalEarth:SOV_A3>USA</NaturalEarth:SOV_A3>
        <NaturalEarth:UIDENT>1506</NaturalEarth:UIDENT>
    </NaturalEarth:10m_railroads>
</gml:featureMember>
```

7. Limiting the elements returned with `maxFeatures` is ok for a sample request. In general, you want to have more control over the number and types of features you want to extract. Indeed, you can filter them with a spatial operator or with alphanumerical filtering on attributes. In the following sample, we use the `bbox` operator to filter the railroad elements that intersect an extent:

```
~$ curl -XGET "http://localhost/geoserver/wfs?service=wfs&version
=1.0.0&request=GetFeature&TypeName=NaturalEarth:10m_railroads&bb
ox=-116.68,36.29,-111.36,39.90" -o getBboxFeature.xml
```

8. The request again returns a single feature but the root element is
FeatureCollection. If your try to extend bbox, more features will
be listed inside it:

```
<wfs:FeatureCollection
...
>
    <gml:boundedBy>
        <gml:null>unknown</gml:null>
    </gml:boundedBy>
    <gml:featureMember>
        <NaturalEarth:10m_railroads fid="10m_railroads.481">
            <NaturalEarth:the_geom>
                <gml:MultiLineString srsName="http://www.opengis.
net/gml/srs/epsg.xml#4326">
                    <gml:lineStringMember>
                        <gml:LineString>
                            <gml:coordinates xmlns:gml="http://
www.opengis.net/gml" decimal="." cs="," ts=" ">-
116.86064613,34.86170075 -116.85924232,34.86536286
                                ...
                            -112.16722572,40.70233796
-112.15178382,40.70752595</gml:coordinates>
                        </gml:LineString>
                    </gml:lineStringMember>
                </gml:MultiLineString>
            </NaturalEarth:the_geom>
            <NaturalEarth:ScaleRank>8</NaturalEarth:ScaleRank>
            <NaturalEarth:FeatureCla>Railroad</
NaturalEarth:FeatureCla>
            <NaturalEarth:SOV_A3>USA</NaturalEarth:SOV_A3>
            <NaturalEarth:UIDENT>49706</NaturalEarth:UIDENT>
        </NaturalEarth:10m_railroads>
    </gml:featureMember>
</wfs:FeatureCollection>
```

What just happened?

You learned how to use WFS for retrieving data with all the geometrical and alphanumerical
details. Combining the retrieval with the capabilities to insert or update data (WFS-T), you
can build an online editing system for vector data.

Delivering raster data

When it comes to raster data, **Web Coverage Service (WCS)** is the equivalent of WFS for delivering the original data. Like vector data, raster data may be rendered in a proper way on a map and you will get the result with WMS and a `GetMap` request. WCS is intended to get a raster data set or its subset in its original form, without any rendering or other processing.

With WCS you don't have a standard format for data delivery; it depends on the original format of your data.

The current release of GeoServer supports the 1.0.0 and 1.1.0 WCS versions.

As with WFS, you can find the full reference for WCS at the OGC repository, `http://www.opengeospatial.org/standards/is`; look for:

◆ OpenGIS Web Coverage Service (WCS) Implementation Specification

Time for action – retrieving raster data

We will use WCS to get raster data, using the sample data shipped with GeoServer. In case you disabled it, as we did in *Chapter 11, Tuning GeoServer in a Production Environment*, you will need to enable the WCS in GeoServer. Like WFS examples, we will use `cUrl` for sending requests:

1. The first operation we will use is `GetCapabilities`. As with WFS, it returns a list of available `featuretype` and operations:

   ```
   ~$ curl -XGET "http://localhost/geoserver/wcs?service=wcs&version=
   1.0.0&request=GetCapabilities" -o getCapabilities.xml
   ```

2. The following lines show you the brief description for a coverage, extracted from the list returned:

   ```
   <wcs:CoverageOfferingBrief>
       <wcs:description>A very rough imagery of North America</
   wcs:description>
       <wcs:name>nurc:Img_Sample</wcs:name>
       <wcs:label>North America sample imagery</wcs:label>
       <wcs:lonLatEnvelope srsName="urn:ogc:def:crs:OGC:1.3:CRS84">
           <gml:pos>-130.85168 20.7052</gml:pos>
           <gml:pos>-62.0054 54.1141</gml:pos>
       </wcs:lonLatEnvelope>
       <wcs:keywords>
           <wcs:keyword>WCS</wcs:keyword>
           <wcs:keyword>worldImageSample</wcs:keyword>
           <wcs:keyword>worldImageSample_Coverage</wcs:keyword>
       </wcs:keywords>
   </wcs:CoverageOfferingBrief>
   ```

3. The `DescribeCoverage` operation lets you get a full description of it:

```
~$ curl -XGET "http://localhost/geoserver/wcs?service=wcs&vers
ion=1.0.0&request=DescribeCoverage&Coverage=nurc:Img_Sample" -o
describeCoverage.xml
```

4. Inside the description, the returned code contains a list of the supported data formats for the output:

```
<wcs:supportedFormats nativeFormat="WorldImage">
  <wcs:formats>GeoTIFF</wcs:formats>
  <wcs:formats>GIF</wcs:formats>
  <wcs:formats>PNG</wcs:formats>
  <wcs:formats>TIFF</wcs:formats>
</wcs:supportedFormats>
```

5. Now we will retrieve `coverage`. The `GetCoverage` operation retrieves it from GeoServer. Unlike the `GetFeatures` operation in WFS, a few parameters are mandatory. You have to specify the bounding box (`bbox`) and the `width` and `height` parameters. The `bbox` operator defines the geometrical extent you want to extract, while `width` and `height` define the image size:

```
~$ curl -XGET "http://localhost/geoserver/wcs?service=w
cs&version=1.0.0&request=GetCoverage&coverage=nurc:Img_
Sample&crs=EPSG:4326&bbox=-130.85168,20.7052,-62.0054,54.1141&widt
h=982&height=597&format=geotiff&bands=1" -o coverage.tiff
```

6. If you open the `coverage.tiff` file with a picture viewer, you will see that it contains the same data as the original coverage:

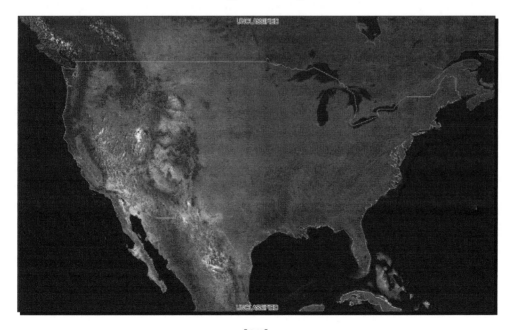

What just happened?

You learned the basics of retrieving raster data. If your project needs to process the raster data on the client side, it is very important that they are not transformed by the map server, as with WMS.

Getting help

Through this book you have learned a lot about web mapping and GeoServer, but being an ultimate reference is far out of this book's scope.

When you are in trouble or simply curious about the new features, there are a lot of online resources that can help you. The project site, `http://geoserver.org`, contains a lot of information about GeoServer. Besides the basic features, you can find descriptions for the community modules that are plugins developed by the contributors to address specific requirements. Maybe you will find something really useful for you.

The project blog, `http://blog.geoserver.org`, announces new releases, ideas, and contributions. Your RSS feed reader can't miss it!

There are two mailing lists, one user oriented and the other for developers that are hosted on `sourceforge.net`. Information and links to the subscription point are at `http://geoserver.org/display/GEOS/Mailing+Lists`.

On both, you can ask for information about the software in general and for specific issues. Many core developers read both the lists and you can get an answer that can save you from wasting your time. As with any other mailing list, following some rules may increase your chances of getting a solution to your problem:

- ◆ **Be specific**: If you write an e-mail stating GeoServer does not seem to work, you can be sure that nobody will reply to you. You should describe a clear sequence to replicate your issue, also giving details about your configuration.

- ◆ **Be polite**: People on the lists are there to help you but are not at your service. Most of the time they will do their best to find a solution for your issue, but sometimes this can't be done. It could be that nobody knows how to solve your issue or it is too complicated to be solved. If your issue requires a lot of coding, you can't expect that someone will start working on it as soon as you post it on the lists.

- ◆ **Be collaborative**: If you have got coding capabilities, you might try to build a patch for the issue and submit it in the source code repository. It will be checked and hopefully committed.

To report an issue you should use the issue tracker `http://jira.codehaus.org/browse/GEOS`.

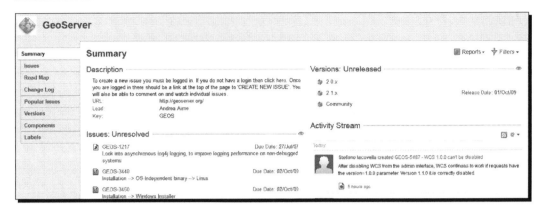

You need to register. It is free and you only have to insert a valid e-mail address, and then you can report a new issue. Browsing for current status is allowed for both registered and anonymous users.

Have a go hero – GeoServer needs you!

We hope you liked GeoServer. It is a valuable piece of software and it comes to you with no license cost, as with any open source project. Several developers, power users, and companies work hard every day to make it a better and more capable product.

If you find it useful you may want to consider giving back some of what you received.

Join the mailing lists and try not only to learn, but also to give back what you learned. GeoServer project is supported by all the people using it; so help to make it better.

Pop quiz - using WFS and WCS

Q1. How can you filter a feature in a WFS `GetFeature` request?
  1. You can only limit the number of features returned with the `maxFeatures` parameter.
  2. You can only filter the features returned by specifying an area of interest with the `bbox` parameter.
  3. You may specify an area of interest with the `bbox` parameter or build a filter on attributes, both alphanumerical and geometrical, with the filter operations in the request body.

Q2. Can you resample raster data with WCS's `GetCoverage` request?

1. No, you can only get data at their native resolution.

2. Yes, but you can only select among the resolutions included in the `DescribeCoverage` response.

3. Yes, using a proper combination of the `bbox`, `width`, and `height` values you can obtain the desired resolution.

Summary

In this final chapter we gave a brief description of WFS and WCS—two different ways to serve spatial data on the Web. But there's much more than this in the GeoServer project.

We can just mention the main features we didn't cover in the book, such as **Web Processing Service (WPS)**, which is a standard protocol for invoking the geospatial processing services, CSS styling, which is an alternative way of simplifying SLD complexity to style your layers, and time support for vector and raster data.

Whatever your needs in serving spatial data, GeoServer has an answer, or will have it soon!

Pop Quiz Answers

Chapter 2, Getting Started with GeoServer

Pop quiz – setting up Java

Q1	3
Q2	3

Pop quiz – GeoServer security

Q1	2
Q2	2

Chapter 4, Accessing Layers

Pop quiz – accessing data

Q1	2
Q2	3

Chapter 5, Adding your Data

Pop quiz – adding data to GeoServer

Q1	3
Q2	2

Pop quiz – adding data

Q1	3
Q2	1

Chapter 6, Styling your Layers

Pop quiz – SLD basic elements

Q1	1
Q2	2

Pop quiz – styling points

Q1	2
Q2	2

Pop quiz – styling lines and polygons

Q1	3
Q2	1
Q3	2

Chapter 7, Creating Simple Maps

Pop quiz – creating mapping apps

Q1	2
Q2	3

Chapter 8, Performance and Caching

Pop quiz – configuring integrated GeoWebCache

Q1	2
Q2	1
Q3	3

Chapter 9, Automating Tasks: GeoServer REST Interface

Pop quiz – reviewing REST operations

Q1	3
Q2	2
Q3	3

Chapter 10, Securing GeoServer before Production

Pop quiz – reviewing security

Q1	2
Q2	3

Chapter 11, Tuning GeoServer in a Production Environment

Pop quiz – production environment

Q1	3
Q2	3

Chapter 12, Going Further: Getting Help and Troubleshooting

Pop quiz – using WFS and WCS

Q1	3
Q2	3

Index

A

About & Status section
about 57, 60
configuration, loading manually 60, 61
contact information 59
GeoServer Logs 59
Server Status 57
additional data sources
exploring 122
MySQL 123
Oracle 122
Adobe Illustrator 95
Apache Tomcat
about 38
configuring, on Ubuntu 45, 46
GeoServer, deploying 49, 50
installing 38
installing, on Ubuntu 42-44
installing, on Windows 38-41
license agreement 42
URL 38
web interface, exploring 47
ArcGIS Online
URL 18
ArcGrid 73, 120
AtomPub format 92
Atom Publishing Protocol. *See* **AtomPub**

B

bbox 90
bug tracker
exploring 61

C

caching defaults
default cached gridsets 214
default layers options 213, 214
direct integration, enabling 212
setting 212
TMS 213
WMS-C 212
WTMS 213
choropleth maps 23
cluster
configuring 297-302
Cluster File System 296
configuration, GeoServer cluster 297-302
configuration, proxy 293, 294, 295
coordinates in decimal degree 10
coordinate systems
about 12
geographic coordinate systems 12
projected coordinate system 12
SRID 13
UTM 12
Web Mercator 13
CQL (Contextual Query Language) filters 91
CSV 73, 96
cURL
about 237
URL 237, 238
custom Google map layer
creating 193
custom gridset
creating 215-218

D

data
about 61
configuring 106
filtering 120
layer groups 69
Layer Preview 61
layers 68
stores 66
styles 69, 70
workspaces 64
data access
layers, securing 278-284
shapefile, creating 278
data publishing, REST interface
layers, working with 261
styles, working with 260
data, REST interface
managing 238
namespaces, working with 238
workspaces, managing 239-245
workspaces, working with 238
data security, GeoServer
group definition 272
roles, defining 276, 277
roles definition 272
user definition 272
user/group services 272
users and groups, creating 272-275
data stores, REST interface
managing 246-251
default cached gridsets 214
default layers options, caching defaults 213, 214
Demo requests interface
about 79
demo requests, exploring 80, 82
projection list, filtering 83, 84
SRS list 83
DescribeCoverage operation 311
digital elevation model (DEM) 120
direct integration 212
Disk Quota, GeoWebCache
configuring 209-211
DMZ 295

E

ellipsoid 10
emacs 128
EPSG Geodetic Parameter Registry 14
EPSG registry
about 14
exploring 14
URL 14
European Petroleum Survey Group. *See* **EPSG**
external GeoWebCache
using 231, 232
external WFS, vector data sources
configuring 107
external WMS, raster data sources
configuring 121

F

featuretype element 307
feature types, REST interface
about 252
PostGIS table, adding 256-259
shapefile, adding 254-256
Firebug 90
Firefox 90

G

GDAL output 99
geographic coordinate systems 12
Geography Markup Language (GML)
about 306
reference 306
geoid 10
GeoJSON
about 97
parsing 97
geometrical shapes
representing 14
GeoRSS
using, with OpenLayers 199
GeoRSS format 93
GeoServer 9
about 31, 32, 295
additional data sources 122

basic security, implementing 51, 52
bug tracker 61
data, configuring 105
data security 271
deploying, on Tomcat 49, 50
installation options 48
integrating, with OpenLayers 196-199
layers, styling 127
MySQL, adding 123
Oracle, adding 122
output options 98
proxy, configuring 293-295
raster data sources, configuring 120
REST 236
REST interface 236
sample maps, creating with Google Maps API
        179
security settings 268
service faults, avoiding 295, 296
unused services, disabling 291, 292
URL 48, 312
vector data sources, configuring 106
GeoServer bundled styles
viewing 130-132
GeoServer cluster
configuring 297-302
GeoServer Demos
about 79
demo requests, exploring 80-83
GeoServer interface
about 55, 56
About & Status 57
data 61
Demos 79
global security settings 77
Security 76
services 70
settings 73
Tile Caching 76
GeoServer Logs 59
GeoTIFF 67, 120
GeoWebCache
about 55
caching defaults, setting 212
Disk Quota, configuring 209-211
exploring 206

external GeoWebCache, using 231
gridsets, configuring 215
storage, configuring 206-209
tile layers, configuring 218
URL 206
GetFeatureInfo freemarker template
using 99, 100
GetFeature operation 307
GetFeature request 291
GetMap request 288, 290
GIF format 92
GIS
about 7, 8
coordinate systems 12
geometrical shapes 14
raster data 16
GIS software 9
GitHub project 192
GlassFish 38
global security settings, GeoServer interface 77
global settings, GeoServer interface
about 73
enable Global Services 74
logging configuration, changing 74
logging level, creating 75
logging Profile 74
Log location 74
Log to StdOut 74
Proxy Base URL 74
Verbose reporting 73
GML2 (compressed GZIP) 97
GML3 73
gml:coordinates element 308
GML (plain text) 96
Google 13
Google basemap
customizing 189
Google Earth 26
Google Maps 13
Google Maps API
about 180
click event, intercepting 193, 194
GeoServer layer, adding as base layer 185-187
GeoServer layer, adding as overlay 180-184
pre-calculated maps, using 187-189
user, interacting 193

Graphics Interchange Format. *See* GIF
gridsets
   about 215
   configuring 215
   custom gridset, creating 215-218
group definition 272
Gtopo30 121

H

httpd 292

I

ImageMap 101
ImageMosaic 121
Inkscape
   about 95
   URL 95
installation
   Apache Tomcat 38
   GeoServer 48
   Java 32
installation, native JAI 288-290
interface settings, GeoServer
   about 73
   global 73
   JAI 75
issue tracker
   URL 312

J

JAI 58, 75, 288
JAI-IO package 289
Java
   runtime parameters, configuring 286-288
   tuning 286
Java Advanced Imaging. *See* JAI
Java installation
   about 32
   JRE, installing on Ubuntu 36, 38
   JRE, installing on Windows 35
   JRE/JDK installation, checking on Ubuntu 34
   JRE/JDK installation, checking on Windows 32, 33
Java Naming and Directory Interface (JNDI) 67
Java Virtual Machine (JVM) 58

Java Runtime Environment. *See* JRE
JBoss 38
JDK (Java Development Kit) 32
Jetty 292
JPEG format 94
JRE
   about 32
   installing, on Ubuntu 36, 38
   installing, on Windows 35
JRE (Java Runtime Environment) 32
JRE/JDK installation
   cheking, on Ubuntu 34
   cheking, on Windows 32, 33
JSON 73
JVM
   runtime parameters, optimizing for 286-288

K

KML (Plain) format 94
KML preview 63, 64
KMZ (Compressed) format 94

L

labels
   adding 160
   lines, labeling 163-165
   points, labeling 161, 162
   polygons, labeling 166, 167
   styling 166
latitude 9
layer groups 69
Layer Preview
   about 61
   KML preview 63, 64
   OpenLayers preview 62, 63
layers
   about 68
   grouping 176, 177
   styling 176
layers, REST interface
   managing 262, 263
LeafLet
   about 88
   exploring 201
   URL 88
   using, with GeoServer layers 201, 202

lineString element 308
linestring symbols
   about 146
   border, adding 148
   centerline, adding 148
   dashed lines, using 151, 152
   dashing lines and markers, mixing 153, 154
   hatching, using 149, 150
   simple line style, creating 146, 147
longitude 9

M

map
   building 17, 18
   colors and shading 19
   symbols 18
memory usage 58
MySQL
   about 123
   adding, in GeoServer 124
   URL 107

N

namespace URI, REST interface 238
native JAI
   installing 288-290
notepad++ 128

O

OGR output 99
online resources, GeoServer 312
Open Geospatial Consortium (OGC)
   about 16
   URL 16
OpenJDK 32
OpenLayers
   about 88
   filtering 91
   GeoRSS, using with 199, 200
   integrating, with GeoServer 196-199
   options, exploring 89, 90
   tiles, working with 90, 91
   using 196
OpenLayers preview 62, 63
Open Source Geospatial Foundation (OSGeo) 88

OpenStreetMap
   about 20
   URL 20
   using 21, 22
Oracle
   about 122
   adding, in GeoServer 122, 123
Oracle Java™ JRE 32
Oracle Locator 122
Oracle Spatial 122
Out Of Memory (OOM) 287
output options, GeoServer
   GDAL 99
   OGR 99
   TEXT/HTML 99

P

Parallel Garbage Collector 287
PDF format 95
pdf Reflect option, WMS Reflector
   exploring 103
PgAdmin 120
PNG format 95
PointSymbolizer 101
point symbols
   angles and transparency, dealing with 140
   composing 146
   external graphics, using 144, 145
   simple point style, creating 134-137
   simple shapes, composing 141-143
   stroke value, adding 137-139
   working with 134
polygon symbols
   graphic filling, using 157
   hatching, using 158-160
   simple polygon style, creating 155, 156
   working with 155
polyline 15
PostGIS
   about 110
   data, loading 116-118
   data, publishing in GeoServer 119
   installing 110, 114, 115
PostgreSQL
   installing 110-113

pre-calculated maps, Google Maps API
    custom Google map layer, creating 193
    GeoServer cached layer, adding as overlay 187-189
    Google basemap, customizing 189-192
    using 187
Processing Service (WPS) 314
project blog
    URL 312
projected coordinate system 12
projection
    about 10
    classifying 11
properties file, vector data sources
    configuring 106
proportional maps 25
proxy
    configuring 293-295
    setting 292
Python
    URL 237

Q

QGIS 128
    URL 128

R

raster data
    about 14
    delivering 310
    drawbacks 17
    retrieving 310-312
    used, for modeling real world 16
raster data sources
    about 120
    ArcGrid 120
    configuring 120
    external WMS, configuring 121
    GeoTiff 120
    Gtopo30 121
    ImageMosaic 121
    WorldImage 121
raster formats 67
RDBMS 296
real world
    modeling, raster data used 16

Reflector 87
REpresentational State Transfer. *See* REST
Requests library
    installing 237, 238
Resource Cache 59
REST
    about 236
    Requests library, installing 237, 238
    using 236, 237
REST interface, GeoServer
    data, managing 238
    data, publishing 260
roles definition 272
root account 270
rules, mailing list 312
runtime parameter
    optimizing, for JVM 286-288

S

sample maps, building
    Google Maps API, exploring 180
    Leaflet, exploring 201
    OpenLayers, using 196
security, GeoServer
    data access 277
    implementing 51, 52
    security settings, improving 52
security settings, GeoServer interface
    about 268
    catalog security 78
    data 78
    groups 77
    master password, changing 270, 271
    roles 77
    services security 79
    strong encryption, enabling 269, 270
    users 77
seeding 227
Server Status
    about 57
    configuration and catalog 59
    connections 58
    JAI 58
    JVM 58
    locks 58
    memory usage 58

resource cache 59
update sequence 58
service faults
avoiding 295, 296
services
about 70
WCS 73
WFS 73
WMS 71
Shapefile 73, 98
spatial data
about 8
sphere, projecting on plane 10, 11
world, measuring 9
spatial reference system. *See* **SRS**
spatial reference system identifier. *See* **SRID**
sphere
projecting, on sphere 10
SRID 13
SRS 13
SRS list
filtering 83, 84
standard structure, style
exploring 129
GeoServer bundled styles, viewing 130-132
storage, GeoWebCache
configuring 206-209
stores
about 66
data formats 67
Styled Layer Descriptor (SLD)
about 29, 127, 128
URL 128
styles
about 69
data, loading 133
editing 128
standard structure, exploring 129
styles, REST interface
adding 260, 261
managing 260
SVG format 95

T

TEXT/HTML 99
thematic mapping
about 168

choropleth road map 172
roads, classifying 169, 171
thematic maps
about 23
building 26-28
choropleth maps 23
proportional maps 25
TIFF format 95
tile caching 76
tile layers
client, building for tiger county layer 227
configuring 218, 219
configuring, for caching 219, 220
seeding 227-230
using, with OpenLayers 221-227
tiles, OpenLayers
working with 90
TMS (Tiled Map Services) 213
Tomcat. *See* **Apache Tomcat 286**
Tomcat web interface
exploring 47
Transactional Web Feature Service (WFS-T) 58
Transverse Mercator projection 12

U

Ubuntu
Apache Tomcat 7.x, installing 42-44
downloading 36
JRE, installing 36-38
JRE/JDK installation, checking 34
Tomcat, configuring 45, 46
United States Geological Survey (USGS) 121
Universal Transverse Mercator system. *See* **UTM system**
unused services
disabling 291, 292
user definition 272
user/group services 272
UTM system 12

V

vector data
about 14
delivering 306
retrieving 306-309

vector data formats
 about 67
 PostGIS 67
 properties 67
 shapefile 67
 WFS 67
vector data sources
 about 106
 configuring 106
 external WFS, configuring 107
 PostGIS, using 110
 properties file, adding 106
 shapefiles, adding 107=109
vector data store connections 58
vi 128
visibility, setting
 about 173
 thematic roads map, enhancing 173-175

W

WCS
 about 58, 291, 310
 reference 310
 using 310
Web Coverage Service. *See* **WCS**
Web Feature Server 73
Web Feature Service. *See* **WFS**
Web Mapping Service. *See* **WMS**
Web Mapping Services Cached. *See* **WMS-C**
Web Map Server 71
Web Map Service 58
Web Mercator 13
well-known text (WKT) representation 13
WFS
 about 73, 88, 96, 291
 reference 306
 using 306
WFS output formats
 CSV 96
 GeoJSON 97
 GML2 (compressed GZIP) 97
 GML (plain text) 96
 Shapefile 98
WFS-T 291

Windows
 Apache Tomcat 7.x, installing 38-41
 JRE, installing 35
 JRE/JDK installation, checking 32, 33
WMS
 about 71, 291
 SRS list, limiting 71, 72
WMS-C 212
WMS output formats
 AtomPub 92
 exploring 92
 GeoRSS 93
 GIF 92
 JPEG 94
 KML (Plain) 94
 KMZ (Compressed) 94
 PDF 95
 PNG 95
 SVG 95
 TIFF 95
WMS Reflector
 pdf Reflect option, exploring 103
 using 101, 102
WMTS (Web Map Tiled Services) 213
workspace, REST interface
 about 238
 managing 239-245
workspaces
 about 64
 creating 65, 66
world
 measuring 9
 representing 17
WorldImage 67, 121

Thank you for buying
GeoServer Beginner's Guide

About Packt Publishing

Packt, pronounced 'packed', published its first book "*Mastering phpMyAdmin for Effective MySQL Management*" in April 2004 and subsequently continued to specialize in publishing highly focused books on specific technologies and solutions.

Our books and publications share the experiences of your fellow IT professionals in adapting and customizing today's systems, applications, and frameworks. Our solution based books give you the knowledge and power to customize the software and technologies you're using to get the job done. Packt books are more specific and less general than the IT books you have seen in the past. Our unique business model allows us to bring you more focused information, giving you more of what you need to know, and less of what you don't.

Packt is a modern, yet unique publishing company, which focuses on producing quality, cutting-edge books for communities of developers, administrators, and newbies alike. For more information, please visit our website: www.packtpub.com.

About Packt Open Source

In 2010, Packt launched two new brands, Packt Open Source and Packt Enterprise, in order to continue its focus on specialization. This book is part of the Packt Open Source brand, home to books published on software built around Open Source licences, and offering information to anybody from advanced developers to budding web designers. The Open Source brand also runs Packt's Open Source Royalty Scheme, by which Packt gives a royalty to each Open Source project about whose software a book is sold.

Writing for Packt

We welcome all inquiries from people who are interested in authoring. Book proposals should be sent to author@packtpub.com. If your book idea is still at an early stage and you would like to discuss it first before writing a formal book proposal, contact us; one of our commissioning editors will get in touch with you.

We're not just looking for published authors; if you have strong technical skills but no writing experience, our experienced editors can help you develop a writing career, or simply get some additional reward for your expertise.

OpenLayers 2.10 Beginner's Guide

ISBN: 978-1-84951-412-5   Paperback: 372 pages

Create, optimize, and deploy stunning cross-browser web maps with the OpenLayers JavaScript web-mapping library

1. Learn how to use OpenLayers through explanation and example

2. Create dynamic web map mashups using Google Maps and other third-party APIs

3. Customize your map's functionality and appearance

4. Deploy your maps and improve page loading times

Python Geospatial Development

ISBN: 978-1-84951-154-4   Paperback: 508 pages

Build a complete and sophisticated mapping application from scratch using Python tools for GIS development

1. Build applications for GIS development using Python

2. Analyze and visualize Geo-Spatial data

3. Comprehensive coverage of key GIS concepts

4. Recommended best practices for storing spatial data in a database

5. Draw maps, place data points onto a map, and interact with maps

Please check **www.PacktPub.com** for information on our titles

Java 7 New Features Cookbook

ISBN: 978-1-84968-562-7   Paperback: 384 pages

Over 100 comprehensive recipes to get you
up-to-speed with all the exciting new features
of Java 7

1. Comprehensive coverage of the new features of
   Java 7 organized around easy-to-follow recipes

2. Covers exciting features such as the try-with-
   resources block, the monitoring of directory events,
   asynchronous IO and new GUI enhancements,
   and more

3. A learn-by-example based approach that focuses on
   key concepts to provide the foundation to solve real
   world problems

JBoss AS 5 Development

ISBN: 978-1-84719-682-8   Paperback: 416 pages

Develop, deploy, and secure Java applications on this
robust, open source application server

1. A complete guide for JBoss developers covering
   everything from basic installation to creating,
   debugging, and securing Java EE applications on this
   popular, award-winning JBoss application server

2. Master the most important areas of Java Enterprise
   programming including EJB 3.0, web services, the
   security framework, and more

3. Starts with the basics of JBoss AS and moves on to
   cover important advanced topics with the help of
   easy-to-understand practical examples

Please check **www.PacktPub.com** for information on our titles

Made in the USA
Middletown, DE
16 March 2017